KARLIEN VANDERHEYDEN

IGNACE DECROIX   STIJN VIAENE

Digital at Heart

HOW TO LEAD A HUMAN-CENTRIC DIGITAL TRANSFORMATION

Lannoo
Campus

CONTENTS

INTRODUCTION 7

CHAPTER 1
VIGILANT LEADERSHIP 27

VIGILANT LEADERS 29
STIMULATING CURIOSITY 30
UNMASKING BIASES AND NOISE 47
MASTERING INFORMATION OVERLOAD 62
ENERGY SCAN FOR VIGILANT LEADERSHIP 71
CHECKLIST FOR VIGILANT LEADERSHIP 72

CHAPTER 2
VOYAGER LEADERSHIP 75

VOYAGER LEADERS 77
CO-CREATING FOR INNOVATION 78
EMBRACING VULNERABILITY AND AUTHENTICITY 99
BUILDING UPON DIVERSITY AND INCLUSION 113
ENERGY SCAN FOR VOYAGER LEADERSHIP 130
CHECKLIST FOR VOYAGER LEADERSHIP 131

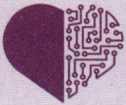

CHAPTER 3
VISIONARY LEADERSHIP

135

VISIONARY LEADERS   137
CRAFTING ORGANISATIONAL AND INDIVIDUAL PURPOSE   138
HARNESSING THE POWER OF STORYTELLING   158
EMBRACING RISK WITH CONFIDENCE   173
DEVELOPING PARTNERSHIPS   187
ENERGY SCAN FOR VISIONARY LEADERSHIP   198
CHECKLIST FOR VISIONARY LEADERSHIP   199

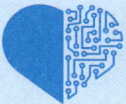

CHAPTER 4
VESTED LEADERSHIP

203

VESTED LEADERS   205
BUILDING A CHANGE COALITION   206
COPING WITH CHANGE FATIGUE   219
BREAKING DOWN SILOS   232
GIVING AND RECEIVING FEEDBACK   247
ENERGY SCAN FOR VESTED LEADERSHIP   260
CHECKLIST FOR VESTED LEADERSHIP   261

CHAPTER 5
THE COMBINED POWER OF
DIGITAL LEADERS

265

REFERENCE LIST   289
NOTES   313

INTRODUCTION

The year is 2049. The world around us is transforming relentlessly. Let's take a look at what the future could look like.

The working-from-home narrative has strengthened. The metaverse considerably changed how people collaborate inside and outside of work and, now more than ever, society is truly digitally immersed. Where employees previously switched between home and company offices, they now connect and interact by means of virtual reality. People are no longer limited by physical constraints, either by what their body allows or what their environment dictates. Limitations are off and the rules of work have changed in other ways as well. Whereas many people initially saw their job tasks being automated and some people worked alongside robot colleagues, shop-floor workers now operate semi-autonomous robots – almost exact replicas of themselves – from a home-based control centre. Furthermore, the increasing interconnectivity between company and industry data lakes have made product flows more transparent. Warehouse prices now fluctuate on a minute-to-minute basis, always highlighting a fair and transparent price setting.

AI has vastly augmented most occupations, helping people work more efficiently and productively. Smartphones have become relics of the past. The microchip[1], implanted into people's brains, provides constant access to information projected onto the retina of the eye by a minuscule lens. There's no longer a need to take pictures either as everything is being tracked, recorded, and stored for easy access. People can easily scroll through the past and find that one exact moment and project it wherever they want. Completely new occupations and industries have been created: recently, rockets started leaving the Earth's atmosphere daily and various sizeable organisations now send people, robots, and materials into outer space to support the first attempts at colonising other planets and also to support the burgeoning space mining industry. Highways still stand, for now, but they are gradually being reclaimed by nature. Traffic is regulated according to multiple sky layers, each dedicated to a specific class of air vehicle. We have entered a new era.

Some futurists advocate for a technological utopia and convey an optimistic and potentially even transhumanist future to inspire people. "Why would we want to stop here?", they think. Others, more sceptically, suggest that we should stay realistic and not get ahead of ourselves. On the other hand, there are those who stress the risks humanity could face – painting Terminatoresque, dystopian images of a dramatic, apocalyptic moment when machines take over. Technological singularity, for example, represents a, currently hypothetical, point where an artificial superintelligence surpasses human intelligence, which will result in a fundamental redefining of our human existence. Some people mostly stress the positive outcomes (such as advanced medical treatment and economic growth); others are more likely to stress the negative outcomes and risk (such as job displacement and ethical dilemmas). Despite coming from often competing views, all groups have valid points and remarks. But it is up to us to choose the outcome. *"The future is not yet set in stone. The future is what we make it,"* write professor of organisational behaviour Nicky Dries and colleagues.[2]

Let's time warp back to the present. Our little Blue Planet is at the edge of multiple large-scale changes: globalisation, technological innovation, geopolitical instability, and demographic shifts. We are in the era of the always-on transformation.[3] People must adapt constantly and brace against the impact of such ruthless disruptive forces. So must companies. For them, it's truly transform or die. They are up against the digital world, a ferocious beast that has barely stretched its muscles and eagerly eyes the ring – hungry for the first round.

ding ding, goes the bell.

Digital technologies are disrupting society, and organisations and employees are hit by alternating left jabs of complexity and right jabs of volatility. Unexpectedly, you are hit by two frontal kicks of turbulence – the rules have changed, or rather, your opponent doesn't follow any rules. They don't need to. You freeze in front of this monstrosity of an opponent, as making winning choices feels more difficult than ever.

ding ding, round two has started.

You engage in this dance, nonetheless. Data and digital technology can be deployed to boost efficiency. Emerging technologies overhaul everything from supply chains and manufacturing to research and development. They are engines of innovation and revenue growth. You understand that this opponent will allow you to hone your skills; that you are offered unprecedented opportunities to develop new products, new services, and potentially even reimagine your entire business. But you need to keep up; the sweat is at your temples, your breath heavy.

ding ding, round three – did you catch your breath?

Your key competitors are no longer the sole source of threat and disruption. New market entrants pop up from anywhere and everywhere – often from far beyond your industry or business model. These disrupters don't just nibble at existing businesses either; they nimbly introduce far superior and more agile models. Let's not forget the mighty cutting-edge tech behemoths now trying to expand their reach, preying.

Can they be stopped?

Outcome 1

Round by round, you find your rhythm. The punches of complexity and volatility no longer catch you off guard; in fact, you have started to anticipate them. Your eyes sparkle and a smile spreads on your face – you're learning how to dance with this digital beast. Each challenge, each jab sharpens your skills, and with every blow you take, you come back stronger.

Digital tools are now no longer a threatening opponent; instead, they are your sparring partners. As you master various tools – automation, AI, ... –, your organisation is becoming more and more innovative, customer-centric, and resilient.

The bell rings for the final round, and this time you are standing tall, proud and victorious.

Outcome 2

You survive, round after round, managing to block the worst of punches. Some jabs land, and though they sting, you keep on fighting. Your organisation has adopted certain digital technologies, but the transformation is wearing you down, making you feel unbalanced.

Some areas of the business thrive, but others are lagging behind, still burdened by legacy systems and a resistant group of employees.

As the bell rings for a final round, you remain standing, neither defeated nor triumphant. It's clear to the crowd that you've made progress, but there's work to be done still – the match isn't over, and you know that your next steps will determine whether you win or just continue to fight in place.

Outcome 3
The relentless barrage of punches and kicks has become overwhelming. You clutch your groin as the beast's unpredictability exposes every weakness in your strategy and company culture.

Unprepared for the relentless pace of change, teams falter, unable to adapt. Technologies are implemented, but without a clear vision or purpose. Confusion and frustration have risen exponentially. As round after round passes, the business loses momentum, inertia is on the horizon.

You're in the wrong weight division, you realise. When the final uppercut comes, the lights go out, and the canvas welcomes you. The count to ten starts. *ding ding*, game over.

Has digital pushed you against the ropes, worn you out, and left you standing with your gloves up? Do you feel battered and bruised, or excited and still energised? Can you do anything but parry the punches, jabs, and hooks as they come?

The rules of the game have changed. Jack Welch, former chairman and CEO of GE, voiced the implications eloquently: *"When the rate of change inside an institution becomes slower than the rate of change outside, the end is in sight."*[4] Similarly, "A time of turbulence is a dangerous time," management thinker Peter Drucker once said, "but its greatest danger is a temptation to deny reality".[5] Entering the ring and engaging in a potentially scary dance is one thing; coping effectively and flourishing is an entirely different story. But how?

TURBULENCE AS THE 21ST CENTURY NEW NORMAL

Disruption has been a recurring phenomenon since the dawn of the industrial age. In his 1892 landmark book *Degeneration*, physician and social critic Max Nordau wrote that the unnaturally accelerated demand of industrial life offers people little to no breathing space. And while it took several generations to perfect the steam engine to power the first Industrial Revolution, it takes significantly less time to develop and implement digital technologies. To survive today's business complexity, companies must possess flexibility; they need to routinely explore and exploit opportunities faster than their rivals. This is what we call **Organisational Agility** – defined by John Coleman, as

> "Creating an adaptable organisation with a higher possibility to drive disruption in society, the industry, and the marketplace [...]. It looks like a pattern of constructive collaboration between people with diverse perspectives [and] feels like increased humanity, authenticity, leadership, and engagement, and overall caring more about [...] meaningful-shared-purpose, value, understanding needs and wants, outside-in-thinking, and more."[6]

Organisational agility is a prerequisite for successful digital transformation.[7] Stijn Viaene defines this as follows[8]: "Digital transformation is a process of organisational change that leverages digital technology. It is a response to shifts in an organisation's business environment driven by a continuous stream of digital opportunities and challenges. We deliberately frame digital transformation not as a tactic, but as a strategic, holistic endeavour – an end-to-end effort that spans the entire value chain and is both inward and outward-looking. Digital technology plays a dual role in the process, as digital transformation is about organisation-wide change both in response to and with the help of digital technologies." Digital transformation is continuous in nature. It results in successive waves of transformation rather than discrete projects or programs.

A new wave of technologies has arrived while many companies are still struggling to master previous ones. Currently, 91% of organisations are engaged in digital initiatives[9,] with 71% of organisations aiming to increase their company's tech investments over the next few years. In the case of specific technologies, such as chatbots and large language models, up to 85% of organisations expect to invest significantly[10.] George Westerman, MIT Sloan senior lecturer, and Didier Bonnet, affiliate professor at IMD Business School, discuss how digital transformations become increasingly complex. Whereas 85% of companies underwent a transformation in the past decade[11], nearly 74% failed to improve business performance.[12] And approximately half of companies that undertake transformations fail.[13] It's of little surprise then that 93% of companies consider digital transformation the most important training topic to invest in.[14]

CHANGE: WHAT'S IN A NAME?

Business transformations are often built around structural elements – new processes, facilities, policies, and – of course – technologies. However, author and CEO Timothy R. Clark writes that *"Agile's core technology isn't technical or mechanical. It's cultural."*[15]

Change invites hidden fears, anxieties, and insecurities into your company. The author Tony Schwartz sees change as something *"[...] where resistance tends to arise – cognitively in the form of fixed beliefs, deeply held assumptions and blind spots; and emotionally, in the form of the fear and insecurity that change engenders. All of this rolls up into our mindset, which reflects how we see the world, what we believe, and how that makes us feel."*[16] You don't just need to transform your processes and technologies; as a result, you also need to transform your people. This internal shift – what people think and how they feel – must be a cornerstone of your strategy.

INDUSTRY 4.0 TOWARDS 5.0

Historically, industry has evolved in various waves of revolutions. The Fourth Industrial Revolution, the one we are currently witnessing, is more popularly referred to as 'Industry 4.0'. Originating from a German government industrialisation strategy, and publicly introduced in 2011 at the Hannover Fair, this revolution is highlighted by a strong aspirational nature that originally aimed to integrate new and emerging technologies in the manufacturing process to maximise productivity, efficiency, and overall interconnectivity. In contrast to its predecessors, Industry 4.0 is happening on an unprecedented scale and at exponential speed and has now left the confines of manufacturing to include changes in value chains and the industrial ecosystem. Whereas we have not yet fully experienced its disruptive properties and broader impacts, key enabling technologies are already vast and plenty, and ever-more diversely applied, most often in an interconnected manner:

— **The family of Extended Reality (XR)** – Assisted reality, augmented reality, virtual reality, holography, and the Metaverse. XR encompasses technologies that blend the physical and digital worlds to enhance or create immersive experiences.

— **Big Data and Big Data Analytics.** Examining extremely large and complex datasets to uncover hidden patterns and correlations to derive insights, enabling data-driven decision making.

— **Cybersecurity.** Focuses on protecting computer systems, networks, and sensitive data from digital attacks and unauthorised access.

— **Autonomous Robots and Cobots.** Designed to work alongside humans, enhancing productivity and safety by automating repetitive or dangerous tasks.

— **Digital Twins.** Simulates real-world entities in a virtual manner, allowing for analysis, monitoring, and optimisation.

— **Internet of Things.** Networks of interconnected physical devices embedded with sensors and software that empower them to collect and exchange data.

— **Blockchain and Decentralisation principles.** Ensures secure, transparent, and immutable record-keeping without a central authority, promoting trustless transactions.

— **5G and 6G.** Advanced mobile networks, aimed at offering faster speeds, lower latency, and greater capacity. Considered a crucial backbone for other advanced applications, such as IoT, autonomous vehicles, and more.

— **Other waves of new, frontier technologies will continue to emerge as forces of disruption and transformation (e.g., cloud computing).**

People often assume that digital transformation is solely a technical challenge. That's understandable. After all, digital is mentioned first, isn't it? Industry 4.0 is therefore often considered to be a technology-centric movement, with people eyeing automation as a way to increase system efficiency and safety by reducing human involvement. Such an approach, however, might lead to disappointment. The role of people becomes more, not less, important as more powerful technology engulfs society. Developing automation and introducing new technologies without consideration for people, however, is expected to result in new, potentially catastrophic failures.

Recently, Industry 5.0 offers a fresh perspective. Where previous industrial revolutions emphasised the economics aspects of growth, Industry 5.0 recognises the power of industry to achieve societal goals, by making production respect the boundaries of our planet, and placing the wellbeing of employees at the centre of the production process. Considering this, Industry 5.0 consists of 3 core pillars, being **sustainability**, **resilience**, and **human-centrism**. Overall, it aims to blend the creativity of human experts with efficient, accurate, and intelligent machines, illustrating a strong trend of people interacting and collaborating with technology, and suggesting a symbiotic ecosystem of our two main protagonists: the human and the machine. Although it might read like kicking in an open door, George Westerman states that *"Technology produces nothing for a company on its own."* Yet, we seem to have forgotten this. He writes,

> "The real challenge is changing the business using technology. In other words, when [people] think about digital transformation, transformation is tougher and arguably more important than digital. In the face of constantly evolving technologies and fast-moving startups, it can be tempting to think that a strategy focused on keeping up with technical innovation will provide a competitive edge. However, focusing only on digital and not transformation sets you up for failure. You need the leadership capability to innovate – and execute – on the options that technology enables."[17]

While digital technologies are crucial for any digital transformation process, it's still your people who make the place. Humans and machines are combinatorial in this regard and the challenges of work and digital transformation require companies to reflect on and optimise the constantly evolving options of work automation. Silvia Lehnis, head of data, analytics, and AI at UBDS writes,

"As technologists, we are often attracted to logic, structure and systems thinking. Code it in once, and it is done. A rule the system follows
beautifully until you change it. But when we release new systems, new
features, or fully transform organisations, that kind of thinking has limited reach. We rely on people to change their behaviour, to start using
new systems and processes, to start planning differently [...] Humans
are at the core of transformations, yet we do not act rationally or take
to change easily. New systems that are not used, or are not used right,
do not deliver the expected return on investment. Staff spend time
re-training, raising support tickets, asking others for help, or avoiding
new systems, which negate the expected benefits that come with a
digital transformation."[18]

Because digital transformation touches upon the daily life of many stakeholders,
people *"can be either the greatest inhibitors or the greatest enablers of transformation
success"*.[19] In times of change and transformation, employees across the entire chain
of command experience a wide variety of emotions, ranging from positive (e.g. excitement, trust, and curiosity) to negative (e.g. fear, insecurity, and resistance).

SELF-TRANSFORMATION VS. BUSINESS TRANSFORMATION

Business transformations are challenging to cope with for various reasons. First,
unlike self-transformation projects, business transformations are more likely to
be imposed. Secondly, businesses tend to wait too long, so transformations often
happen in crisis mode and in a reactive rather than proactive manner. This doesn't
really create an attractive environment to work in. Third, if the urgency is considerable, there is only a short-term, often superficial, focus. Fourth, change efforts
lose momentum. There is a tendency to consider the implementation of a specific
technological tool the endpoint of the journey, while this is most often the actual
starting point of true operational change – where tasks are being redefined; where
people now – indeed – have to work together with or alongside a technological
partner; where the story of change is now actively happening and reshaping (part
of) the work environment.

In an already turbulent world, employees require a different work culture – one in
which they can change their thoughts and behaviours. When you are around people who are not willing to change, chances are you will be less inclined to change
yourself. But if you find yourself surrounded by change-supporting colleagues, you
are more likely to support change as well. This is what we call social contagion: the
emotions and behaviours you observe in your surroundings profoundly influence

you.[20] Transformation expert Jim Hemerling hammers just one thing: putting people first. In other words, a **human-centric** approach.

In striving for an agile organisation, leaders will stumble upon various people-related challenges. This is why we wrote this book:

> Digital transformation impacts and involves people from all layers of the company in different and profound ways. We need human-centric digital transformation.

After all, your colleagues define how a place looks, feels, and behaves. They are fundamental. In other words, if you want to be successful in this transformation process, you must change people's **hearts** (*"Why am I doing this job?"*), **heads** (*"How do I look at my job?"*), and **hands** (*"How am I doing my job?"*).[21]

REVAMPING LEADERSHIP MINDSET AND CAPABILITIES

Can you expect your colleagues to be agile when they are swimming in fear? Can you and your colleagues give candid feedback, explore unconventional ideas, and dissent without being ridiculed? Or have these acts of agility already become sources of punished vulnerability (e.g. criticism, embarrassment, discouragement, silencing, shaming, trivialising, bullying, intimidation)? When you notice that colleagues don't ask questions or admit mistakes, don't dare to explore ideas, let alone challenge the status quo, it is time to act. Timothy R. Clark states,

> "If you drop agile tools and processes into a legacy culture that punishes the very acts of vulnerability required to be agile, you will fail."[22]

Alongside an organisation-wide struggle, employees also struggle to change behaviours and mindset. George Westerman and Didier Bonnet identified two capabilities that can help companies in becoming digital masters.
— **Digital capability** empowers organisations to change existing processes and products and improve or create new business models.
— **Leadership capability** is envisioning and driving organisational change in systematic and profitable ways.

There is a growing fear that the gap between the digital masters and their competitors is increasing. George Westerman and Didier Bonnet surveyed 1300 executives in more than 750 global organisations in 2018 and concluded that,

> "Only 38% of them told us that their companies had the digital capability needed to become digital masters, and only 35% said they had the leadership capability to do so."

The New Leadership Playbook for the Digital Age – the result of a global executive study that set out to explore how the changing nature of competition, work, and society is influencing the future of leadership – states that,

> "[Leaders] around the world are out of touch with what it will take to win, and to lead, in the digital economy. Digitalisation, upstart competitors, the need for breakneck speed and agility, and an increasingly diverse and demanding workforce require more from leaders than what most can offer [...] The need for change is urgent, and time is running out for leaders who are holding on to old ways of working and leading [i.e. command and control], [...] that may have worked in the past but now stymie the talents of employees throughout their organisations."[23]

The results of a global survey of 1500 executives, conducted by Harvard leadership professor and change expert Linda A. Hill and colleagues, concluded,

> "More troubling, though, was that fewer than half of our participants think that they or other senior executives at their organisations have the right mindset and skills to lead in the digital era. Those closer to the nuts and bolts of digital functions – the chief technology officers, chief information officers, and chief digital officers – feel more confident about their own capabilities but less so about those of their colleagues in other functional areas."[24]

Hill and colleagues supplemented this with,

> "Leaders must be comfortable moving forward with ambiguous and incomplete information [...] and must learn to see their decisions and actions as working hypotheses that they can only validate by collecting feedback [...] as expeditiously as possible. Leaders will be blindsided if they rely only on their past experience or expertise when making decisions [...] and need to adopt holistic thinking and stay open to the

unexpected. [As such,] they must learn to stretch their 'own imagination and creativity' to envision what the future could be for the company and its stakeholders, anticipate possible scenarios, and prepare to adapt to whatever unfolds."[25]

Does this mean that everything is terrible these days? Of course not. Some companies already embrace new ways of working and leading. Their employees aim for transparency, authenticity, collaboration, and empathy. Leaders understand the strength of purpose and connectivity, and value curiosity, trust, and digital savviness; colleagues are customer and employee obsessed. But they also admit that no one is competent across the complete set of required skills, attributes, and capabilities. In this new way of working,

> "Teams don't simply rearrange the relationships between leaders and followers; they unleash the talents of every person to cultivate communities of leaders [across the divides]. [...] The primary leadership challenge in the digital economy, however, isn't simply to adopt a group of [digital technologies and] behaviours [...]. The deeper challenge is to develop a new mindset that anchors, informs, and advances these [digital technologies] and behaviours."[26]

Building on this, one might want to consider the example of W.L. Gore (famous for its waterproof GORE-TEX fabric): as a result of its cultural principles that revolve around the notion of freedom, the company is considered a nimble organisation, *"a company filled with people who feel it is their job to lead and to step forward, propose new ideas, and translate them into action"*.[27] Companies need increased awareness to ask better questions; the habit of constantly scanning outside of the industry; a hunger to search growth models; and an ambition to follow through on new pathways. Rather than taking pride in creating the old there must also be accountability for transforming the old and, ultimately, achieving strategic congruence between the two. However, to get there, to a state where everyone feels they can be a leader, a mindset shift is also required.

THE 4-V DIGITAL TRANSFORMATION LEADERSHIP MODEL

To help you reimagine what it means to lead in the digital economy, the 4-V digital transformation leadership model was developed at Vlerick Business School by Professor Stijn Viaene.[28] It outlines four digital transformation practice areas and associated leadership activities. These areas – Vigilant, Voyager, Visionary, and Vested – need to be cultivated and balanced for organisations to develop and maintain digital-age organisational agility. The model provides guidance by defining the progress that digitally transforming organisations and their leaders need to strive for in each practice area. The model was developed using extensive and longitudinal action-design research methodology.

To make your digital transformation successful, the model states that you require a combination of these leadership activities to cope with the aspects of novelty, ambiguity, and uncertainty.[29] The framework of the model will be used in this book to highlight and discuss a selection of useful skills and insights that these leaders can build on and hone to diagnose, envision, and mobilise transformational change.

THE 4-V MODEL

As an organisation-wide phenomenon, digital transformation inevitably spans multiple contexts within an organisation. The model identifies four primary contexts, or practice areas, for studying digital leaders within organisations undergoing such transformation. Each context is defined by two key dimensions of organisational tension – transformational purpose and scope – that influence the digital transformation mandate of leaders, as well as the criteria for judging its success.

The first dimension, transformational purpose, involves a tension – exploiting versus exploring. Transformational purpose qualifies whether progress with the introduction of a new way of working by digital transformation leaders is sought in the space of the organisation's exploration agility or exploitation agility. The ability to effectively transform the organisation's exploitation and exploration is critical to organisational agility and long-term success. The second dimension, transformational scope, involves another tension – thinking versus action. Transformational scope qualifies the latitude afforded to digital transformation leaders in seeking to push the edge of the thinkable or the actionable with the introduction of new, digital-savvy, agile ways of working. While it is important to think big and demonstrate audacity of thought, it is equally important to balance this with pragmatism to ensure digital transformations are implementable and can lead to real, tangible change.

Plotting these two dimensions of organisational tension on a pair of non-quantitative axes produces four distinct quadrants, each corresponding to a context in which the notion of effectiveness or success is different.

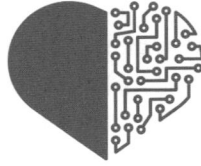

The **Vigilant leader** is always alert, curious and attentive to techno-logical advances, changing customer behaviour, competitor moves, market disruptions and new entrants, and – as such – is ready to respond when necessary. They operate well in ambiguous and tur-bulent situations. They are sharp-eyed, fascinated, and circumspect. Their watchful demeanour helps the company act quickly at the earliest, most feeble signs of opportunities and threats. The Vig-ilant leader, in sum, enables the company to make sense of what is happening beyond the periphery of the organisation, business model, or industry. As a result, Vigilant leaders decode the turbu-lent environment and make it easier for everyone to see interesting future world scenarios. In short, Vigilant leaders help realise digital transformation by:

— Keeping people **alert** for new digital-age threats and opportuni-ties beyond the boundaries of the organization or sector
— Helping people make sense of what new digital opportunities and threats **could mean** for them
— **Inspiring** people to explore new ways of working powered by dig-ital technologies

The **Voyager leader** is an entrepreneur who connects and teams people up to make ideas tangible. They bundle diversity and creativity to show opportunity at work and, in doing so, turn the abstract into something real. Voyager leaders invent new ways to propel the business forward and make it battle-ready by suiting up with a concrete mode of implementation. To make this succeed, Voyager leaders don't assume that the way things have always been done is the best way to do them. They place a high value on learning and capturing lessons from experimentation. The cycle of learning is pragmatically adopted as an imperative to guarantee rapid and lean iterations between thinking and acting. In short Voyager leaders help realise digital transformation by:

— Bundling together the diversity and creativity of individuals into an entrepreneurial **team**
— Exploring solutions by efficiently progressing through a steadily paced process of **build-measure-learn** feedback cycles
— Using empirical **feedback** from customers and other stakeholders to drive forward the exploration of solutions

The **Visionary leader** welcomes the Vigilant leader's vigilance as inspiration to turn the "what is" into an image of "what could be", and then paint a picture of the company's "to be" state (i.e. "what should be") from a strategic point of view. They combine weak signals, ideas, and experiments with great imagination and foresight into a winning business aspiration. Great visionaries tell engaging and energising stories of the organisation in the digital age. Rather than focusing on the financial and performance narratives – which often feel empty for most employees – the Visionary leader aligns purpose, principles, and profit. Through their stories, Visionary leaders nurture a shared focus and commitment to the company, advocating the adoption of digital technologies to attain a competitive edge and capture business value at scale. They choose to compete with an ecosystem lens as they understand the innovation potential associated with digital partnerships, collaborations, and overall co-creation. In short, Visionary leaders help realise digital transformation by:

— Telling a purposeful and inspirational transformative story of **competitive** advantage, advocating the empowering use of digital technologies
— Boldly rethinking the organization's core **capabilities** and operating model for achieving digital-age customer-centricity
— Envisioning success by combining the organization's critical digital assets and those of ecosystem **partners**

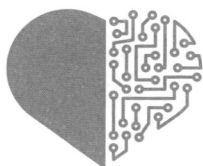

The **Vested leader** enables the company to move beyond experiments and visionary tales and, steadily and progressively, turn these into a productive, yet flexible, organisational machinery. They put the entire organisation on a roadmap to successful digital transformation by creating organisational mechanisms to swiftly mobilise skills and resources from a variety of disciplines and bring them together to plan, develop, improve, and redevelop organisational capabilities. Vested leaders of the digital era are champions of crowdsourcing. They deploy a different concept of what a company is by focusing much more on self-learning and fostering networks. In doing so, they take a clear step back from outdated learning practices, the deeply ingrained command-and-control organisations, and both design and promote an agile architecture that builds on employee empowerment. Briefly, Vested leaders help realise digital transformation by:

— Keeping the **entire** organization, rather than individual elements, on a roadmap to successful digital transformation
— **Mobilizing** the right skills and resources for timely exploration and exploitation
— Facilitating the **learning** and adoption of digital technologies, work and organizing practices at scale for an empowered workforce

TRANSFORMATIONAL PURPOSE

	TRANSFORMATIONAL SCOPE		
	Vigilant leadership context	**Visionary** leadership context	Pushing the edge of the thinkable
	Voyager leadership context	**Vested** leadership context	Pushing the edge of the actionable
	Agility in exploration capacity	Agility in exploitation capacity	

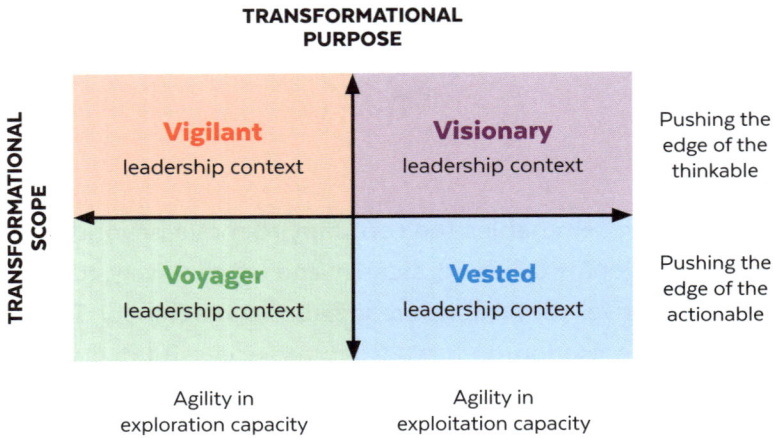

Figure. The digital transformation leadership profiles.

In successful organisations, people at all levels within the organisation can take on these different leadership roles. One person might even take up multiple roles. Considering this, each leadership type represents a social network or coalition of individuals spread across the organisation. It is, however, important that people take up such a role because it connects to their strengths and because these activities give them energy. If you're curious about this, we have included a short Energy Scan at the end of each chapter for you. We suggest you fill it out to see which role is more likely to energise you.

The leadership types, however, do not exist in isolation. Instead, they are intrinsically connected and interdependent. The real trick to digital transformation is to connect the leadership types virtuously.

Adapted from: Viaene, S. (2020), "Digital Transformation Know-How", Acco.
Viaene, S., & Sen, K. (2024). Leading digital transformation for organisational agility: a substantive practices-based framework. Working paper 20241212. Vlerick Business School

CONCLUSION

In this book, we have embedded various reflections, exercises, tips and tricks, and potential solutions. Do not jump headfirst into all these tips and tricks, as you might feel overwhelmed. Digital transformation is unlikely to happen overnight. Minor but deliberate tweaks make a massive difference if you allow processes to happen steadily, step-by-step. If you try to do a 180 degree turn instantly, you will invite frustration. Instead, make small changes day by day, week by week and let them compound. If you change 1% every day, or even just 0.01%, that is fine. Habits expert James Clear asserts that real change comes from the compound effect of hundreds of miniscule decisions, which he calls atomic habits. Push that snowball and get things rolling.

Digitally transforming your company is not just about embedding the newest and most fancy technologies out there; neither is it about just streamlining internal processes and policies. The result of any transformation depends on your employees' willingness, how well you succeed in transforming your colleagues' mindsets, and discovering a fundamentally new relationship between people and technology. Through this book, we want to help you and your colleagues build the confidence to get involved in digital transformation, engage with change, and become true protagonists.

Remember, however, to truly achieve digital transformation, an organization must continuously make progress across all four dimensions of the 4V framework — meaning each V-type needs to be addressed in its own right.

So, let's get going!

CHAPTER 1

Vigilant Leadership

TRANSFORMATIONAL PURPOSE

TRANSFORMATIONAL SCOPE

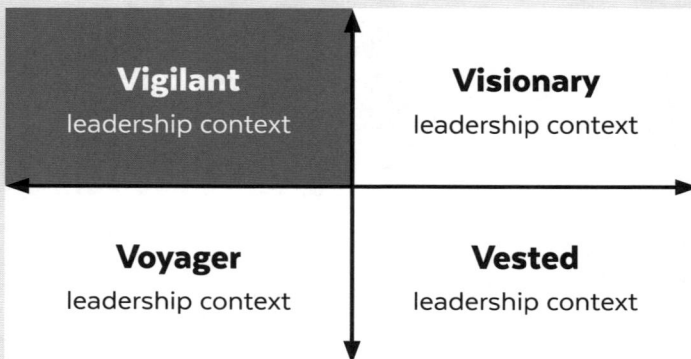

Vigilant leadership context	**Visionary** leadership context
Voyager leadership context	**Vested** leadership context

Pushing the edge of the thinkable

Pushing the edge of the actionable

Agility in exploration capacity

Agility in exploitation capacity

VIGILANT LEADERS

In the context of fostering and striving for a successful digital transformation journey, the Vigilant leader focuses on a core set of jobs to be done.

Vigilant leaders...
— Keep people **alert** for new digital-age threats and opportunities beyond the boundaries of the organization or sector
— Help people **make sense** of what new digital opportunities and threats could mean for them
— **Inspire** people to explore new ways of working powered by digital technologies

To this end, Vigilant leaders put various skills to good use in order to guide colleagues and the company through a *human-centric* process.

In the following chapter, we will introduce you to several digital transformation protagonists and how they build on these skills to foster a meaningful journey for themselves, colleagues and other stakeholders, and the organisation at large.

— Hadrien at GalleryX and how he supported and promoted colleagues' **curiosity** levels to explore for new opportunities;
— The Foresight Team at Fintrix and how their awareness of potential **biases** helped them in boosting the company's vigilance;
— Larry at Digitize Consulting and how his own awareness of **time and information overload** resulted in an organisation where information became digestible and usable once more.

STIMULATING CURIOSITY

HOW CURIOSITY DRIVES ART AND TECH

Introduction

During his studies, Hadrien was thrilled to land an internship at a renowned art gallery – GalleryX – , a perfect blend of his passions for art and business. As he immersed himself in the intricate workings of the art industry, Hadrien became increasingly excited about many still untapped opportunities that could elevate the gallery's profile. His innovative spirit and strong joie de vivre did not go unnoticed for long, leading to a job offer to spearhead GalleryX's innovation strategy.

Hadrien's enthusiasm for digital advancements was boundless; he actively sought the next big thing to propel the gallery forward. Hadrien understood that clients sometimes lack the time or chance to visit in person and many now desire enriched pre- and post-visit experiences. The visitor is key to Hadrien, and he recognises that a new, digital-savvy generation is emerging, demanding fresh and unique art experiences.

His vision includes integrating cutting-edge technologies into the gallery's operations to position it as a top international player. He proposed leveraging technology not just as a tool but as a transformative experience. Technology can act as a useful conversation starter, a marketing tool, and an entirely new way of experiencing art. Digital artworks and artainment are one of his sources for inspiration: augmented reality (AR) would allow paintings to come alive on smartphones, interactive touch walls could engage visitors in dynamic ways, and digital animations could breathe life into deceased artists, making them seem to stroll through the gallery's corridors. For Hadrien, technology is a gateway to redefine how art can be experienced and shared.

The problem at GalleryX

Hadrien faced significant resistance from colleagues who were sceptical or indifferent to adopting such innovations. Many expressed concerns about potential disruptions to established routines and some feared that the gallery's esteemed reputation for high-quality face-to-face interactions would take a hit as well. Others felt overwhelmed by their current workload and dismissed Hadrien's enthusiasm as impractical. This reluctance to embrace new ideas stifled the gallery's potential for growth and innovation. Furthermore, the gallery risked alienating an entirely new generation of art enthusiasts. A critical gap has appeared in the gallery's current approach: without exploring and embracing technological possibilities, they are likely to fall behind.

The art gallery operates in an era of digital turbulence and must seek to understand the changing customer dynamics in order to bridge the client-gallery gap in novel ways. Unfortunately, the majority of ideas to innovate don't seem to gain internal acceptance. Questions arise as to why some organisations appear to be more innovative and proactive than their competitors, and why others are stuck in the status quo. *Curiosity* is a promising path to help us in understanding this.

CURIOSITY: WHAT DOES IT MEAN?

While trying to figure out why some customer service agents stayed in their jobs longer than others, economist Michael Housman stumbled upon an unusual insight. Housman began with the thesis that employees with a history of job-hopping would leave sooner. The data, however, did not support this thesis. The research team also found out that they had collected an entire data set about which internet browser employees used to log in to apply for the job. The researchers did not expect to find any correlation at all – assuming that a browser preference was simply a matter of personal taste – but the results were astounding. Employees who used Mozilla Firefox or Chrome to browse the internet were 15% more likely to stay in their jobs than those who used Internet Explorer or Safari. To ensure that this was not just a coincidence in the data, Housman and his team ran additional analyses for absence, performance, and customer happiness.[30]

"Around here, we don't look backwards for very long. We keep moving forward, opening up new doors and doing new things, because we're curious… and curiosity keeps leading us down new paths"

The Walt Disney Company

Employees who used Firefox or Chrome were not necessarily more tech savvy or knowledgeable about computers. What made the difference was *how* they obtained the browser. If you buy a new PC or laptop, the default browser built into Windows is Microsoft Edge; for MacBook users, Safari is preinstalled. Most people settle for the default, by default.

To get Firefox or Chrome – or any other type of browser, for that matter –, people must refuse to accept the default option and take the initiative instead. Michael Housman and Adam Grant, professor at the Wharton School of the University of Pennsylvania, consider this small act to be "a window into what you do at work".[31] The service agents who accepted the default browsers approached their jobs quite similarly: they followed standard operating procedures for handling customer complaints and stayed on script during sales calls. Firefox and Chrome users, on the other hand, were more likely to seek out novel ways to address customer concerns. The latter group had a higher retention rate because they moulded the jobs according to their preferences.

CURIOSITY AND THE CURSE OF COMFORT

The starting point of passing on the default is **curiosity**. But what is curiosity exactly? In *Atlas of the Heart*, University of Houston professor Brené Brown writes the following,

> "Curiosity is recognising a gap in our knowledge about something that interests us, and becoming emotionally and cognitively invested in closing that gap through exploration and learning".[32]

Curiosity implies a desire for new experiences and an interest in situations from which you may learn. It requires both awareness and daring to be vulnerable. Why is this? Because of its specific nature, curiosity requires us "to surrender to uncertainty. We have to ask questions, admit to not knowing, risk being told that we shouldn't be asking, and, sometimes, make discoveries that lead to discomfort."[33] The other side of the coin means that too much curiosity – and too much vulnerability – might potentially lead to getting hurt.

People sometimes settle for the opposite of curiosity: **certainty**. In organisations where certainty reigns, cultures of protectiveness can be seen. Certainty invites **the curse of comfort**, however. We default to what is familiar and easily accessible, and we prefer to stick to what we know rather than what we can learn. Curious individuals, on the other hand, wonder why a default option exists in the first place and are more likely to show higher levels of perseverance, grit, engagement, and performance. People are even more likely to work on goals that are meaningful to them. Companies, leaders, and employees all benefit from a curious mindset. Jony Ive, the former chief design officer at Apple wrote the following about Steve Jobs:

> "He was without doubt the most inquisitive human I have ever met. His insatiable curiosity was not limited or distracted by his knowledge or expertise, nor was it casual or passive. It was ferocious, energetic, and restless. His curiosity was practiced with intention and rigor. In larger groups our conversations gravitate towards the tangible the measurable. It is more comfortable, far easier and more socially acceptable talking about what is known. Being curious and exploring tentative ideas were far more important to Steve than being socially acceptable. Our curiosity begs that we learn. And for Steve, wanting to learn was far more important than wanting to be right."[34]

Curiosity is often sparked by complex environments that are fraught with uncertainties and difficulties. Consider GalleryX and the changing client-gallery relationship. New environments create turbulence which might elicit feelings of uncertainty. Some people try to resist this or even enter a state of inertia; others are likely to engage with a curious mindset, thinking: "This is an opportunity to explore ideas, develop solutions, and gain fresh and unique insights!"

WHY DOES CURIOSITY MATTER?

Parents know that children are incessant questioners. Consider the never-ending stream of *why's* that makes your kids so delightful and, well, sometimes less delightful. *Why* do they have so many questions?

Kids are on a mission of discovery; everything is new, uncertain, and fascinating. They want to know how things work and are tenacious in their pursuit of answers. Throughout childhood, our brains gradually make sense of all information and form thought patterns on which to rely. But these patterns also keep us from asking *why*, which is often necessary. As we grow older, we don't ask as many questions anymore. That's a pity, of course. Yet, asking *why* helps us to consider a broader range of solutions to the problems at hand.

REFLECTIVE EXERCISE

How often do you ask "why?" in a meeting, in a conversation with friends and family. How frequently do you ask a "childish" never-ending stream of why's? We invite you to ask why something is the way it is proposed or discussed in a meeting. Keep on asking "why?" until you get a satisfying answer.

— Why should we use a certain technology to better serve our "art gallery" customers?

— Why do our customers need a different experience?

— Why would this experience help to create a different relationship with the customers?

— Why...?

Alternatively, you can place a question mark behind your original hypotheses and answers.

Sixty percent of employees struggle to satisfy their curiosity due to daily routines and a too-rigid organisational structure.[35] People are often in performance mode, trying to demonstrate their knowledge, rather than in learning mode. And while employers may value employees' curiosity and creative ideas, the focus of companies on efficiency and risk avoidance unfortunately suffocates learning, curious minds, and creative talents. Companies and leaders must seize the capital that is embedded in employees' minds. After all, it is free. The role of Vigilant leaders to ignite a learning appetite and a healthy dose of curiosity should thus not be underestimated. Curiosity matters in companies for a variety of reasons:

— **Fewer mistakes.** Employees who can nurture their curiosity in a supportive environment dare to seek out and consider alternatives. Overall, they can show more openness and are better equipped to consider external ideas. You are less likely to make errors as you won't just look for information that supports your ideas nor will you neglect contradictory information.

— **Creativity.** Curiosity links to inquisitiveness – which refers to having or showing an interest in learning things. Therefore, it enables you to approach difficult situations more creatively: you set aside preconceived notions, gain new insights into complex issues, and reframe and comprehend problems better.

— **Fewer conflicts.** You can put yourself in the shoes of others and see things from their point of view, helping you to communicate and share information more openly. Teamwork runs more smoothly and effectively as a result.

— **Disruption tolerance.** As transformational change is a product of turbulence and chances are high that (most) jobs will be disrupted at some point, curiosity will stimulate to work with rather than against these changes. For example, at GalleryX, curious employees might be more willing to explore how certain technologies can be integrated into their work, rather than clinging to traditional practices.

— **Augments learning.** When curiosity is nurtured, employees are more likely to approach training and development opportunities with more enthusiasm and openness. Such a curious mindset makes learning more effective and people might be more willing to experiment with their newly acquired knowledge.

DIGGING DEEPER INTO CURIOSITY

In his groundbreaking article "The Psychology of Curiosity"[36], professor of economics and psychology George Loewenstein introduced the *information gap theory*: curiosity is the feeling of deprivation we experience when we identify a gap in our knowledge. When a curious person discovers something fascinating, they want to know how it works.

UNDER-CHALLENGED

As we age, we gradually grow *competent* in some areas. We become skilled through repeated practice and experience, and reach a point where we can seemingly operate certain tasks on autopilot. This reinforces rigid behaviour and fixed thinking, which might lead to disengagement, boredom, and cognitive stagnation. You have probably been there before: which tasks, at work or at home, can you complete with your eyes closed? There is no longer any challenge to the task. To battle this feeling of being *under-challenged*, it might be interesting to look at routine tasks, rigid behaviour, and firm assumptions with a different mindset.

Consider the **beginner's mind.** Buddhists practise *Shoshin* – walking through life without any expectations and unobstructed by prejudices. The concept of Shoshin was introduced in *Zen Mind, Beginner's Mind*[37], a book by Shunryū Suzuki, and was further popularised by Jon Kabat-Zinn, the founding father of mindfulness. You start your morning with fresh eyes. There are zero immediate opinions and responses at the ready; there is no upfront knowledge. You consider yourself a blank page. Considering this, curiosity becomes more than just a desire to learn something new.

The beginner's mind is present in all living beings: consider a baby's face turning sour when tasting a lemon for the first time or your cat's initial trepidation dipping a paw in snow. The older you get, the less likely you are to experience this sensation and the more your experiences are filtered by what you already know. Adults gradually enter a sleeping mode and, sometimes, we might need a mental nudge to reactivate and awaken.

Suzuki wrote that the mind of a beginner has plenty of possibilities, while the mind of an expert has few. The expert frequently engages in expressions of supreme confidence. Philosopher and economist Erik Angner writes that, unfortunately, overconfidence "afflicts most of us much of the time [...]. Sadly, being an expert in one domain does not protect against overconfidence."[38] In fact, overconfidence is considered *the mother of all biases*.[39] In a famous study of clinical psychologists and psychology students, participants gradually received more information about a case. Participants' confidence grew, but the quality of their judgment did not. The "experts" with a PhD didn't do better, either. The experienced mind often only sees the path that has already been walked, while the beginner's mind considers what's new and unexpected. But, how can you experience that mental nudge?

OVER-CHALLENGED

Alongside being under-challenged, you can also experience the exact opposite: being *overly challenged*. You have probably juggled many different "complexities" simultaneously – combining a new job and a new relationship, perhaps while relocating, and more. Such balancing acts impair your sensitivity to context, causing your capacity for awareness to dwindle. If you want to live a healthy curious life, however, Susan David advises people to strike a balance between under-challenge and over-challenge, where comfort exists alongside excitement and stress. People differ in their needs to strike that balance. Whereas some tasks and challenges will have you biting your nails, other tasks might feel more like a joyful walk in the park. Meanwhile, colleagues could experience the exact opposite.

MASTERING "THE CURIOUS WAY"

Vigilant leaders are guardians who understand how a solid sense of curiosity is triggered; that colleagues experience triggers differently – curiosity is a very personal activity, after all –; that colleagues who are overexposed to triggers must cool down; and that a solid learning culture must be established to provide fertile ground for curiosity to flourish. Thus far, only 10% of companies have managed to create such a learning culture, with only 20% of employees demonstrating effective learning behaviours.[40]

BALANCING THE CURIOSITY ZONES

While curiosity cannot be taught, it can be stimulated and fostered. As people's curiosity levels vary, Vigilant leaders must first understand the situation in which colleagues find themselves, before trying to channel curiosity. In light of this, psychologist Daniel Berlyne argued that humans seek the sweet spot between two profoundly unpleasant states:[41]

— Understimulation: situations that lack (sufficient) novelty and complexity
— Overstimulation: situations where (too much) complexity and uncertainty are present

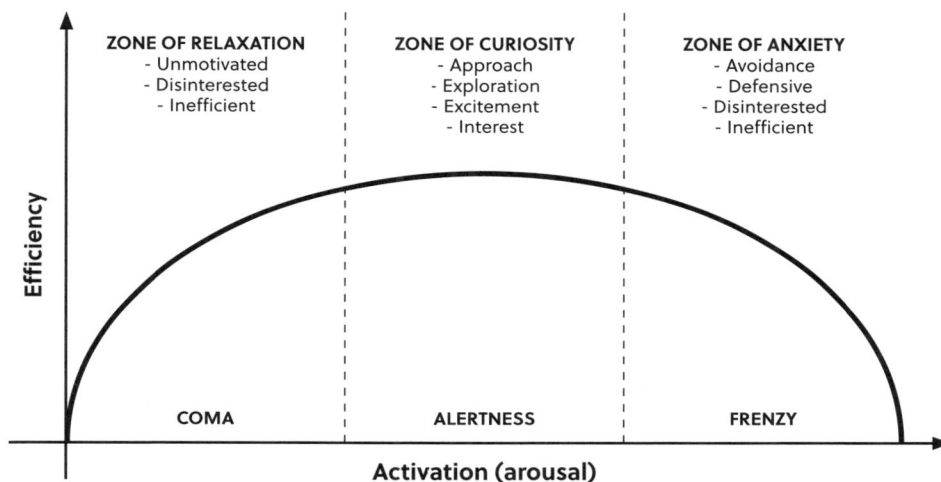

Adapted from: Day, H.I. (1982). Curiosity and the interested explorer. *Performance & Instruction*, 21(4), 19-22.

Three "Zones" of curiosity in which people fit are highlighted: the Zones of Relaxation, Curiosity, and Anxiety.

— *Zone of Relaxation* and excess understimulation: When you sense that your colleagues are in this zone, introduce an intriguing new challenge.

While some people might dread feeling unproductive and inefficient, most productivity methods do advise people to take breaks to maintain their productivity and efficiency in the long run. This helps your brain to get a breather, allows the body to loosen up, and allows reconsideration of the bigger picture. It's important that people can be understimulated every now and then. From there, curiosity can be stimulated again. Let's go back to GalleryX. As a Vigilant leader, you can stimulate colleagues in this Zone of Relaxation to investigate the possibilities of augmented reality in improving the gallery's customer service. Think up front about which aspects of the project might be interesting to prevent people from entering a bored state. For some it might be thinking about completely new opportunities, others might be passionate about solving customer problems with the help of new technology, and so on.

— *Zone of Curiosity* and acceptable stimulation: You are aware when your colleagues are adequately stimulated and will not benefit from additional stimuli.

Colleagues who are already in the Zone of Curiosity do not need an extra push. Still, they can help brainstorm or give feedback on some new ideas. For instance, how can GalleryX make artists more present in the art gallery by using augmented reality and holograms?

— *Zone of Anxiety* and excess overstimulation: When colleagues are rendered immobile, initiating a "cooling-off" period is recommended.

It might happen that people end up being overstimulated at some point because they are engaged in too many tasks at the same time. This isn't necessarily a bad thing, but people cannot remain in the Zone of Anxiety for too long. If this is the case, they are rendered incapacitated and unable to be curious. Here, it is recommended that Vigilant leaders avoid further stimulation and, instead, have people temporarily engage in routine-based and cognitively less demanding activities. It is not advisable to add further stimulation and increase their workload. If people remain too long in this Zone, they will experience frenzy and risk lower levels of happiness, lower productivity, and potentially experience (symptoms of) burnout. The Vigilant leader enters the picture as a result of the ongoing interaction between colleagues and the stimuli in their (professional) environment. They shape the environment accordingly to guarantee relaxation and a healthy state of activation or arousal.

DID YOU KNOW?

In the early 19th century, English romantic poet John Keats coined the term *negative capability*. He used this term to describe famous writers such as William Shakespeare who were able to work within times Fear, Uncertainty and Doubt (FUD). According to Keats, these writers had the ability to accept that they did not have an immediate answer at the ready and instead remained willing, curious, and focused, even when a project was far from the desired end goal.

In the modern context of digital transformation, negative capability can be thought of as an ability to be comfortable with change; to entertain the uncertainty that change invites along the way; and not become anxious by its presence. This ability prevents you from racing prematurely to a more certain, but also suboptimal, conclusion. Those colleagues who master negative capability can facilitate the exploration of new terrain and the discovery of a neighboring possible opportunity because they suspend their judgment and remain open about many possible outcomes. They do not become fixed early on to just one version of success.

THE FIVE-DIMENSIONAL MODEL OF CURIOSITY

People, however, differ and it is no different regarding curiosity. It is worthwhile to try and understand the ways in which people are curious and to what extent they are properly aligned with the demands surrounding them. *How* and *why* is someone curious might be better questions than merely asking whether someone is curious. This simple yes-or-no question discredits the complexity of curiosity and the individual behind it. Research has outlined "the five-dimensional model of curiosity"[42]. Below, we have broken down 25 statements about curiosity into five sections. Rank the statements in each block based on how well they describe you and relate to you – give a five to the statement that describes you best and a 1 to the statement that describes you least.

EXERCISE: WHAT IS YOUR PREFERRED CURIOSITY MINDSET?

1	Thinking about solutions to difficult conceptual problems can keep me awake at night	■				
	I view challenging situations as an opportunity to grow and learn		■			
	I like to learn about the habits of others			■		
	A small doubt doesn't stop me from seeking out new experiences				■	
	The anxiety of doing something new makes me feel excited and alive					■
2	I can spend hours on a single problem because I just can't rest without knowing the answer	■				
	I am always looking for experiences that challenge how I think about myself and the world		■			
	I like finding out why people behave the way they do			■		
	I easily handle the stress that comes from entering certain situations				■	
	Risk taking is exciting to me					■
3	I feel frustrated if I can't figure out the solution to a problem, so I work even harder to solve it	■				
	I seek out situations where it is likely that I will have to think in depth about something		■			
	When other people are having a conversation, I like to find out what it's about			■		
	I don't find it hard to explore new places when I lack confidence in my abilities				■	
	When I have free time, I want to do things that are a little scary					■
4	I work releentlessly at problems that I feel must be solved	■				
	I enjoy learning about subjects that are unfamiliar to me		■			
	When around other people, I like listening to their conversations			■		
	I can function well, even if I am unsure about wether a new experience is safe				■	
	Creating an adventure as I go is much more appealing than a planned adventure					■
5	It frustrates me to not have all the information I need	■				
	I find it fascinating to learn new information		■			
	When people quarrel, I like to know what's going on			■		
	I have no difficulties in concentrating when there is a possibility that I will be surprised				■	
	I love friends who are excitingly unpredictable					■

Adapted from: Kashdan, T., Disabato, D.J., Goodman, F.R., and Naughton, C. (2018), "The Five Dimensions of Curiosity", *Harvard Business Review*.

In which dimensions do you score highest? Did any stand out, or did you score evenly across the board? What does each dimension refer to?

— **Deprivation sensitivity.** You are intellectually engaged to reflect on abstract and complex ideas and solve problems. You experience a certain level of discomfort and want to reduce this feeling of tension. To this end, you seek to eliminate the knowledge gaps by looking for the necessary information.

— **Joyous exploration.** You are open to and triggered by new experiences, knowledge and information; you are likely to engage in initiatives for personal growth and show tenacity in your pursuit; and you find pleasure, meaning, and motivation from this. Unlike deprivation sensitivity, where you might want to avoid a certain (negative) feeling, joyous exploration emerges out of appetite.

— **Social curiosity.** You want to know what other people think and do, and you are easily triggered by talking and listening to others. You are curious about their thoughts and actions. To satisfy your curiosity, you engage in either overt actions (such as observing and asking questions) or covert actions (such as listening in to conversations).

— **Stress tolerance.** You show you are willing to accept the uncertainty and confusion that comes with new complex phenomena. Some people enjoy things that others find stressful. Those colleagues who score high on this, might look forward to or have little problems with unexpected events that are likely to accompany change.

— **Thrill seeking.** You feel a need to hunt for experiences that are novel, intense, and complex. Physical, social, and financial risks trigger you and, in this case, you deliberately increase your anxiety level.

"Free curiosity has greater power to stimulate learning than rigorous coercion. Nevertheless, the free ranging flux of curiosity is channelled by disciple"
St. Augustine of Hippo

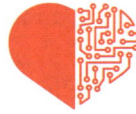

EXERCISE

Which curiosity mindset do you think fits your colleagues when it comes to digital transformation? How do you notice this? Write down your thoughts and impressions.

Now put the words into action. Involve your colleagues to have a conversation about curiosity: you can have your colleague(s) complete the entire survey above or you can choose one or two statements per mindset and have your colleague(s) decide which type of curiosity triggers them most or least. Were you correct in your assumptions?

By knowing people's (preferred) curiosity mindset and the triggers and stimuli they prefer, you can consider the best mindset for specific tasks and projects. If a colleague expresses that they are not easily triggered by social curiosity, you might reconsider sending them to a large conference, for example.

Nurturing curiosity to evolve the company, colleagues, and yourself

Like many other skills and activities, the success of curiosity often depends on how disciplined and engaged we are in embedding it into our daily routine. Below is a comprehensive list of tips and tricks that you can use to nurture curiosity adequately – in the organisation, colleagues, or yourself.

STIMULATE THE ORGANISATION

— *Organise* **"why?", "what if?", and "how could we?" days.** *Form teams of diverse backgrounds (such as levels of expertise, departments, etc.) to explore potential solutions for specific challenges.*

— *Encourage colleagues to broaden their horizons and give them opportunities to take up other roles within the organisation. Provide them with sufficient time and resources to do so. It might be a good idea to consider* **job crafting** *and allow colleagues to co-design their work. An added benefit is that these colleagues are more likely to feel a sense of purpose and meaning in their jobs. Both curiosity and interest are important for our meaning-making.*

- **Demystify learning.** *We often consider learning to only happen in more formal settings. Consequently, we might be unaware of unofficial learning acts and opportunities. Learning also happens outside of books and (online) classes.*
- **Encourage connectivity and engagement.** *Make open-knowledge systems that allow employees to share and access learning resources. This helps to scale learning across teams and departments. Do so in a connected manner where you create opportunities for colleagues to learn from one another.*

STIMULATE THE BEHAVIOUR OF PEOPLE
- *Stimulate a "curiosity mindset" and a learning orientation by **communicating the value of learning.** Pay attention to more than just the endgame and overall performance of employees; consider the entire learning process. Ask: "So, what did you learn?"*
- *Instead of saying "Yes, but", try saying **"yes, and"**. This technique, also known as the "plussing" technique, helps you and others to stay curious and expand on ideas. Although we list "curiosity" and "creativity" as company-wide goals, we frequently reject creative ideas. During brainstorming, create an environment of comfort, wellbeing, and psychological safety. Excessive emotions can stifle creativity. For example, when we fear being mocked by colleagues or our boss, we are less willing to contribute.*
- *Dare to ask about colleagues' **interests outside of work** – perhaps they are reading about topics and exploring questions that could benefit the company.*
- **Prime others.** *Deploy useful and intriguing information to get colleagues interested in something. Curiosity cannot exist without someone being interested and it might be worthwhile to create opportunities where colleagues are exposed to ideas and experiences.*

STIMULATE YOURSELF
- *Create a **curiosity journal.** For example, write down one question per day. After a while, you may notice that your questions grow and develop, and maybe your life even starts to change. Good questions could be, "What meaning can I derive from this experience?", "What did I learn from this conversation?", "Why did I act in such a way?", and so on.*
- *Aim for **inquisitiveness.** As we advance up organisational ladders, we are more inclined to believe we have less to learn. Furthermore, we believe we are expected to talk and provide answers. It's important, however, to recognise that you can always learn from others as well. Still, rather than asking questions, we have a strong tendency to impose our ideas on others. As such, it's worthwhile recognising that you may not always know the answer and demonstrate the value of seeking answers. Encourage yourself to go exploring.*

— Develop *positive learning habits.* *Choose activities that fit your personality, lifestyle, and work schedule. Consider a broad range of activities, such as reading one article each morning, reading one book per month, engaging in 15 minutes of reflective (curiosity) journalling each evening, or scheduling one hour of online learning per week*

— Dare to *"wonder"* around. *You combine the acts of wondering and wandering. Leave your chair and take a curious stroll – visit colleagues and inquire about their activities and how they are doing, with genuine curiosity.*

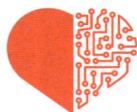

EXERCISE: REFRAMING

Assemble a group of employees to entertain a certain problem with digital transformation your company currently faces.
The challenge? In five minutes, generate 15 different questions that reframe the problem.

Reframing means deliberately shifting the way you define or interpret the problem — challenging the initial assumptions, uncovering hidden angles, or viewing it from entirely different perspectives (e.g. customer-centric, system-level, long-term vs. short-term). The goal is to open up new thinking.

Then, consider which questions helped reveal fresh insights or unexpected pathways for addressing the digital transformation problem.

Together, reflect on why a pathway could be important or meaningful.

The Vigilant leader is the catalyst who activates natural levels of curiosity and builds on them. At GalleryX, Hadrien can embed the learnings and insights from curiosity in various way to stimulate colleagues' – and in the end, the gallery's – levels of curiosity.

STORY CONTINUATION

Hadrien struggled to ignite the curiosity and forward-thinking mindset in his team. The lack of collective curiosity not only hindered GalleryX's growth potential but was also resulting in an alienated customer base. To drive GalleryX forward and keep up with the evolving times, Hadrien had to bridge the gap between the innovative ideas and his colleagues' reluctance. This isn't easy, as Hadrien came to understand. Being a Vigilant leader, he accepted that some internal resistance is normal. Some colleagues are too busy with their core tasks and others are struggling to regain the same level of curiosity that they had when they first entered the industry. It also seems that Hadrien's presence has upset a comfortable status quo within the gallery. Still, fostering a culture of curiosity and openness to technological innovations might be essential if the gallery wants to remain competitive.

Addressing the burning platform at GalleryX

Rather than opting for the classical approach to team meetings, Hadrien decides to arrange a **hands-on workshop**. This includes clear demonstrations that showcase the practical benefits of new technologies like augmented reality. Colleagues can **experience** these innovations firsthand and various interactive sessions allow them to **experiment** with some tools. Hadrien also invited the curator of a recently revamped museum that went all-in on futurism and technology. Their success story was shared on how innovation enhanced both the visitor and employee experience. The curator highlighted how operational efficiency had vastly improved, allowing people to dedicate more time to what really motivates them in their job. This is followed by a "why", "what if", and "how could we"-afternoon, a dedicated safe haven for **brainstorming** to broaden horizons. Hadrien wrote one open-ended **question** on a flipchart: "How can we leverage technology to provide a better customer experience?"

Hadrien noticed that the workshop sparked curiosity with colleagues actively participating. Whenever certain ideas were formulated, Hadrien acted as a true Vigilant leader, striving to keep the discussion as open as possible. Interestingly, while concerns were raised about the impact of technology on existing workflows, not only Hadrien but also others engaged in an open dialogue and entertained potential solutions. Together, three strategic pillars were identified for GalleryX:

— **Enhanced customer experience:** incorporating augmented reality by means of smartphones and glasses, visitors will be provided additional insights into the artwork. One colleague suggested the idea of video-recording artists and having them provide an in-depth discussion of their own art pieces.

— **Enhanced employee experience:** some administrative burdens had been identified, with the gallery now exploring digital cataloging systems to better manage art. Furthermore, people agreed that it might be worthwhile to frequently try to experiment with new art forms and exhibition concepts.

— **Community engagement and building:** many clients are returning customers and it was suggested that people could share their experiences and buy artworks online. An interactive kiosk would capture visitors' feedback. On the one hand, the gallery might benefit from the extra exposure; on the other hand, the gallery might continuously improve its offerings to better match it with clients' preferences.

In line with this, colleagues loved the idea of spending one or more days embedding themselves in the operations of like-minded museums and galleries. They could **explore** different realities, engage in (albeit minor) job crafting, and benefit from both **formal and informal learning opportunities**.

Reflecting on GalleryX's situation, which actions would you take to foster employees' curiosity and stimulate the success of the company's digital transformation journey? How could technology help you drive curiosity?

UNMASKING BIASES AND NOISE

NAVIGATING INNOVATION PITFALLS IN DIGITAL BANKING TRANSFORMATION

Introduction

Fintrix, one of Belgium's leading SMEs in the banking industry embarked on a digital transformation journey with the ambition of **streamlining customers' onboarding processes**. The current process is highly **siloed** as it requires clients to undergo multiple, repetitive steps whenever they seek additional services. Such a **fragmented** approach has not only led to significant customer dissatisfaction but also resulted in the loss of clients to competitors. To address these challenges, Fintrix's leadership established **the "Foresight Team"**, tasked with developing a more comprehensive and client-centric process – one that would, for example, minimise redundant documentation requests. The team's mandate was clear: **monitor** relevant industry trends and **source** innovative ideas that could successfully drive the bank's digital transformation efforts.

The team constantly scans leading technology news channels, frequently attends relevant conferences and technology fairs, and even looks at other key industry players, such as their competitors, to stay up to date with their progress. At first, the Foresight Team eagerly collected information and shared this successfully within the organisation.

The problem at Fintrix

The Foresight Team quickly became entangled in a **web of thought patterns** undermining its effectiveness. While well-intentioned, their non-stop focus on innovation and technology gradually morphed into a case of innovation bias. They **overvalued** novelty without fully considering the bank's unique context or other stakeholders' readiness levels. Furthermore, they didn't always assess whether certain technologies were relevant or practical to implement in their specific situation. The team constantly eyed other banks' technology adoption and considered this a benchmark against which to pit themselves. Soon, the sheer volume of new concepts and technologies started to **overwhelm** employees. Colleagues now struggled with these wild and often radical ideas. Instead of fostering a culture of innovation and curiosity, a culture of dread had appeared, and instead of being inspired, people were now anxious and fearful.

A particularly vivid example can be seen in how the team handled the developments in Generative AI and chatbots. Eager to showcase the potential, the Foresight Team particularly highlighted the technology's potential to transform client interactions by providing more personalised recommendations without needing a human touch. Employees froze mid-activity.

Customers voiced concerns as well. They wondered why Fintrix was so **slow** in adopting technologies while other industry players already appeared to reap significant benefits and offered some impressive new use cases and tools. The bank's leadership now grappled with balancing the need for innovation with the risk of pushing away important stakeholders and employees being hesitant to engage further.

SYSTEMS 1 AND 2

The world teems with information. Vigilant leaders are tasked to scan their company's environment, spot interesting changes and trends, and communicate the most important ones back to the company in a concise, well-formulated manner. In doing so, they can employ the less-is-more or less-is-better effect: humans prefer a small, concise set of information to a larger set of ungrouped information. The path to the less-is-more/better effect is perilous, though. You risk getting tangled in your own thinking patterns and those of the organisation.

In situations like that, we risk succumbing to errors in our judgments and decision making. In *Thinking, Fast and Slow*, Daniel Kahneman distinguished between two ways of thinking – System 1 (our fast lane) and System 2 (our slow lane). Your **fast thinking** (intuitive, automatic, associative, implicit) can be extremely beneficial. It enables you to make quick decisions and complete tasks with ease. For example, imagine that you would have to carefully think and reflect each morning on how to make a good cup of coffee. This would cost you an incredible amount of time and mental bandwidth. Here, you can make good use of your System 1.

WATCH OUT: TRAINED INCAPACITY

When you drive in the fast lane, your mind operates in a default mode. Often accredited to limitation economist Thorstein Veblen, trained incapacity discusses how experts' overconfidence leads them to ignore important contextual information. They do not have the ability and flexibility to override the default mode. As a result, the more familiar you are with a topic, the more likely you are to revert to your default mode and pull a prefabricated solution from memory rather than adapt and respond to the new information in front of you.[43]

However, in many cases, System 1 does not suffice, and System 2 is much needed: your **slow thinking** (deliberate, thoughtful, and rational) often takes precedence. For example, when you try to solve a conflict with a client, you can't just go for a solution that worked with a previous client. In this case, we need to press "pause" and go from System 1 to System 2. In other cases, we can go from System 2 to System 1. A good example here is when you learn to ride a bike: at first, you must consciously *think*, reminding yourself to maintain balance, and to steer left when you want to go left. This is a shaky period in which people frequently hit the ground and scrape their knees and palms. After a while, however, we automate our thinking, and riding a bike happens intuitively. It requires less and less mental effort. There is a downside to System 1 though. People are frequently subjected to errors in their judgments and decision making. This opens the door to two key concepts: *bias* and *noise*.

BIAS AND NOISE

Bias is the average error in our judgments. If you look at many judgments, and the errors in those judgments all follow the same direction, that is bias. **Noise** is the variability of error. If you look at multiple judgments, and the errors in those judgments follow numerous different directions, that is noise. In the case of bias, you might be able to predict the outcome (*in favour* or *against*). In the case of noise, however, this is almost impossible because you are battling a problem of variability.

A good example of noise is found in the judicial system. Judges should be interchangeable. They should give identical sentences in identical cases. When they don't, there is system noise. We find the same dynamics in medicine, with underwriters in insurance, and in many other functions. This illustrates noise on a meta-level.

There can also be noise on the individual level. It happens, for instance, when people are presented with the same problem twice, and they give different answers. Or it happens when people see the same problem under different conditions; the conditions shouldn't matter, but they do. For instance, it's worse to be a defendant on hot days or close to lunch time. Sentences are known to vary with the outside temperature or how hungry a judge is. Therefore, *noise awareness* is crucial.

As illustrated, people in the same profession are likely to make distinct *professional* judgments; and, one person can also evaluate the same case differently at different times. This leads to two conclusions: first, there is noise *between* people and, second, there is noise *within* people. But where does noise come from? Three sources can be identified.

— **Circumstances or "occasion noise".** Consider the following examples: *weather* – how does a rainy day affect your mood? Are you grumpier? *Fatigue* – how do you engage with colleagues after a horrible night's sleep? *Hunger* – have you ever rushed through a meeting and made decisions, without giving them due consideration, because you were hungry? Have you noticed how you tend to take your time for more deliberate thought after a nice lunch? Over time, colleagues might attribute your behaviour to your character instead of realising that certain contextual factors impact your behaviour. To solve this, it's important to engage in a bidirectional exercise to become more aware of circumstantial impact. This makes us more considerate towards one another.

— **General tendencies or "level noise".** This refers to the broad variability in how individuals assess certain situations. What is their baseline? For instance, some judges tend to be more lenient in the courtroom, while others are consistently harsher in their rulings. Similarly, evaluators in performance reviews may differ as well: one might be more generous, offering high praise, while another might focus strictly on flaws, highlighting weaknesses and offering lower scores as a result. In organisations, this variability of course results in inconsistent and often unfair outcomes and decision-making.

— **Assessment patterns.** Have you ever had a doctor's appointment where the doctor seems dismissive of your ailments? Did you seek a second opinion and did that doctor regard your ailments as a top priority to investigate? This is possible because of *rigidity*. Experts in all industries can at one point be blinded by tunnel vision – over the course of our careers, we see a lot of different cases and, as such, we develop our own patterns of analysis. This isn't necessarily a problem, as long as we do not blindly accept these patterns as blueprints for the future.

Noise does not come without consequences. First and foremost, mistakes will be made. If one colleague prices an insurance policy too high, and someone else rates it too low, we might reason, "But they cancel each other's mistakes, right?" Not really. If you price your policy too high, you will lose a customer; if you price it too low, you undercharge. Either way, you lose. Secondly, fairness and credibility are impacted. If you receive a low rating from one person and a high rating from another during a performance review, not only the credibility of the involved parties suffers, but procedures are now also perceived as somewhat dubious.

A bias, on the other hand, is a tendency to lean one way or the other; to unknowingly act upon certain assumptions. Biases could cause you to deviate from rational standards and have you jeopardise a neutral point of view. For example, your company's sales forecasts may be consistently optimistic, or your investment decisions may be overly cautious; perhaps you underestimate the amount of work to be done for a project, or you prefer to hire people whose names sound familiar. Maybe you don't assign complex projects to a colleague who has a lesser degree. Inadvertently, we discriminate against others and treat them differently. Surprisingly, we are even biased towards our own objectivity!

Luckily, there is one significant advantage to this: unlike noise, biases make your actions and decisions somewhat *predictable*.

People categorise objects, experiences, people, and ideas. Some information and ideas will feel like your allies. They fit your mental categories. Consequently, you want those ideas to succeed and to be defended. These categories allow us to have "snap judgments" or "quick gut decisions". For example, when you meet someone new, you almost certainly have your analysis at the ready. They gave you a firm handshake and have a pleasant smile – these characteristics fit "the nice and professional guy" category. The majority of these judgments are based on simple cues in your environment. Here, you filter out information that appears unimportant. However, just because something is unimportant to your predefined mental categories, this does not mean it is of no importance and not worth paying attention to. In other words, you battle against data that doesn't fit your categories. They are the enemy. Such a mindset happens unconsciously and makes your thinking processes unreliable – even when you believe you are objective and fair-minded.

DID YOU KNOW?

Orchestras began to use blind auditions in the 1970s. Until then, women made up less than 10% of orchestra players in the United States. This was not due to poor musicianship, but rather to how women were perceived. During auditions, the use of curtains rendered gender invisible. The proportion of women in orchestras has risen to nearly 40% in recent years[44].

Attitudes toward gender and diversity were not altered, however; rather, it was made impossible to consider these and instead focus on true talent, regardless of appearance.

Nonetheless, the fast lane is not necessarily a bad lane to drive in. It helps us in plenty of cases where we do not need to consciously process every detail in our environment – every facial expression, every conversation, every... We simply cannot. We would be trapped in an infinite loop of *analysis paralysis*. People *need* that fast lane, that System 1, to function properly without sacrificing all mental energy. Chess masters thrive in this fast lane. Through repeated training and skill, they have developed the incredible ability to glance at a game in progress and instantly know the next dozen moves. Doctors who perform surgery frequently rely on their extensive training and education to react quickly to prevent the worst from happening.

This fast thinking can also be inaccurate, unfortunately. In the fast lane, you are less likely to pay attention to the world as it is *right now*. Stemming from this context-insensitivity, people might overvalue readily available information while undervaluing subtleties that require extra effort to uncover. Instead of *seeing* what is happening, we *think* what is taking place. As a consequence of habitual thinking – *we have always thought this way, why change?* – you remain rigid in your thinking. In the slow lane, you are grounded and curious and as a result, you can see past your (hidden) biases, assumptions, and motivations. You venture out, map the terrain, and look for obstacles in order to become acquainted with your surroundings and comprehend reality *as it is*. When you come across information that contradicts your mental categories, you are less likely to retaliate and, instead, you itch to put your beliefs to the test. This is likely to produce better judgment.

ANCHORING TRAP

Recall the last time you went (grocery) shopping. Did you notice any products on sale? Not only was the discounted price displayed, but also the original "anchor" price, correct? You'll get a great buy, it seems.

The anchoring trap not only makes it hard for us to resist short-term payoffs (that might negatively affect long-term outcomes), it also steers us in the wrong direction: you give disproportionate weight to the first bit of information you receive. This could be information or data that you seek at work, hear from others, or even the original question you asked. That first piece of information acts as an anchor that dominates your thinking and decision-making.

WATCH OUT

Have you found yourself saying, "The competition is doing this, so we should do the same"? You have run into a trap where your competition is your anchor.

As a result of the anchoring trap, you could see things only from the perspective of your industry or stick to benchmarks that use old definitions that might no longer fit current realities. By acquiring additional input and comparing it with your own reasoning, you can cut the anchor before it drags you to the bottom of the ocean. In the case of Vigilant leaders, it might be extremely difficult to convince colleagues about new ideas, such as chatbots, because people are quick to compare with what they have today. At Fintrix, employees might reason, "Why would we even use a chatbot? Personal relations with our customers are key." All new ideas will then be offset against this one line of thinking. Preferably, you also allow colleagues to individually reflect on new ideas, so they don't fall prey to others' anchors.

CONFIRMATION BIAS AND OPTIMISM BIAS

At Fintrix, your manager has asked you to investigate two technologies that the bank is considering implementing: Artificial Intelligence and blockchain. Your previous job was at a successful scale-up that creates blockchain solutions for banks, fintech companies, and logistics providers.

You are tempted to seek out information that confirms your preferred narrative – this is confirmation bias in action. The risk for Vigilant leaders is to accept information that confirms their beliefs and ignore and discredit information that doesn't. Confirmation bias carries multiple risks: first, we fail to understand subtleties and start thinking in gross generalisations; second, we become slaves of superficial consistency. *Fixed* thinking settles in.

In times of digital transformation, confirmation bias is often intensified by optimism bias: a tendency to be overly optimistic about something new, its applications, while failing to recognise limitations and weaknesses. Excessive optimism evolves into wishful thinking. To remain critical and adaptive, instead, it might be worthwhile to employ a devil's advocate, someone who challenges your perspective and tests the strength of your arguments. When you, for instance, research the use of Generative AI and chatbots at Fintrix, do not only look for the potential benefits of chatbots and AI, but also search for the potential downsides of implementing these tools.

SURVIVORSHIP BIAS

Survivorship bias occurs when we prefer people, companies, or technologies that "made it", and overlook those that didn't. This might have you reach incorrect conclusions. Don't just read about the most profitable new companies or the most successful people. Also study those who stumbled and failed.

While tempting, the biographies of successful people should not automatically be regarded as blueprints for success. Survivorship bias in this regard is deceptive and plays tricks on the mind. For every successful person and company, a thousand others may have failed – the stairs to the top are littered with those who did not make it. For Captain Jack Sparrow lovers: *"Dead men tell no tales."* Or do they? It's recommended to seek advice, also from those who "failed". Their input could be more valuable because they are more likely to have reflected on what led to their demise. There's much to be learned from these stories

STATUS QUO TRAP AND THE SUNK COST FALLACY

Business transformations go in against our preference for safety, comfort, and tranquility. This is termed the status quo bias. Anything that might be slightly disruptive is likely to be met with caution, suspicion, or even active resistance. After all, what is different is better kept at a distance, right?

Whenever you make a decision, you weigh the possible gains and losses against the current situation, the status quo. Moving away from a comfortable baseline is considered a loss. There are several factors at work here:
— People avoid feelings of loss and regret.
— People wonder about the potential costs of changing things.
— People are reluctant to commit to something unknown.

The status quo trap evolves into inertia and appears in businesses where perfectionism dominates and where mistakes are blasphemy. Companies that allow (and encourage) employees to make mistakes, on the other hand, tend to be more innovative. Psychological inertia and the status quo trap are also caused by the vast amount of information available, the numerous trends and developments, and simply not knowing where to look first, let alone knowing where and how to begin. Start a process of change gradually so your colleagues can grow accustomed to its constant presence. This might help colleagues break free from the status quo trap and thaw the frost that is impeding your company's machinery.

The status quo trap is oftentimes linked to the *sunk cost fallacy* (more commonly referred to as the *escalation of commitment*), or a tendency to keep pursuing a course of action because you have already invested resources. Instead, it could be very rewarding to oftentimes consider whether a certain made investment is still likely to benefit you in the future. One fascinating paradox is that we oftentimes experience inertia *whilst* moving forward. However, the direction we move towards might no longer be the correct one. It's crucial to regularly check whether initial judgments are still aligned with reality – such as moving market dynamics and changing customer demands.

CHOICE OVERLOAD
When you are presented with too many options or too much information, you could experience analysis paralysis. This could even result in decision fatigue and anxiety.

In a well-known study at Columbia University, a research team set up a booth of jam samples.[45] Throughout the study, researchers alternated between two offers: a selection of 24 different jams and a selection of only six jams. Several intriguing observations were made. The booth with 24 samples enticed 60% of passers-by to stop. This was only 40% in the case of the booth with six samples. So, you'd think "More is better!" However… In the case of the 24 options, 3% of those that stopped purchased a jar 1.9%, while 30% of those who stopped at the other booth actually purchased a jar (13.2%). It seems, when you give people a lot of options, they make fewer decisions. Choice overload boils down to this: while some variety is beneficial, too much is overwhelming.

Choice overload connects to anxiety. Choices cause *mental anguish* (especially when we want to make the best decision possible) and cause *disappointment* (the more options we have, the more likely we will be disappointed as we are less likely to feel we made the best decision. The other options could have been better, couldn't they?). The Vigilant leader can apply Hick's Law here: "To make quick decisions, reduce the number of choices." Make an unbiased preselection and reduce the number of options available to your colleagues. Fewer options lead to less complexity, which leads to more consideration and higher engagement.

THE SWISS POCKETKNIFE

Over 150 biases are identified in the meantime, so whether we want it or not, all of us operate based on biases, preferences, and prejudices. No one can maintain a consistent state of neutrality. Fortunately, while biases are "devilishly hard to eliminate", professor of law Joan Williams writes, "It's not as difficult to interrupt."[46] On top of that, we have to deal with the dangers of noise – the variability in our decision-making. Luckily, there are ways to slow down and investigate our beliefs and assumptions. By taking the time to pause, even if only for a brief moment, you might end up saving a lot of time by preventing issues.

Decision hygiene refers to a set of procedures to save time and increase decision accuracy whenever you engage with a new situation or a new piece of information. Consider the Swiss pocketknife: most people always grab one preferred tool in the pocketknife. This tool wears out over time and becomes dull and rusted. It's crucial to also consider the other viable options.

TIPS AND TRICKS TO COPE WITH NOISE AND BIASES

— **Aggregate.** Whenever multiple stakeholders are involved, don't just assign judgment to one team member. Instead, allow people to make judgments independently and take the average.
— **Take a mental walk.** When you face decisions, walk through your thought process, and put your assumptions to the test. This activates your System 2.
— **Pen and paper.** Define potential biases and noise ahead of time. Which ones do you think will come and play? Writing them down creates awareness and establishes accountability.

- **Outward-in perspective.** Take an outside-in approach. Examine the problem from various angles. Embrace diverse perspectives and invite others to your thought process: how does it appear to your colleagues, the customer, to your business partners?
- **Challenge network.** Bounce ideas off a trusted party. Are you able to defend an idea in front of your kids who barrage you with many *why's*? Obtain multiple opinions. And overall, remain open to feedback.
- **Protect your misfits, protects against superstars and the "dark triad".** Every team requires at least one misfit: someone who thinks differently, sees opportunities where others don't, and who isn't fond of the status quo. These rebels are oftentimes labelled as dangerous antagonists. But that rebel, according to Innovation and Change Catalyst Simone van Neerven, can be your key to successful innovation. They counter *herd thinking* and promote organisational agility. In other words, they are well-suited to digital transformation. However! We must also protect the company culture from excessive misfit behaviour. These misfits could show "superstar" behaviour. You know those superstars who act toxically, disrespectfully, and no one dares call them out on it?
- **Contextualise questions.** Rethink your feedback sourcing. When you ask people to rate something on a scale from 1 to 5, you open the door wide for noise. Even when you provide a clear-cut definition of the topic (for example, "great relationship skill"), people will interpret it differently. It may be useful to replace some absolute scales with relative scales – for example, "How would you describe our performance this year compared to last year's performance?"

These tips and tricks might help you actively engage with **open-minded thinking.** Unconscious noise and biases may not go away completely, but you are now better positioned to understand them and their impact. And you are armed to identify them. This helps you to be more confident that the decisions you make are not taken from a blind spot.

For Vigilant leaders this means that they receive and process information objectively before sending it deeper into the company. Vigilant leaders always consider these questions:

- Is the data objective? Did I use my anti-noise and anti-bias skills to filter incoming data?
- Will the information properly inspire colleagues? Which kind of information do they need?

WATCH OUT: AUTOMATED BIASES

With the recent pushes toward more automation and AI-driven decision-making, research on algorithmic bias shows that it is critical to first improve the quality of our own human judgments. Most algorithms are – for now – still written by humans. If those humans are biased and noise-unaware, can we really expect an algorithm to be free of bias?

Research of Luke Haliburton[47] and colleagues uncovers (the risks of) labeler bias in machine learning (ML) annotation tasks. This refers to the systematic errors that are introduced into datasets due to human subjectivism and inconsistencies. This can significantly affect the traning of ML models and result in innacurate predictions or unfair outcomes.

It's therefore often recommended to employ a diverse set of people for tasks like these.

Furthermore, Vigilant leaders remain alert about how they communicate the information to colleagues. Vigilant leaders can share information efficiently by being particularly wary of two risks.

— **Stop information dumping.** Channel the raw data. More is rarely better. Employees rarely have the time to process all information, and when they do try, they are most likely cruising in the fast lane.
— **Stop standardised communication.** How you communicate should be tailored to the recipient. Recognise that colleagues absorb information in different ways: some may be persuaded and inspired by numbers and percentages; others may be put off by that.

EXERCISE: THE NOISE AUDIT

To inform yourself about biases and noise, and avoid their full impact, it might be interesting to create one (or more) artificial situation(s) in which multiple colleagues (unknowingly) look at the same case. You can, for example, create a case where people have to evaluate a potential new colleague or new client.

It's not your ambition here to get to the right answer. You want to gather and combine the opinions of various people and spot the differences in their answers and judgments. As you will notice, your colleagues are likely to make differing judgments, decisions, and evaluations. The variability can be quite low, with almost certainly some sense of bias present (which allows you to predict the direction of the bias), or the variability can be quite large.

Continue organising noise audits. Obtain colleagues' independent judgments first, then aggregate and discuss them.

STORY CONTINUATION

As the Foresight Team got tangled up in the dangers of innovation bias and others, they reported on **technology for technology's sake.** While a technology pilot in one sector was delivering amazing results, this didn't necessarily mean that it **fitted** Fintrix's reality. The case of Generative AI and chatbots was the final straw for many employees and the Foresight Team, shocked by the loud negative reactions, decided to take a step back and carefully examine where things had gone wrong.

Addressing the burning platform at Fintrix: part one

First, they recognised how a **common frame of reference** was missing – a clear map that aligned Fintrix's internal capabilities with external trends. This framework should be present if they want to successfully filter out technologies that are not a good fit; without the framework, it was impossible for the Foresight Team to ask the right questions and protect themselves against extreme behaviours – such as challenging the status quo in such a way that it had become toxic. Starting from this framework provided the team with a crucial, yet painful insight: many, if not most, previously gathered technologies were, while impressive, completely irrelevant. Second, the Foresight Team relied upon simple pen and paper (flipcharts, in this case) to write down potential biases that might have influenced and perhaps still does influence their judgment. Together, they **identified** a few bigger culprits:

— **Choice overload and survivorship bias** resulted in having collected too much random and noisy information.
— **Confirmation bias** resulted in the Foresight Team's voice dominating the discussion.

While on the right track with the chatbot idea, they had to acknowledge that too much harm had already been done: they had activated colleagues' status quo bias, resulting in people being unwilling to change.

Addressing the burning platform at Fintrix: part two

To address these challenges, the Foresight Team took several corrective actions. They recruited a challenge network, consisting of Julian and Augustina. Augustina is deeply familiar with Fintrix's technical operations and Julian always has good insights regarding the tone of the customer and employee. Together, they could be considered a perfect blend to counter the Foresight Teams' confirmation bias. From now on, no information would be conveyed further into the company without first receiving a passing grade from this challenge network.

They somewhat act as gatekeepers, first vetting a clear fit between external innovation and internal capability and, if needed, closing the gate if a potential flood risks Fintrix's operational efficiency. In some special cases, Julian and Augustina had the **option to expand** the challenge network, including **internal and external stakeholders**, whose main tasks are to question assumptions, test ideas against real-world scenarios, and provide honest feedback. By aggregating more independent judgments, this also meant that colleagues were now presented with a more balanced and less biased selection of technologies and trends. This streamlined and well-curated body of information made it possible for Fintrix to construct stories to motivate colleagues and embrace innovation.

Reflecting on Fintrix' situation, how would you **handle the dangers of bias and noise** to stimulate the success of the company's digital transformation journey? Is there any way technology could help you?

MASTERING INFORMATION OVERLOAD

CUTTING THROUGH THE NOISE: STREAMLINING TECH COMMUNICATION AND SHARING

Introduction

Larry has always been passionate about technology. With natural curiosity and an unrelenting drive to be at the forefront of innovation, he built a career around his love of tech and gadgets. After ten years in IT consulting, Larry finally secured his dream job as a technology scout at Digitize Consulting, a leading firm specialised in digital transformation for the financial services industry.

In this role, Larry is tasked by Vivian – founder and CEO – with inspiring other colleagues about the vast potential of new technologies. He considers himself a catalyst for innovation and change. His role is clear: in an industry where staying on top of technological advancements makes or breaks a company, Larry ensures that Digitize Consulting remains market leader in most of EMEA.

Whenever colleagues ask for Larry's whereabouts, similar responses are heard: "Larry is at a technology fair" or "He's working from home today, following various online inspiration sessions." Larry even managed to secure some funds to attend technology safaris at regional innovation hubs Shenzhen and Silicon Valley. On the rare occasions he is found behind his office desk, Larry is all over the internet, searching for the newest and most fancy technological applications. He sends out emails daily packed with reports, links, and QR codes, each one detailing another new trend he discovered. More recently, he organises "Tech-over-Lunch with Larry" (TELL) sessions, designed to be informal yet informative, encouraging colleagues to sacrifice their lunch breaks for a dose of tech inspiration. Additionally, Larry proposes the idea for video content, further expanding the channels through which he disseminates information.

The problem at Digitize Consulting

While Larry's intentions are commendable, the sheer **volume and frequency** of these communications overwhelm his colleagues at Digitize Consulting. Instead of being seen as valuable, Larry's messages are now perceived as spam, with people being bombarded by information. Not only do people now ignore Larry and his messages, they also **ignore and miss** those critical insights that could drive innovation. Meanwhile, Larry still pushes out mails, documents, and now even videos on a daily basis – **unaware** that these messages have no recipients left.

Researchers compared the time it took to search the library for an answer to the time it took to "Google it"[48]. They discovered that *googling* the answer takes around seven minutes, whereas offline searching takes 22 minutes. Put another way, every time you *google* something, you gain about 15 minutes. This light-speed access to information, however, invited a paradox: our society has access to more information than ever before, but while the response time – the time to receive information – decreased significantly, the hit rate didn't increase in tandem. More recently, the surge of generative AI-based tools such as ChatGPT provided us with even faster access to new content generated by a seemingly intelligent agent. In contrast to standard search engines, this content is now processed on demand and tailored to our specific question. While the hit rate seems stronger than before, questions do arise about the credibility and correctness of the output we are provided with.

The World Health Organization coined the term *infodemic*[49]. Everywhere we look, information comes at us – sometimes we explicitly ask for it; oftentimes we do not. Our brain is not made to process so many stimuli in such a short time span, and these excess stimuli generate mental friction. We consider ourselves *Homo Informatici* while, instead, we have become servants of that very information – we *are* the data, some even say. It's crucial to focus on *digital nutrition*. Psychologist Jocelyn Brewer outlines three aspects:[50]
— Being mindful and aware of your digital usage.
— Considering the meaningfulness of what you're participating in digitally.
— Being moderate with it.

This section is centred around one question: "How do you ensure that the right information reaches the right person at the right time without causing feelings of overload?" Vigilant leaders that gather too much information are not necessarily a bad thing. Trouble looms when they bombard colleagues with that information.

THE INFORMATION DILEMMA

Just like a dragon is said to hoard gold and treasure, humans have the habit of hoarding information. We collect information in the hope that it will be useful in the future; because we want to play it safe and get all the information out there; because it allows us to verify the accuracy and validity of previously acquired information. Several factors are at work here:

— Collecting information indicates our commitment to rationalism and competence.
— Information helps us in justifying decision-making.
— Information acts as a currency to establish and nourish our reputation.
— Collecting information helps us build and maintain social relationships (for example, to anticipate future interactions).

The human brain is a meaning-making machine that constantly wants to make sense of all the bits and bytes headed its way: sights, sounds, experiences, flashy billboards on your way home, hundreds of shows on all those streaming services, the numerous emails hitting your inbox. You name it.

Multiple terms have emerged that describe our perilous information situation: data asphyxiation, data smog and data delirium, info glut and info pollution. Although information and data are regarded as valuable resources – "the oil of the digital economy" – the sheer volume causes stress, job dissatisfaction, and physical illness. By now, we are all caught in the crossfire of information streams.

While the growing field of data science enables companies to find signals in the unfathomable volumes of data,[51] companies struggle to communicate the critical insights gleaned from that data. Such circumstances necessitate the deployment of coping mechanisms:

— Create a personal database to **store information** for future reference without ever looking at it.
— **Ignore** information.
— **Prioritise** information based on its importance, frequently considering the sequence of deadlines ahead.
— **Skim** through the received material and **discard** anything that appears to be unimportant.
— **Delegate** the information to another person.

The dilemma is obvious: we receive so much information but not enough of the right information. Vigilant leaders rise to the occasion. They protect against information floods and prevent colleagues from being overly exposed to *Information Fatigue Syndrome (IFS)*. The number of people suffering from IFS has severely increased and thus it is high time to reconsider the value of information and how we use it.

Colleen Sinclair, professor specialised in intergroup and interpersonal relation-ships, advises us to remind ourselves of the importance of value and accuracy in what we share with others before we share it[52]. Take a step back to allow the brain to catch up with your emotions. Sometimes you share things based on gut reactions (the fast lane) rather than based on the conclusions of critical thinking (the slow lane). In addition, be honest about your biases, Sinclair says. Remember, while most people believe others are biased, they are often confident that they themselves are not. We are less critical of ourselves when it comes to handling (mis)information.

HUMAN COGNITIVE CAPACITY: "HELP, I'M CRAZY BUSY"

In the story of information overload, information isn't the only culprit. It is fre-quently accompanied by its partner in crime: time. People are oftentimes stuck in a climate of interactions that relentlessly draw their energy. Does the following ring a bell? "You spend a significant amount of time in meetings every day but feel like nothing has been accomplished.[53] "Time poverty" – a term coined by social scientists – is real.

In the end, people automatically respond "busy", when they are asked how things are going at work. We often voice and display how "hard" we are working and that we are multitasking. And why wouldn't we? When others perceive us as being busy, they think we are important, admirable, and impressive people. *Busyness*[54], as it stands, is now a virtue, but is also a far cry from the past, where leisure rather than work was a signifier of dominant social status.

However, merely using the word "busy", might already invite consequences: stress hormones rise and the executive function in the prefrontal cortex declines. This, in turn, negatively impacts our capacity for memory, judgment, and impulse control and, what's more, the brain areas that are linked to anger and anxiety light up. The resulting exhaustion, in turn, leads to increasing health problems, absenteeism, and turnover.

In other words, people's ability to absorb and engage with information is limited; and often their time to do so is limited as well. When you exceed those limits, you are likely to feel overloaded; your brain has too many tabs open. Recall that amaz-ing feeling you get after closing all your browser tabs on your computer after a long day? Isn't it wonderful? It's as if the world goes silent and calm for a moment. *Ruthless meeting efficiency* is necessary. At Netflix, for example, meetings cannot exceed 30 minutes and meetings that would be one-way are replaced by other ways of information sharing[55]. When they want interaction, colleagues are expected to review material in advance. Ask yourself as a Vigilant: what is this meeting for? Is this the best way to reach out to my colleagues? What's my role?

Lack of information handling and time management affect decision-making. Whenever you engage with too much information, your attention and focus drop. As a result, you make decisions based on only a subset of the total information available. The decision-making process becomes flawed. Less is more when it comes to *cognitive information overload*. An increase in input results in a decrease in output, and whenever the quantity of to-be-processed information increases, it becomes more difficult to achieve quality. The Vigilant leader, however, believes that "more becomes more once I filter the more".

COMMUNICATING WITH VIGILANCE

Handling information is about more than just considering people's cognitive capacity. First, the way you present information is significant; secondly, how you frame the information and make it relevant to your colleagues' context matters too.

American consulting engineer Willard Brinton described the last-mile problem of conveying information in his seminal work *Graphic Methods for Presenting Facts* (1914) more than a century ago,

> "Time after time it happens that some ignorant member of a committee will upset the carefully-thought-out plan of a man who knows the facts, simply because the man with the facts cannot present his facts readily enough to overcome the opposition."[56]

How do we overcome this? There are several tricks that can help your information hit the right spot:

— **Relevance and relatability.** Share relevant information. Find out what is important to others, not what feels important to you. A first step could be to stay up to date on what is important to others. The quality reporting in your company could perhaps be done in the future with the help of Artificial Intelligence. In that case, it's crucial for the Vigilant leader to understand which information to provide colleagues with. How can you make it *relatable*? Do you need to provide examples of other industry players that already use Artificial Intelligence? Or do you need to explain how they can trust such new systems? Inquire.

— **Technology.** Use technology to your advantage but don't rush into using any tool that seems "hot". Consult colleagues to determine which knowledge sharing tools (i.e., platforms, protocols, or apps) best suit their work style and habits. Together, you can avoid technology overload – prevent the use of too many tools and platforms in parallel.

— **Communicating.** People often have access to and rely on all sorts of insider information that others – for example, their colleagues – don't have. This "curse of knowledge" might be linked to your job, or your expertise and experience. In itself, this *curse* doesn't do any harm. However, when we are unaware that others don't have a similar knowledge base, our message remains rather abstract. While you might see a clear picture presented, someone else could end up being confused. Following *Made to Stick* by Chip and Dan Heath, your communication benefits from bringing a message that is simple (strip your message to the core), concrete (refrain from high-level noun, e.g. *high -performance*, when possible, and credible (provide tangible proof through details, statistics, or testimonials).

In addition to information quality, Vigilant leaders also consider the timing of "throwing" information – regularly interrupting colleagues with information is not acceptable.

As a vigilant leader it is important to find ways to effectively communicate your ideas, e.g. through a platform or through a focused meeting. Interrupting the work of colleagues every time you have an idea might have a negative effect. Constantly having people shift between tasks (even if it is just a mental distraction) lowers satisfaction and productivity. Over and above this, people feel drained and are overstimulated.

THE ZEIGARNIK EFFECT AND CONTAMINATED TIME

When we leave tasks unfinished, something curious happens in our brains. Psychologist Roma Kumar[57] explains that the brain stores received information in the sensory memory – where information is received through our five senses – for a very brief period of time, before moving it to our short-term memory. While most short-term memories are quickly forgotten, this is not the case for incomplete tasks. Instead, your brain constantly rehearses tasks to keep that information active: in other words, it reminds us of those emails, that article, the customer. Once the task is completed, however, you will easily forget about it. Have you wondered why so many television dramas, for example, use cliffhangers? This phenomenon has a name: the *Zeigarnik effect*. Russian psychologist Bluma Zeigarnik noticed how waiters seemed to have better memories of unpaid orders. Once the bill was paid, the waiters suddenly found it difficult to remember the exact details of the order. The information had left their short-term memory. Zeigarnik proposed that failing to complete a task creates underlying cognitive tension, which causes you to mentally return to it.[58] This insight also casts new light on the concept of *multitasking*, referred to by sociologists as *contaminated time*.

As a Vigilant, when you interrupt the work of colleagues, it is highly likely that they are not focused on your message but try to listen to you while finishing the task they are working on. It is your responsibility to get your message across by taking the context into account.

DID YOU KNOW?

Sociologists have a name for what you "get" when you multitask: contaminated time. You might feel productive and efficient when you scroll through Instagram while hitting the gym or walking your dog, or when you respond to emails during a family dinner. But are you? This is counterproductive. Contaminated time is time when you are not present. You try to combine too many things. A study by Ruth Ogden and colleagues found that technology is secretly stealing around 60% of our spare time.[59]

Vigilant leaders are, for example, aware of the ideal moment to share certain information, are front-runners in leading highly effective and to-the-point meetings (if those meetings are necessary in the first place), and make sure that, by communicating in a focused way, others are not overloaded.

STORY CONTINUATION

For Digitize Consulting to succeed, it is essential that the issue of information overload is addressed. Larry's role as Technology Scout is vital, but the timing of his dissemination of information must be recalibrated to ensure that his insights do not land on deaf ears. When Larry was having lunch with his close colleague Alejandra – whom he affectionately called Alex –, he confided in her, expressing his frustrations about feeling unappreciated in his new role. He mentioned how colleagues had become creative in avoiding his TELL-sessions, ignoring his well-researched remarks during meetings, and he swore he even saw some people rolling their eyes just earlier that day.

Alex, never one to shy away from honesty, responded gently but firmly, "Larry, are you really surprised? You're overwhelming us. It's not just the volume of information, but the frequency too. You're sending daily emails and hosting weekly lunch sessions. And now you are adding videos to the mix too? We have our own jobs, our own challenges – sometimes **it's just too much.**" Her words hit Larry hard, but they also opened his eyes. He realised that in his enthusiasm, he had **lost sight** of his colleagues' needs and their own working lives. Determined to make a change for the better, Larry decides to approach his role with a new perspective: as of now he will aim for **content relevance and relatability**, leverage technology in a good manner, and adapt his communication style.

Addressing the burning platform at Digitize Consulting: Part One

First, Larry recognised that he had to start by **understanding** what was truly important to colleagues. He started to actively listen to them to stay updated on their needs and priorities. Rather than focusing on what he found exciting, he learned that sharing relevant and relatable information was key. For instance, while he is fascinated by the potential of Artificial Intelligence (AI) in quality reporting, his colleagues are less concerned about the technicalities of this technology. Instead, their experiences show them that clients are struggling with practically using and trusting such systems. By **listening** to colleagues and understanding this nuance, Larry can now provide concrete examples of other industry players that use AI successfully but also explain the relationship between advanced technologies and end-users' trust.

Secondly, Larry learned that using technology was indeed advantageous, but some caution might be necessary. He had been quick in adopting many tools, platforms, and strategies to share information, which contributed to the overload that colleagues experienced. Now, he first **consulted** with colleagues to determine which knowledge-sharing tools best suited their work styles and habits. By **aligning** on one well-chosen platform, Larry further prevents a recurring struggle issue within many organisations – technology overload.

Third, as technology scout, Larry struggled with the 'curse of knowledge' – while he, indeed, had access to insider information and an often deeper understanding of the technologies he was advocating for, a **knowledge gap** was present which made his communications abstract. To overcome this, Larry paid additional attention to making his messages simple and concrete by stripping them down to their essence. Especially high-level jargon was avoided. He backed up this information with some visuals, such as statistics, and clear testimonials.

Addressing the burning platform at Digitize Consulting: Part Two

As part of his new approach, Larry restructured his TELL-sessions. Rather than holding them weekly, he opted for one highly focused session each month. This gave him time to refine content, align it properly with the specific interests and challenges of colleagues, and even bring in some guest speakers who could respond to any questions people might have. By reducing the frequency – and therefore also the overload – he ensured that each session had become **meaningful, engaging, and truly beneficial.**

On a more practical level, Larry also **prioritised relevance and timing** – "Is this information really necessary for people?". Before sending out any communication, Larry would run his content through a chatbot to condense and streamline it further and, in doing so, make sure that the message was concise and to the point.

Through these changes, Larry found a **new balance**. He continued to be a valuable source of technological insights for Digitize Consulting and he did so in a way that was considerate of people's time and attention. "Quality of quantity" had become his modus operandi. Soon Larry noticed how he had gained the appreciation of colleagues and how his job became effective again in assisting both Digitize Consulting and its clients in driving digital transformation forward. His ability as a Vigilant leader to share relevant, relatable, and well-timed information transformed his role from that of an enthusiastic but overwhelming presence into a strategic asset for the company.

Reflecting on Digitize Consulting's situation and Larry's approach, how would you **further reduce information overload** and better the company's chances for a successful digital transformation journey? How could you use technology to help you out?

ENERGY SCAN FOR VIGILANT DIGITAL TRANSFORMATION LEADERSHIP

The Vigilant leader is always alert, curious and attentive to technological advances, changing customer behaviours, competitor moves, market disruptions, and new entrants, and – as such – is ready to respond when necessary. They operate well in ambiguous and turbulent situations. They are sharp-eyed, fascinated, and open to different perspectives. Their watchful behaviour helps the company act quickly on the earliest, weakest signs of digital opportunities and threats. The Vigilant leader, in sum, enables the company to make sense of what is happening beyond the periphery of the organisation, business model, or industry. As a result, Vigilant leaders decode the turbulent environment and make it easier for everyone to see interesting future world scenarios linked to digital technologies. They make sense of new information and stimulate people to open up for new alternatives.

Do you want to find out which of the Vigilant leader skills give you and your colleagues energy? Take this short test.

1 = never 2 = rarely 3 = sometimes 4 = very often 5 = always

Questions	Your response (1 – 5)
I am always open to different thoughts and contexts	
I enjoy looking for different perspectives	
I like making sense of new information	
I enjoy stimulating people to see alternatives	
I enjoy turning people's fear of the unknown into interest	
I like to question common practices in the company	
I enjoy finding out about new technological opportunities	
I enjoy acting on the gaps in my/our knowledge	

Total score:

CHECKLIST FOR VIGILANT DIGITAL TRANSFORMATION LEADERSHIP

If you now wonder whether signs of Vested digital transformation leadership can be spotted within your company, you can reflect on the following set of statements:

At [your company name], we *are curious*, *as we ...*

regularly ask 'why?'	
are wary of the curse of comfort and don't settle for the default.	
challenge colleagues according to their curiosity levels.	
understand people's preferred curiosity mindset.	
value others' creativity and curiosity.	
remain open to and stimulate learning experiences.	
adopt a beginner's mind.	
stimulate the organisation, the people, and the self.	
embed curiosity into our daily routines.	
embark on journeys of discovery.	

... remain vigilant for bias and noise, as we ...

recognise bias and noise	
understand where noise could come from.	
foster noise awareness in the organisation.	
watch out for signals of habitual thinking.	
identify the potential biases at play in any context.	
interrupt biases.	
engage open-minded.	
slow down and investigate.	
increase decision accuracy by means of decision hygiene.	

... manage time and information, as we ...

protect against the information fatigue syndrome.	
correctly interpret the value of information.	
know when (not) to send information.	
know how (not) to send information.	
respect people's time and respect their capacity to engage.	
avoid contaminated time.	

CHAPTER 2

Voyager Leadership

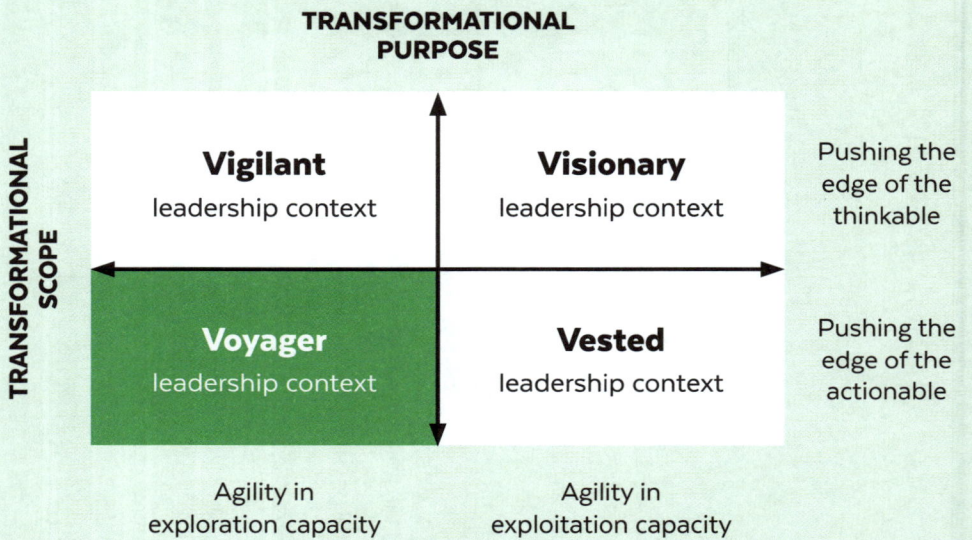

TRANSFORMATIONAL PURPOSE

TRANSFORMATIONAL SCOPE

Vigilant
leadership context

Visionary
leadership context

Voyager
leadership context

Vested
leadership context

Pushing the edge of the thinkable

Pushing the edge of the actionable

Agility in exploration capacity

Agility in exploitation capacity

VOYAGER LEADERS

In the context of fostering and striving for a successful digital transformation journey, the Voyager leader focuses on a core set of tasks.

Voyager leaders...
— Bundle together the diversity and creativity of individuals into an entrepreneurial **team**
— Explore solutions by efficiently progressing through a steadily paced process of **build-measure-learn** feedback cycles
— Use empirical **feedback** from customers and other stakeholders to drive forward the exploration of solutions

To this end, Voyager leaders put various skills to good use in order to guide colleagues and the company through a *human-centric* process.

In this chapter, we will introduce you to several digital transformation protagonists and how they build on these skills to foster a meaningful journey for themselves, colleagues and other stakeholders, and the organisation at large.

— Julio at SupplyTech and how recalibrating their understanding of **co-creation** helped them reconnect to customers and other stakeholders;
— Jonathan at NexTalent, who dared to portray **vulnerability** and role-modelled **authentic** leadership;
— Bram at Innovora and how his new understanding of diversity supported him in fostering **inclusive teamwork** within and outside the company.

CO-CREATING FOR INNOVATION

FROM ISOLATION TO INNOVATION

Introduction

In the rapidly evolving world of supply chain and logistics, SupplyTech has built its reputation on being a forward-thinking technology provider, committed to **proactively addressing** the pressing needs of modern supply chains. Operating within a fiercely competitive industry, marked by complex operations, fluctuating demand patterns, and intricate global networks, the company has consistently focused on leveraging cutting-edge technologies to streamline supply chain processes for its clients. Recognising the potential of artificial intelligence, SupplyTech was particularly keen to exploit generative AI's capability for knowledge and insight generation. GenAI promised a more dynamic solution than previous technology, capable of learning from vast amounts of data, generating unique responses, and adapting on the spot. As such, SupplyTech set its sights on creating PlanBot – a generative AI-powered assistant designed to reimagine the role of supply chain planners. The tool would serve as an **intelligent co-pilot** for planners, empowering them with real-time insights, suggesting optimised solutions, and functioning as a proactive teammate to make faster, more-informed decisions. SupplyTech's vision was rooted in the promise that GenAI could be the solution to many of the industry's complexities.

Overall, PlanBot symbolised a bold new step forward, aiming to automate complex planning tasks while augmenting human capabilities. With a team of **highly skilled in-house AI-specialists and engineers**, SupplyTech started to design a tool they believed would revolutionise supply chain management and change how planners approach their daily operations.

The problem at SupplyTech

However, despite the immense potential of GenAI and significant investments, PlanBot's launch revealed a **critical flaw** in SupplyTech's approach. The chatbot, although a testament to the company's technological know-how, **failed to resonate** commercially. SupplyTech's sales team faced immediate resistance from potential customers, who found PlanBot lacked practical utility, with capabilities that fell short of addressing the **nuanced challenges** they faced daily. PlanBot's design, developed in a silo with little input from real-world users, resulted in a product that wasn't properly **aligned** with the everyday needs of the intended end-users: supply chain planners.

Feedback from customers highlighted a broad range of issues: PlanBot's features were unrefined, failing to provide the real-time, actionable insights planners needed (and were promised). The tool's interface was described as cumbersome, leading to frustration rather than efficiency. Instead of simplifying planners' work, PlanBot added unnecessary complexity. Planners who did try to integrate PlanBot into their workflow quickly reverted to tried-and-tested tools, resulting in clients **abandoning** the tool even when offered at reduced rates.

This misstep was more than a product failure; it heavily damaged SupplyTech's reputation. Clients began to view SupplyTech as **out of touch** with the practical needs of the industry, resulting in a significant loss of trust. Many wondered why SupplyTech did not co-create with other stakeholders in developing its new solution. It cast doubt on the company's credibility as a leader in supply chain technology, raising further questions about its approach to innovation and product development.

CO-CREATION

The complexities seen in today's marketplace require businesses to entertain innovative solutions. In parallel, customers now view the world through a digital lens. People's expectations are rewired digitally, and their experience demands heighten.

> "Not only must a company offer high-quality products or services, but the way they deliver them to the customer matters much more today than in the past".[60]

At the same time, customers don't just want your products and services imposed on them; instead, they want to collaborate in building and improving products; they want to be heard, share their ideas and inspiration – all in all, to (re)shape their own experience. They want to play a more active role in your business. Professors C.K. Prahalad and Venkat Ramaswamy coined the term *co-creation* to describe this type of relationship[61].

Within a business context, **co-creation** refers to a collaborative process where businesses include outsiders in the ideation and development process. Through collaboration, co-creation encourages innovation by tapping into the **collective creativity** of these stakeholders. This helps businesses approach issues from a fresh perspective and, ultimately, distill better products and services that are likely to be more customised and tailored to the individual. While we might think in terms of our direct customers, many stakeholders can be approached and invited to join efforts: cross-industry partnerships often have companies from different sectors collaborate on new technologies or services; supplier collaboration involves suppliers in product designs; and employee-driven innovations benefit from employees' unique positions to identify improvements or come up with entirely new ideas.

Rather than your business acting as a sole creator of products and services, the co-creation process invites internal and external input and engagement, often resulting in more innovative, effective, and especially more customer-focused solutions. These acts of shared value creation are beneficial in many ways. Co-creation is likely to foster a sense of shared ownership and creates a win-win dynamic where you enhance customer loyalty, improve product-market fit, and potentially even lower your development costs.

How can you make co-creation successful?
— **Know the why:** understand the core purpose behind any initiative for co-creation. This clarity helps you in guiding most activities and decisions, and might ensure that any such efforts are aligned with the objectives of the project.
— **Take extreme ownership:** make sure someone takes full responsibility, both for the successes and the failures. This level of commitment drives accountability and motivates people to do their best.
— **Bring together the right people:** assemble a diverse group of stakeholders, such as end-users, experts, and others who bring their own perspectives and skills. Diversity could help to foster innovation.
— **Facilitate conversation:** actively manage discussions to ensure that they stay focused on the goal. Preferably, good facilitation prevents dominant voices from overshadowing the discussion.

- **Use creativity tools and design thinking activities:** tools like brainstorming, sketching, and mind mapping can help you in your creative thinking and ideation.
- **Maintain a bias towards action:** prioritise doing and experimenting over a too extensive planning approach. This helps you to accelerate learning and ensures that the project moves forward.
- **Learn from failing:** failures are opportunities to learn and derive insights from which to iterate. If you allow such mindset to settle itself, you are more likely to reduce the stigma that is often associated with setbacks and, instead, you might encourage a culture of experimentation.
- **Prototyping is the new research:** prototypes can help you test hypotheses and gather feedback quickly, providing you with more direct and actionable insights than traditional research methods.
- **Make co-creation sustainable:** institutionalise co-creation as a recurring element of your company's business strategy. Install formal processes, training, and support structures to ensure that co-creation can thrive in the long term.

Nonetheless, it's not always easy for companies to engage in these activities. Co-creation invites various challenges. In a more traditional management framework, hierarchy equals control. It is difficult to hand over some of that control, particularly if it's to employees and customers. For many organisations, strategic planning and design often remain closely guarded secrets due to intellectual property concerns. Furthermore, you might struggle with fluently coordinating the input from so many diverse stakeholders and align it with your strategic objectives. While openness matters, so does focus. We highlight two important stakeholders below: your customers and your employees.

STAKEHOLDER: CUSTOMERS

The digital economy puts the customer in the driving seat. If handled properly, engaging with customers might result in several innovative benefits, such as exponential learning and rapid idea generation. When customers are allowed to express their creativity and be directly involved in product development or service design, your offerings are more likely to be aligned with their needs and preferences. You can source their engagement by means of **feedback channels** where you collect and act upon customer feedback, by **crowdsourcing** ideas by inviting customers to suggest new features and improvements, and by **beta testing** where you allow customers to test prototypes and early product versions. Digital open innovation platforms, in this regard, are often favoured to enable a customer-centric co-creation journey:

- **LEGO** listened not only to investors, but also approached local communities, customers, and employees. Through its Lego Ideas platform, you can submit designs for new LEGO sets. Popular submissions might even be produced and sold, with the creator enjoying a fair share of the profits[62].

— **Starbucks** launched the open innovation "My Starbucks Idea" platform, which can be considered a customer participation experiment. Even though the platform is retired now, it allowed customers to share their ideas and suggestions to make the company's products better. In its first five years, the platform received over 150 000 ideas, and Starbucks put hundreds to good use[63].

— With 'co-create **IKEA**', the retailer sends out an open invitation to "create a better everyday life for the many people, together"[64]. The company aims to open up its product development and enrich its product innovation by collaborating actively with consumers, third-party designers, students, and more.

Even though the emphasis on customers has been present for decades, true value is now often attributed to the total stakeholder experience. For now, however, only 11% of companies take a comprehensive stakeholder perspective into consideration.[65] As such, a more intimate and dynamic understanding and collaboration is necessary, with more stakeholders than just your direct customers. For example, your employee experience and expectations are also essential. Why is that?

STAKEHOLDER: EMPLOYEE EXPERIENCE AND EXPECTATIONS

MIT Sloan senior lecturer George Westerman wrote that "employee experience has expanded from a single element to its own set of elements since employees make the business and have first-hand insights [...], employee pain points can be valuable cues on where you can improve the business. If you innovate the work experience, you make the whole company better, including the customer experience".[66]

Remember former GE CEO Jack Welch's statement – "When the rate of change inside an institution becomes slower than the rate of change outside, the end is in sight"? In this case, however, the inside impacts the outside: when the employee experience (inside) is lacking, the customer experience (outside) is expected to follow. Linda Hill and colleagues phrase it in the following way:

> "Workers [...] expect to be heard and to help develop their organisations' plans and solutions collaboratively. They take the responsibility that comes with "co-creation" seriously, with younger generations of employees ready to be judged on their creativity as much as their expertise."[67]

Companies usually consider how their customers influence reputation – consider social media's role in this – but are less likely to consider employees. Certain aspects such as employee job satisfaction, however, impact an employee's willingness to recommend the company. Your employees have the power to act as your reputation advocates, and it's up to Voyager leaders to make sure they truly are and can be.

REFLECTION

To what extent is your company currently engaged in digital value creation with different stakeholder groups? Consider the following in the context of PlanBot:

— **Employees:** for example, marketing teams can help you with insights into customer preferences, branding, and positioning; R&D teams possess the in-depth knowledge of PlanBot's technical capabilities and limitations; and so on.

— **Customers and end-users:** often considered the most critical external stakeholder, they provide hands-on feedback into how PlanBot might fit the daily operations. Building on their feedback is likely to ensure that the bot solves what it needs to solve.

— **Communities and user groups:** engaging with industry communities, forums, or user groups can provide you access to a wealth of collective knowledge, as well as help you reach out to early adopters who might be more willing to test PlanBot. Their collaboration can boost product relevance.

— **Industry experts and consultants:** in the case of SupplyTech, experts in supply chain management, AI, and related fields will bring a strategic perspective to co-creation, helping to forecast industry trends, recommend best practices, and more.

— **Technology and innovation partners:** certain key players might be specialised in AI, data analytics, or software integration that SupplyTech doesn't yet master. This could help in accelerating PlanBot's product's development and ensure that the bot used the latest technologies in the most effective manner.

— ...

Companies can uncover new sources of value by connecting to a broad set of stakeholders. This might help them to tap into new markets, foster stronger relationships, and increase their standing with customers.

Which other stakeholder groups can you identify in your network?

UNLOCKING CO-CREATION

Co-creation is not about magical or divine interventions; instead, it is about trial and error where creativity is offered the right opportunities and the right context to flourish, and where businesses adopt *epistemic humility*, or "the realisation that our knowledge is always provisional and incomplete – and that it might require revision in light of new evidence,"[68] as professor of practical philosophy Erik Angner wrote. Voyager leaders, in this regard, play an important role in nurturing and stimulating such a collective creativity-supporting environment. A good way to start doing this is by unlocking creativity at the level of the individual.

UNLOCKING CREATIVITY: TIPS AND TRICKS FOR THE INDIVIDUAL

People are not always as creative as they would want to be. Only 25% of people currently feel that they are able to unleash their own creative potential.[69] Sometimes, we suffer from fixed patterns of thought and behaviour that undermine creativity. Consider, for example, whether you feel it is important or not to always agree with colleagues and bosses; whether you always see obstacles to new ideas; whether you catch yourself consistently thinking that something won't work, before having tried it.[70] People can take certain steps to escape this.

— **Frame the problem and take a step back.** Joseph Grenny, author and co-founder of Crucial Learning, states that when you give yourself a compelling unsolved problem, the brain becomes slightly triggered or irritated.[71] This creates subsurface cognitive irritation and stimulates creativity. If you want your unconscious mind to do some heavy lifting, carry round a piece of paper with a meticulously articulated problem or statement. If you want to further increase cognitive irritation, engage in a first (probably unsatisfactory) round of finding a solution. The act of walking away from a problem is crucial, however. Your unconscious brain will churn in the background, drawing on a broader range of mental resources, experiences, and creative connections.

— **Don't force your epiphanies.** Sometimes your brain feels toasted because of the cumulative stress of your job and life in general. It will then be very difficult to come up with innovative ideas. Time management coach Elizabeth Grace Saunders advises you not to force your creativity. You might trigger a fight-or-flight response instead, which has you operate from your primal – and least creative – part of the brain. Sometimes it's better to simply say, "I'll see what happens" rather than "I must be creative right now."

— **Trigger your "diffuse-thinking" state.** In the "focused-thinking" state, you work via established neurological pathways. In the diffuse-thinking state, the brain operates rather loosely and tries to make connections between different parts of your brain. To get into this state, walk, nap, eat, or take any other type of break – your brain opens to new possibilities. The combination of stepping away from your screen and positioning yourself in a happy place (for example, sitting in the sun during summer or going for a drink in a coffee shop during winter) works like a charm. Maybe museums or bookshops are better for you. Dare to find out what lifts your creative spirit!

— **Follow your curiosity.** When you notice a passing curiosity – whether at work, while walking the streets of your hometown, or while on vacation – honour it and engage. Something tickled your brain. The sensation is a sign that your unconscious mind wants to explore a new path. This can range from meeting a new person to reading a book. These unexpected tickles could surprise you: some might seemingly have little value, but their relevance can reveal itself months or years later. Suddenly, they are sources of inspiration.

DID YOU KNOW?

The London Philharmonic Orchestra's composition of the 50 greatest pieces of classical music included six pieces by Mozart[72], five by Beethoven, and three by Bach*. Pablo Picasso's opus includes over 1800 paintings, 1200 sculptures, 2800 ceramics, and 12000 drawings. How many of these artistic creations are you familiar with? People's most original output, their most original ideas, come from the period when they also produce the largest volume of work, according to psychologist Dean Simonton[73]. The famous adage, "quality over quantity", is thus not always true. Those ideas that are strange mutations, dead ends, or complete failures have a worthwhile cost. They generate a greater number of ideas.

Dean Kamen, a well-known technological whiz, says "You gotta kiss a lot of frogs before you find a prince." People who come up with novel and successful ideas are not necessarily better than their peers in their fields. They likely brought forth a greater volume of work, which provided them with more variety and a higher chance of originality. "The odds of producing an influential or successful idea are a positive function of the total ideas generated," Dean Simonton concludes.

*Mozart composed more than 600 pieces before his death at age 35; Beethoven produced 650; and Bach wrote more than 1000 pieces.

— **Keep a shoebox.** Gather your thoughts and experiences – anything you come across. Take notes (in a notebook, in a note-taking app on your phone, or on sticky notes on your desk), use voice memos to record, create a simple "ideas" Google form. Gathering and organising information increases the likelihood that you will retain most of it. This, in turn, could help you conjure fertile connections over time. Encourage colleagues to submit ideas for improving processes, redesigning products, and optimising the overall workplace.

— **Engage in uncomfortable conversation.** While we do not expect you to switch sides after a conversation with people of different opinions, you can gain valuable insights. It's worthwhile to invite different perspectives from lives you may never live. A confrontation with other realities helps you to approach situations from a different angle. However, this necessitates a shift in how we tend to approach our conversations. In an episode on PBS, Adam Grant mentions that people tend to argue about what they themselves find interesting rather than listening to the other and considering what the other might find interesting or convincing.[74]

UNLOCKING CREATIVITY: TIPS AND TRICKS FOR THE COMPANY

Even though individuals can stimulate their creativity, a study on workplace creativity revealed that 75% of employees experience growing pressures to be productive rather than showcasing their creativity.[75] Quite astonishingly, the study also highlighted that, in parallel, employees are expected to think increasingly creatively on the job. While lack of time is seen as the biggest barrier to creativity, Voyager leaders are a positive force to provide fertile grounds for creativity to flourish.

— **Reward persistence.** Creativity is rarely a single brilliant spark followed by a straightforward path of execution. Ed Catmull, founder of Pixar, compared early ideas to ugly babies that need to be protected from being judged too early[76]. This is where it usually goes wrong in companies: any idea that does not show immediate promise is killed quickly. In the words of Kevin Ashton, a British technology pioneer, "Creation is a long journey, where most turns are wrong, and most ends are dead. The most important thing creators do is work. The most important thing they don't do is quit."[77] Creation demands engagement, every single day. "Ideas are fragile. If they were resolved, they would not be ideas, they would be products,"[78] writes Jony Ive, former chief design officer at Apple.

— **Examine hostage situations.** Sometimes, teams might be creatively blocked. This might be due to over-relying on following certain rules too systematically. Voyager leaders, as a result, ought to identify and remove the limitations that these procedures impose. Additionally, people sometimes struggle with a self-limiting belief regarding their capacity of being an idea generator. Voyager leaders help determine whether colleagues hold themselves back. If needed, they coach and support.

— **Encourage colleagues to explore.** While deep expertise is crucial to creativity, it's rarely enough. If you look at any great body of creative work, you might notice how various insights come from outside the original domain. Interdisciplinary thinking matters. Charles Darwin, for example, spent years studying fossils and thinking about evolution. But it was a 40-year-old economics essay by Thomas Malthus that inspired Darwin's theory of natural selection.[79] It's important, however, that you provide employees with an environment of psychological safety, where leaders illustrate similar behaviours and both encourage and empower people to explore unexpected directions and take risks.

— **Brainstorm.** Merely generating many ideas is unlikely to be sufficient. Voyager leaders improve colleagues' ability to understand creativity and stress the importance of gathering input from friends, colleagues, customers, and partners. The combination of expertise, exploration, and collaboration leads to most breakthrough ideas. Seek detailed feedback from stakeholders (co-creators, potential customers, clients, and others). No matter how brilliant you are, you are probably less brilliant than the full force of a multi-stakeholder co-creation process. It is critical, on the one hand, to involve peers for idea development purposes and, on the other hand, to stimulate a process where colleagues **alternate between solo thinking and group thinking.** Brainstorm with colleagues, go for a drink with a friend, and engage with stakeholders. You will have the opportunity to talk through your ideas to stimulate and challenge your thinking.

However, don't just follow the standard method where you *brainstorm for answers*. People are conditioned to keep the answers and solutions coming. This phenomenon is strongly visible in most classrooms. Students are judged by how well they answer questions. Yet teachers universally agree that few students ask questions because they have internalised a fear of asking questions in class. Questioners are considered pesky; their questions suggest that others haven't quite figured out things. People become masters at keeping questions to themselves, solely voicing answers. Perhaps we might try and brainstorm for questions every now and then?

— **Question bursts.** Teams can use a different lens to investigate issues – Hal Gregersen, senior lecturer at MIT's Sloan School of Management, proposes *question bursts*[80]. Underpinning this is a broader recognition that reframing problems into fresh questions yields novel, even transformative, insights. Gregersen devised several steps:

EXERCISE

Set the stage. Select a challenge that your team cares deeply about. Invite people to help you reflect on the problem. It is advisable to include two or three people who have no direct experience with the problem. Give yourself a couple of minutes to lay out the problem to the participants, how solving it would change things, and to explain why you are stuck.

Start the brainstorm by saying, "Everyone, let's forget about answers today and, instead, come up with new questions we can ask about this problem."

Brainstorm the questions. Set a timer and spend four minutes collectively generating as many questions as possible. The time pressure helps participants stick to the "questions only" rule. Aim for at least 15 questions. Emphasise quantity rather than quality. Redirect anyone who suggests an answer or tries to display their knowledge. These acts cripple a group's capability. Write every question down verbatim to prevent censoring.

Identify the quest. The exercise is likely to produce at least one question that successfully reframes the problem, providing a new angle to solve it. Study the questions that were jotted down and look for those that suggest new pathways. Expand those and generate follow-up questions. You can work via the "five whys" sequence developed by Sakichi Toyoda, founder of Toyota Industries. Why is the question important and meaningful? Why haven't I done this in the past? And so on.

THE LOST ART OF LISTENING

In order to make co-creation successful, Voyager leaders need to make sure people listen to each other. Boris Groysberg and Robin Abrahams, respectively professor of Business Administration and research associate at Harvard Business School, mention that "While listening is a skill universally lauded, it's rarely, if ever, explicitly taught as such, outside of training for therapists."[81] Our focus on talking, rather than listening, is also visible in business schools, for example. Oral communication skills, like presenting, are deemed priorities of the workplace environment and are embedded as learning goals. But even in places and professions where listening is a key skill, things go wrong. It's common for doctors to interrupt patients within 11 seconds, while a patient – on average – needs 29 seconds to describe some of their symptoms.[82] At work, 94% of managers who evaluate themselves as good listeners are rated the worst listeners by their employees.[83]

DID YOU KNOW?

Research from Neil MacLaren and colleagues (2020) considered whether a person's speaking time predicts their emergence as leader. Some even argued for a "babble hypothesis"[84] – which suggests that only the quantity of speaking and not the quality determines whether people attribute emergent leader status to a speech-dominant individual.

It is highly likely that you consider yourself a good listener. Unfortunately, we are as skilled in assessing our listening skills as we are in assessing driving skills: we all think we score above average. You might recognise yourself in the following:
— Not talking when others are speaking.
— Signalling that you are listening. This can be through facial expressions, nodding, and verbal sounds (the "hmm-hmm").
— Being able to repeat what the other person just said.

While the above-mentioned behaviours are often considered illustrative of good listening, they fall short of what a good listener should truly be doing. The elements of listening are as follows:

THE FOUR LEVELS OF LISTENING

As a Voyager leader, you need to be able to listen fully to the members of your entrepreneurial team to learn from their ideas and findings. In addition, you can help your team members listen to each other. Customers also need to be listened to. They can provide you with very useful information on your digital ideas if you listen to what is on their mind. Senior MIT lecturer Otto Scharmer[85] identified four levels of listening and their impact on communication and collaboration.
— **Level 1: basic listening.** This is passive listening, or downloading, with little interest in what is being said. It is listening to confirm what you already know. You listen politely, without being completely present.

— **Level 2: factual listening.** You pay attention to the content and open yourself to new information. You seek to broaden your knowledge but remain on an intellectual level.

— **Level 3: empathetic listening.** The connection goes beyond the facts and you enter into a real dialogue. You empathise with the speaker and try to understand their emotions and experiences. This form of listening fosters connection and mutual understanding. It entails being fully present, not judging the message of the speaker and attempting to understand the other person's point of view rather than solving the issue.

— **Level 4: generative listening.** This way of listening makes collective creativity possible. A dialogue that is not just interesting but transformative is created. You are connected to a shared project and the potential future. This level of listening is characterised by curiosity and courage. There is mutual trust and you are permitted to use your intuition. As a Voyager leader, the challenge is to engage in level 3 and level 4 listening. This kind of listening is a prerequisite in order to co-create successfully. It is also important to train your team members in empathetic and generative listening if you want them to develop innovative and useful digital solutions.

ACTIVE LISTENING

In practice, it is not easy to listen attentively. Often, you start searching for responses before the speaker has finished talking. You might interrupt them to share personal, often similar, experiences. Although it might appear as if you are listening, this is rarely true: you think about other things, are distracted by to-do lists, or have already formulated an answer. Psychologists William Miller and Stephen Rollnick call this phenomenon *the righting reflex* – your innate desire to fix problems and offer answers.[86] As a result of this reflex, you hear only part of what your conversational partner is saying. Sometimes we should just *WAIT* and wonder, *Why Am I Talking*? Ernest Hemingway said, "You need two years to learn how to talk but 50 to learn how to be silent."

EXERCISE: AN INVITATION TO LISTEN

Think back to the last time you felt someone was fully listening to you. How did that feel? When was the last time you dedicated yourself to a conversation? Are there times when you listen more? If so,

— **When** did you do this?
— **Why** did you do this?
— **How** did you do this?

We invite you to take up the task and, when the opportunity presents itself, to get rid of all external and internal distractions and to completely commit yourself to the person in front of you and their story.

The human brain has the capacity to process 300 words per minute, while you can only speak around 120 words a minute. And you think about four times faster than other people talk. It is not surprising that you sometimes drift off during a conversation. As you are reading this sentence, dozens of thoughts might be going through your mind right now – *What will I eat for lunch? How will I respond to that email?*

"SAWUBONA!"

Whenever you interact with someone in an empathic, non-judgmental, and attentive way, they become less anxious and less defensive. Adam Grant states that people then feel a certain pressure to think more deeply about what they are saying, which encourages them to explore their own ideas and opinions more deeply, to recognise nuances, and to share more openly.

While many communicators talk to make themselves seem intelligent, great listeners try to make their audiences feel intelligent. You might think, "I will talk less next time!", but listening well is more than a matter of talking less and being silent. The Zulu, the largest ethnic group in South Africa, greet each other by saying, "Sawubona!", which literally translates to, "I see you!" This brings the other person into existence. They signal that they accept and validate them.

Listening is a skill in which you push and pull information to help yourself and others progress faster; in which you ask and respond; and in which you not only pay attention to the words, but also to tone and body language. The best listeners are those who periodically ask questions that promote discovery and insights. The questions they pose are gentle challengers of assumptions. These techniques can help to nurture your listening skills:

— **Establish receptivity.** Minimise external distractions (i.e. noise, interruptions) and internal distractions (i.e. set an intention to deliberately focus on this person, in this moment, on this topic). Communicate beforehand that you are open to talk about concerns and issues that might be important to them. Make it clear that their (personal) agenda matters. A good listener makes the other person feel supported and conveys confidence in them.

— **Leave prejudices and assumptions aside.** Listening is an act of empathy in which you attempt to see the world from a different perspective. This requires awareness of your prejudices and refraining from making assumptions.

— **Start with interest.** Do not judge the other person's status or ideas; do not try to prove your ideas and status. Instead, be genuinely interested from the start. Be curious and consider listening an opportunity for free education. All people have stories, experiences, and ideas. Allow yourself to discover these insights and try to learn from them.

— **Be aware of nonverbal cues.** Your and other people's behaviours – eye contact, tone, social cues, body language, nodding, and more – during a conversation are telling. They express motivation and emotion. Be attentive, show that you listen – smile, make eye contact, and nod. Consider what their body language conveys – do they seem stressed, tense, perhaps sad, or happy and open?

— **Slow down and Practise the Pause.** Give others the time to finish their story. Allow pauses and silences. Show your conversational partner that what they say is important.

— **Reflect.** Summarise what your conversational partner said, repeat their ideas and and ask whether this is correct to confirm that you were listening. Do not completely rephrase it in your own words as this increases the mental load on both parties.

— **W.A.I.T.** Wonder, "Why Am I Talking"?

Listening is more complex than we might think. In a world focused on problem-solving, we need to create awareness and show empathy by listening and observing; to synthesise input; and to sometimes delay talking and acting. Boris Groysberg and Robin Abrahams advise you to not think of yourself as a good or bad listener, but rather to evaluate yourself on the subskills mentioned above.

EXERCISE: THE LISTENING CIRCLE

The benefits of listening are not limited to one-on-one conversations with your colleagues. The same benefits can also appear in group conversations. The Listening Circle is a method for improving listening in companies.

Gather a group of colleagues and place their chairs in a circle. Find an interesting object that serves as a strong and present symbol in the room – a teddy bear, a peculiar coffee mug, perhaps a small plant.

In the listening circle, only one person at a time can hold the object. The object serves as a reminder to others that it is not yet their turn to start talking. Once you have finished talking, put the object on the floor, signalling that you have finished. Repeat the process.

CO-CREATION WITH EXTERNAL STAKEHOLDERS

Voyager leaders stimulate co-creation within their own entrepreneurial team. They use the diversity in the team to come up with creative solutions. Next to their entrepreneurial team they can also co-create with external stakeholders. Some examples are:

— FedEx was confronted with a live tissue transport problem for organ donation[87]. These donations had to be completed flawlessly and on time. FedEx worked with various stakeholders to solve this issue (surgery scheduling staff, surgeons, patients, and medical device suppliers). The co-creation resulted in SenseAware, a sophisticated package technology that tracks the location of the live tissue, but also the temperature, pressure, and humidity.

— IBM partnered with shipping giant Maersk to co-create TradeLens, a blockchain-based platform that modernises global trade by offering real-time visibility and reducing overall inefficiencies in the shipping industry[88]. While discontinued, the platform brought together multiple stakeholders, such as shippers, authorities, port operators, and more, to track shipments and share data in a secure manner.

— Philips is known to co-create health-technology solutions with hospitals and healthcare providers to improve patient care[89]. This partnership allows the company to develop technologies that meet the specific needs of professionals, such as AI-driven diagnostic tools, patient monitoring systems, and connected medical devices. Philips actively joins forces with clinicians to guarantee that its innovations are both user-friendly and practical.

While these might be excellent examples of co-creation, such collaborations also entail some risks. Co-creation programmes with customers have proven to be a difficult value-creating activity, particularly since the rise of social media. When you invite customers to participate in brainstorming sessions for advertising taglines or product ideas, you bring out the best in customers, but also the worst – and sometimes customers *hijack* these sessions. It's therefore important to consider two things before you embark on such co-creation strategy. First, you must have prior experience with creativity and co-creation in the workplace. For example, your employees may want to feel at ease with the concept and its processes. Second, you must have identified a (major) issue that your company cannot solve on its own.

WHAT COULD CO-CREATION AT SUPPLYTECH LOOK LIKE?

Julio and the SupplyTech team will need to engage with product managers, developers, customer service representatives, and salespeople with direct insights into customer feedback and technological capabilities. Furthermore, their key external stakeholders include supply chain professionals, customers and their (potential) users, and perhaps even other technology partners. It might also be of interest to SupplyTech to consult academic experts.

Given the nature of PlanBot, a digital platform might prove to be worthwhile. Julio can think of implementing an online collaboration tool or a dedicated portal where stakeholders can submit ideas, feedback, and potentially engage in discussions. Physically, SupplyTech can think of hosting workshops or setting up innovation labs, providing a space where stakeholders can meet and prototype. This might be particularly interesting when PlanBot can be demonstrated and interacted with. PlanBot's stakeholders might be interested in joining regular hackathons, design sprints, and feedback sessions as these activities are often designed to brainstorm on new features, troubleshoot problems, and explore innovative ways to integrate PlanBot into user workflows. Additionally, SupplyTech can think in terms of organising interactive webinars and training sessions to help, for example, end users better understand the tool's capabilities. What's more, such interactions are often fertile grounds to sprout and collect feedback.

By focusing on these interactions, stakeholders are more likely to gain a sense of ownership and be more willing to invest in the product's success. Additionally, they might benefit from the various networking opportunities with peers and industry experts. Current PlanBot users could even enjoy greater satisfaction and loyalty as they notice how their input helps in shaping the product. Doing so helps Supply-Tech to smooth over any frustrations that users might currently have.

THE DO'S AND DON'TS OF CO-CREATION

Still, there are some clear *do's* and *don'ts* of co-creation. Stefan Stern, Edelman's ex-director of strategy, provides us with some great pointers.[90]

Do's	Don'ts
Look for the outliers: rejecters, extreme users, hackers, and bloggers.	Don't interact solely with professional opinion leaders.
Be open-minded about who to recruit. This could be a schoolteacher, a skydiver, anyone. Any variable can be a valuable design variable.	Don't just recruit your typical stakeholder profile. Their ideas are likely very similar, reducing the originality in your creative process.
Build a strong (online) community where people can share ideas, build on each other's work, give critique and praise, and perhaps compete. Consider it a web that expands in size over time and where stakeholders can interact directly with one another.	Don't underestimate the effort required to keep such communities engaged. Don't wear them out with repetitiveness and a never-ending stream of polls. Don't let your community grow too large too quickly. Nurture your creative stakeholders gradually.
Consider alternatives to monetary incentives as a motivator. Invite your top creators to the company, for example, and bring them together. Encourage people to constantly come up with new ways to add value.	Don't criticise stupid-sounding ideas. While they may not be what you want or are looking for, these suggestions were made in an attempt to help you.
Invite all levels of the company and confront them with customers who are modifying and customising products. Challenge their assumptions.	Do not present a co-created idea to product teams and label it as a finished product. Instead, do involve them in the co-creation process.
Involve users from the start. If you want to develop better syringes, involve nurses. They have extensive knowledge on the product.	Do not involve users only in one stage. Allow involvement throughout the entire process, from ideation to development and beyond.
Creating new experiences for your end users begs you to create better experiences for your internal players. Make sure that everyone involved is rewarded with a good experience.	Do not only consider how reality might change for your customers, but also think about how employees might experience a new reality.

REFLECTION

Do you recognise any of these do's and don'ts when it comes to entertaining digital transformation in your company? Are there some clear do's that you engage in, or are there some don'ts that have ensnared the company?
— What are your three favourite do's that you want to try out and embed in the company?
— How would you deal with them?

New ideas, products, and services must be meaningful to the customer and other stakeholders to achieve successful *customer-centric value creation*. According to John Pfeil, an emeritus innovation facilitator, these ideas, products, and services must meet an important and relevant need in a novel way. As such, listen to *the Voice of the Customer* – their needs, insights, and ideas can help your company create new products that are truly relevant to your stakeholders. At LEGO, for example, they regularly engage children in the process of character development, storytelling, and providing feedback on new play set ideas. Mads Nipper, former head of marketing and product development liked to say, "Kids will never lie to you about whether something's fun or not."[91] The first advantage of co-creation is thus *relevance*. The second advantage is the *breadth of perspective*. If you explore from a limited perspective and thus see only a portion of the opportunity, you blindly walk into a dangerous pitfall of the ideation phase. Wouldn't it be a waste of your time and resources if you focused on a part of the opportunity that wasn't really that important to your stakeholders? Co-creation enables you to investigate and define all critical aspects of an opportunity. A third advantage is *stretching* – as different points of view interact, co-creation sets off a chain reaction of creativity and ideation: when you hear an idea that you would never have thought of yourself, it sparks a new wave of ideas. What's more, co-creation is likely to foster a sense of *shared ownership* – the fourth advantage.

STORY CONTINUATION

Facing **severe backlash** on the initial release of PlanBot, the company's leadership took a bold step back to reassess their approach and list the tool's shortcomings. They recognised that the original PlanBot **failed to meet industry needs and standards** because key stakeholders were not invited to the table and, instead, a siloed innovation process was preferred. Acknowledging this, SupplyTech pivoted and now embraces co-creation. In response, and together with various stakeholders, the company strives to ensure that the chatbot still evolves into a valuable tool for supply chain planners. Leadership also appointed Julio as partnership liaison to oversee this change.

Addressing the burning platform at SupplyTech

To embrace co-creation, SupplyTech hosts a series of activities to source stakeholders' ideas, suggestions, and needs.

— By organising stakeholder workshops, the company invites supply chain managers and directors, logistics coordinators, and planners to distil new features for PlanBot. In doing so, SupplyTech is better positioned to understand the daily struggles of customers. Any feedback on real-world use cases and pain points are integrated directly into the development process.
— Pilot programmes allow external customers to test beta versions of PlanBot in safe sandbox environments. This offers PlanBot invaluable feedback on how the tool can be improved in real-time, resulting in a much more user-centric tool that is tailored to individual needs.
— SupplyTech worked closely with clients' actual end-users – those planners and operators whose daily life would be impacted by PlanBot. The company considered their input as critical in reshaping the chatbot's user interface, making it more intuitive, accessible, and attractive. A more sleek conversational design was introduced and SupplyTech has loved the suggestions of some planners to allow for custom commands integration.

Learning from these co-creation and brainstorming activities, SupplyTech was able to introduce several key innovations that transformed the chatbot into a highly effective tool. By co-creating, SupplyTech is now positioned to develop industry-specific versions of its bot. The company also benefited from direct access to certain customers' real-world data and scenarios. This helped SupplyTech to fine-tune the tool's ability to make intelligent recommendations based on specific dynamics within certain supply chains.

This shift to co-creation didn't only improve PlanBot's functionalities and market-fit; it also transformed SupplyTech's relationship with the market. As the organisation now adopts a more **transparent communication strategy** – sharing progress updates – and integrating stakeholder feedback, customers' trust is actively being rebuilt. Customers greatly appreciate SupplyTech's proactivity and are eager to share success stories and testimonials about their co-creation journeys.

PlanBot's turnaround underscores the power of co-creation and stakeholder collaboration in driving successful innovation. SupplyTech learned that developing a product in **isolation**, no matter how advanced the technology, does not guarantee success. By **engaging** with several stakeholders, the company was better able to **align** its product with real-world needs, improve functionality, and ultimately regain the trust of the market. Active co-creation is now the cornerstone of SupplyTech's strategy.

Reflecting on SupplyTech's situation, how would you, as a Voyager leader, use co-creation to enhance the chance of PlanBot's success? Could the use of technology help?

EMBRACING VULNERABILITY AND AUTHENTICITY

EMPOWERING TRANSFORMATION THROUGH VULNERABILITY AND AUTHENTICITY

Introduction

Jonathan was brought into NexTalent, a recruitment company, to drive a major digital transformation initiative. The company's traditional model relied heavily on manual processes for identifying and matching job candidates with the requirements of client companies. Yet the industry was being engulfed by digital platforms, automation, and unique user experiences.

To maintain competitive advantage, gain that extra edge over others, and remain relevant in an increasingly digital space, NexTalent's leadership strived to **innovate and explore** new digital value propositions. Jonathan was mandated to steer this change by leveraging technologies to increase overall efficiency and company attractiveness.

Jonathan established the Digital Services Lab (DSL) at NexTalent **to facilitate** this transformation. The lab was meant to serve multiple purposes:

— A safe zone for experimentation, where employees could explore new ideas without any fear of failure.
— A process innovation hub, aimed at creating more efficient workflows for the recruitment process.
— A training ground for digital savviness, cultivating the necessary skills and mindset for the digital future.

The problem at NexTalent

Quite soon after the DSL's launch, transformation efforts stalled, and Jonathan's leadership style revealed cracks. The DSL did not become the creative, collaborative hub it was envisioned to be. Jonathan had positioned himself as **overly controlling** in his management of the lab and its processes. Rather than allowing the DSL to be a space for experimentation, Jonathan had assumed **strict control** over key decisions – such as who would participate in projects, which external providers could or could not be contacted, and which tools were used. Jonathan had decided himself that the first lighthouse project would be to develop and launch a smart mobile application that connects job seekers with possible mentors for career guidance and networking, enhancing the overall job search experience by means of valuable insights and professional advice. Jonathan had commissioned the actual development of the app to GoWithCode (GWC), a fast-growing start-up across the street.

This bred a sense of **mistrust** and an overall **reluctance** to take initiatives. Employees mostly feared repercussions if they made any decisions or even suggestions that diverged from Jonathan's preferences. A **culture of control** had settled in with people having become passive, waiting for directives rather than taking ownership. While Jonathan had gathered an expert project team – consisting of Jan Plirus (job coaching and placement), Anaïs Bruy (marketing), Carol Stefans (data science), and Maria Mendoza (information systems), they didn't dare to push the project forward and always ran to Jonathan for guidance and approval. The relationship with GWC had gone sour as well, as these stakeholders were used to fast sprints yet continuously hit a wall whenever some decisions had to be taken by, who they expected to be, the project owners.

CULTURE OPEN TO EMOTIONS

We live in a world where competition reigns supreme from childhood. Kids strive for top grades and sports victories, while adults are bombarded with management literature on "How to win a customer" or "How to win a pitch". But life encompasses more than just winning and celebrating victories. People face setbacks, experience losses, and sometimes fail. Losing is an intrinsic part of the human experience. Silicon Valley humanist Tim Leberecht wrote, "I lose therefore I am."[92] However, while failure happens all around us, society has restricted the space for experiencing and expressing it without facing any social stigma. Still, defeat and loss are not mere bumps in the road that we should ignore; they are the very basis of our collective human experience.

This stigmatisation also extended into the workplace, where discussions about vulnerabilities, difficulties, and failures are often ignored or consciously shoved aside. Many companies aim for higher employee satisfaction and stronger performance, all while being concerned about employee wellbeing, yet frequently fail to recognise the critical role certain less-celebrated emotions play in achieving these goals. The reluctance to embrace vulnerability and the hesitancy to share emotions create an environment where making mistakes is discouraged. Have we lost the art of losing gracefully?

As a Voyager leader, you want to explore solutions through a build-measure-learn-feedback cycle. This means you need to allow vulnerability. Your team members need to dare to speak up when things are not working; they should be able to share how they feel about the process and the difficulties they encounter. The late professor of management Sigal Barsade pointed out that many organisations neglect employees' emotional wellbeing, not fully understanding how pivotal certain emotions are in fostering the right culture. This suggests that it could be worthwhile to shift towards acknowledging and valuing the full spectrum of human emotions.

The affective renaissance and emotional culture

When leaders don't take emotions into account, they neglect a vital part of the organisation. Emotions are more than just noise or a nuisance. They are rich data sources – communicated verbally and nonverbally (i.e., facial expressions, vocal tone, and body language) – that reveal how colleagues feel, what they think, and how they might behave. Emotions are crucial for a variety of reasons,

> "Emotions influence not just employee wellness and engagement, but also business outcomes such a productivity and profitability [...]. The type of emotional culture organisations or departments have – for example, whether it's based on caring, optimism, or anxiety – predicts many important work outcomes, including employee absenteeism, teamwork, burnout, satisfaction, [feeling safe], and objective performance outcomes like operating costs."[93]

Emotional culture reflects the perspective and values of leadership. Changing a company's emotional culture is not always about grand company-wide declarations but rather also about the small gestures. Even the littlest acts of support contribute to a culture of care and compassion. Consider giving a compliment.

When people receive a compliment every now and then, they are likely to feel more competent and trust in their own capacities grows. This feeling of competence is, according to the theory on self-determination, one of our core needs for remaining intrinsically motivated. Especially now that people work more from home and interact less, they feel more out of touch with their performance. As Voyager leaders work in a rapidly changing environment in which they explore solutions with their team, supporting colleagues with small gestures helps to stay motivated in this process. Bart Soenens, professor at the University of Ghent, provides three tips.[94]

— **Relate your compliments to the process instead of to the person.** By focusing on the actions people take and the efforts they put in, you are more likely to encourage a growth mindset, compared to when you focus on attributing certain successes to their inherent traits. It is particularly empowering if you are reinforced by the idea that your skills and abilities can be developed through dedication and hard work.

— **Don't save a compliment until something is finished.** Recognise things as they happen. This helps to sustain motivation and engagement throughout projects. Furthermore, it shows that all parts of the process are valuable. This is especially crucial in longer-term projects where end results take time to materialise.

— **Refrain from abusing compliments to get something out of it.** Compliments should be given freely and sincerely, not as a tool for manipulation to achieve hidden agendas. When you use a compliment in an authentic manner, you are more likely to build a genuine connection. People are perfectly capable of discerning between a compliment that is meant to encourage or a compliment with certain strings attached.

Historically, *armoured leaders* achieved their positions by virtue of experience and in-depth knowledge. They were expected to provide certainty; to provide answers. They had to exude an aura of knowing the most in the workplace and employees felt very little independence because of it. Many leaders recognise themselves in the following words by Peter Bregman, CEO of Bregman Partners,

> "I see myself as someone who can manage a lot of stress. Who can get a tremendous amount accomplished in a day. Who can work long hours and pull through in clutch moments. Who doesn't give up in the face of problems, but works tirelessly until they are solved. [...] most leaders I know feel the same way. We have to – our companies, our employees, our clients, our families – they all rely on us [...]."[95]

Colleagues in leadership positions often act like superheroes. Not necessarily because they want to, but because they have to; it is expected. We have established a certain sociocultural expectation of managers over the years where they must be perfect, in control, strong, always correct, and knowledgeable[96] – such superhuman behaviour, however, is counterproductive.

Firstly, it's unsustainable. At some point, reality is likely to catch up. With an armoured management mindset, you'd feel responsible for all output and be convinced that your colleagues expect you to know everything. This is of course worrisome as there is simply too much information around us to know and master. Secondly, employees need to feel connected with you. They want to help you. And when you allow them to, they feel inspired. The armoured mindset, however, sees colleagues dissuaded from voicing opinions and ideas; their sense of independence is taken away; and they are discouraged from thinking for themselves. Why is this? Maybe colleagues believe that their boss is the only one with the authority to make decisions and solve problems? Maybe they fear being blamed for mistakes? A new mindset, on the other hand, challenges colleagues to come up with answers themselves.

Breaking through that armoured management routine of "I have to know it all" – is not easy though. It demands courage, self-awareness, acknowledgement of weakness, and a shift towards vulnerability. It demands strength and bravery; it demands daring leadership.
— **Armoured leadership** is characterised by people's reliance on control, defensiveness, and fear of vulnerability to maintain authority. They tend to suppress emotions and install rigid boundaries. Such self-protection mechanisms often lead to a culture where employees are discouraged to voice ideas, make mistakes, or take initiative.
— **Daring leadership** is grounded in openness and willingness to be vulnerable. Leaders embrace transparency, admit mistakes, and encourage employees to bring their whole selves to work rather than only their best selves. They create a culture where people feel safe to take risks, share opinions, and can grow.

VULNERABILITY: FROM WEAKNESS TO STRENGTH

The concept of vulnerability is derived from the Latin word *vulnus,* or *wound,* which expresses our "capacity to be open to a variety of wounds"[97]. Vulnerability is often seen as synonymous with powerlessness, dependency, and feeling exposed. Across many cultures, we were raised with the belief that being vulnerable is being weak. Therefore, it's often frowned upon. However, Rumi, a famous 13th century Sufi mystic and poet wrote, "The wound is where the light enters you." So, let's take a step back from this prejudice – what does vulnerability embody? And can you benefit from it?

Instead of seeing vulnerability as a lamentable weakness that must be overcome, Brené Brown defined it as "the emotion that we experience during times of uncertainty, risk, and emotional exposure".[98] Vulnerability is the ability to show people you are not perfect, that you make mistakes, and that you don't have all the answers. It is showing that you want to rely on others to move forward together. It's empowering colleagues to make decisions themselves. And it's also the thrill you feel on your first day at a new job; excitement about a new project; or speaking out against disrespect in toxic cultures. Vulnerability is about showing compassion for others, about allowing emotion.

Vulnerability is not the same as letting everything out, though. Discipline and self-awareness are still needed to understand what you can share and with whom. Nonetheless, having your feelings and experiences acknowledged, both by yourself and others, is vital. Emotions provide insights into what motivates people and how you can help them improve their performance.

Three distinct types of vulnerability exist: **personal, relational**, and **external** vulnerability. While personal and relational vulnerability focus on the individual and the relationships we have with other people, external vulnerability focuses on your company's stance towards the outside world. External vulnerability adds an extra dimension for the Voyager leader to consider.

PERSONAL VULNERABILITY

As cracks appear in a seemingly perfect façade, openness to external input filters through. This is advantageous. First, people are more likely to acquire information that is useful for projects and personal growth. Adam Grant invites you to think more like a scientist, starting from hypotheses. If you, for example, must take a decision, consider this a hypothesis to be researched. It's wise to wear *the scientist's goggles* to look at your assumptions about work, and more. You may come to fresh and healthy perspectives. Working via the concept of *hypotheses-antitheses-theses* makes you more flexible in your thinking and creates awareness that making mistakes is not necessarily bad. It sounds contradictory, but there is real *joy in being wrong*.

Also dare to be the idiot in the room: if you do not understand something, ask questions until you do. Most likely some other people in the room will quietly thank you. Consider how Jonathan takes complete control over the Digital Services Lab at NexTalent. Instead, he might want to accept being – sometimes – the idiot in the room. A true Voyager leader shows some vulnerability by asking questions and trying to understand other people's ideas.

WATCH OUT: EMOTIONAL LEAKAGE

Colleagues who are practically oriented might believe that bottling and suppressing emotions gives control. You can hear them say, with the best intentions, "Think positive!", "Let's get on with it", and "Move on!". They consider themselves more productive because of it.

While they feel in control, suppressed emotions will get out – somehow, sometime. As this is unintended, psychologists call this emotional leakage. This leak can be a flow of magma, showing the first signs of a volcanic eruption of bottled-up emotions. Now imagine your entire company is filled with people who could erupt.

When leaders don't push their own thoughts and are willing to entertain different perspectives, they create an atmosphere of openness and honesty. If, instead, a leader never shares emotions, the conviction emerges that they are inauthentic and only talk to promote themselves. When a leader reveals their personal side, their colleagues will perceive the leader's words as more authentic.

RELATIONAL VULNERABILITY

Vulnerability also relates to how we rely on others and the understanding that, without trusting the relationships we have, and the expertise others hold, we are likely to continue a path of perfectionism and control. External vulnerability additionally suggests that vulnerability can be understood as our capacity to relate to others in an authentic manner. Therefore, we can see vulnerability as a pre-condition to connect with others. If people don't act from such a position and instead walk a path of control, they are more likely to burden themselves and stifle other people's growth. To move towards a practice where you mentor and value others, you can, for example, stimulate input and idea generation rather than presenting too many of your own ideas. At NexTalent, Jonathan could try to stimulate his project team to take ownership.

WATCH OUT: OVERDOING VULNERABILITY

Vulnerability increases trust and fosters a connection between colleagues, but too much vulnerability undermines you.

To balance over- and under-sharing it is recommended to be selectively vulnerable and open up to others while respecting boundaries.

Vulnerability is not unidirectional, however. It must be owned by you, your colleagues, customers, and all stakeholders. One of the key aspects of vulnerability is the fact that it is a two-way street. Colleagues should not bug you about the smallest details and decisions. This pulls you back into old leadership styles where you might get stuck micromanaging. While you might work on being more open, colleagues might still expect you to have all the answers – because of your seniority, your higher salary, or any other reason. What can you do to counter this?

— **Predefine** your new style and define what changes for colleagues. If they do not know what is expected from them, how can they feel, let alone be, empowered?
— **Show openness and acceptance towards ideas.** This shows that you are serious about your new way of working. Vulnerability is multidirectional and colleagues should also learn to share ideas openly. Do not give your own answers/ ideas immediately but let others do the thinking. Provide feedback instead.
— **Address your feelings before you become emotionally leaky.** We all have off-days. If you are in a bad mood, your colleagues will pick up on it and might think they are the cause. It's best to say, "I'm having a bad day, but it is not because of you. The last thing I want is to make yours worse as well." No additional details necessary.
— **Be absent from some operational meetings.** If you are overly present, colleagues will look to you for decisions, denying their own empowerment. As a leader, voice your opinion and ideas only at the end of a meeting. Do remain aware that if you push your ideas as the only viable solution each time, you do not empower.
— **Create a safe environment to make mistakes.** Colleagues might experience quite unpleasant consequences to honest mistakes. They did not expect that to happen, but it did. In some companies, the immediate response is to blame. Is it in yours?
— **Stimulate the law of reciprocity.** Rather than allowing a "chicken or egg" dilemma – who goes first? – dare to be the first one to showcase (some) vulnerability.

— **Trust someone.** Have someone close to give you advice and guidance. Someone to call after a meeting and ask, "How did that go? How did I do?". A Voyager leader builds on their feedback capacities.

EXERCISE: EMBRACE THE FUCK-UP

Some organisations organise "failure festivals" where employees and managers stand up and talk about their mistakes to share lessons learned. Some publicly admit that they don't have all the answers, which empowers their team to take more ownership.

In a less grand manner, you can also opt for a so-called "failure wall", which is a tool that encourages learning from mistakes in a constructive manner. Generally, you create a physical or virtual space to share failures, mistakes, and lessons learned from projects and tasks.

Not only do you promote learning through more transparency and open discussions, you might also foster a growth mindset by discussing setbacks. This, in turn, stimulates innovation and collaboration.

Once you establish a level playing field and everyone's value is recognised, decisions are more likely to be taken collectively. Considering all this, relational vulnerability revolves around two notions: on the one hand, it's about overcoming one's need to bolster professionalism by understanding that being vulnerable can also be a source of power; on the other hand, it's about letting go of the cultural ideas of a strong managerial solitude by favouring a vulnerable relationship with others.[99] In the exercise below, we invite you to find out how culture is defined in your team – is it *armoured* or is it *daring*? Perhaps ask your colleagues to fill it out and compare the results.

EXERICSE: ARMOURED VS. DARING DIGITAL TRANSFORMATION LEADERSHIP

Armoured leadership													Daring Leadership
We continue our experiment and/or blame others	-5	-4	-3	-2	-1	0	1	2	3	4	5		We stop the experiment
We try to manage/control problematic behaviours	-5	-4	-3	-2	-1	0	1	2	3	4	5		We address the fears and feelings that show up during change
We get stuck by setbacks/disappointments/failures and put time in reassuring the contribution of team members	-5	-4	-3	-2	-1	0	1	2	3	4	5		We learn from setbacks/failures and discuss with team members what we learned
We shame and blame	-5	-4	-3	-2	-1	0	1	2	3	4	5		We learn and take accountability
We aim for perfection and nurture fear	-5	-4	-3	-2	-1	0	1	2	3	4	5		We learn and grow
We avoid tough conversations, including giving honest and productive feedback	-5	-4	-3	-2	-1	0	1	2	3	4	5		We hold tough conversations, including giving honest and productive feedback
We don't take the time to celebrate	-5	-4	-3	-2	-1	0	1	2	3	4	5		We celebrate milestones
We know and we are right	-5	-4	-3	-2	-1	0	1	2	3	4	5		We are learners and we get it right
We critisise others/the system to protect ourselves	-5	-4	-3	-2	-1	0	1	2	3	4	5		We make contributions and take risks
We collect gold stars for ourselves	-5	-4	-3	-2	-1	0	1	2	3	4	5		We give gold stars
We zigzag and avoid challenging conversations	-5	-4	-3	-2	-1	0	1	2	3	4	5		We do straight talking and take action
Total score =													

How did your team score? The closer you are to -55, the more *armoured leadership* is present in your team. The closer you are to +55, the more *daring leadership* is present in your team. Is there a difference between how your team scores and the rest of the organisation?

On which aspects can you still improve?

EXTERNAL VULNERABILITY

External vulnerability is the exposure and openness of an individual or company to outside influences and changes that might be beyond their direct control. Consider certain economic fluctuations, actions from competitors, changes in regulation, and – of course – technological advancements. If fostered correctly, external vulnerability can be deployed as a tool for strategic awareness and readiness for interactions. Voyager leaders, in this regard, embrace their company's position of external vulnerability to navigate the organisation through certain uncertainties in a more effective manner, leveraging new opportunities.

DID YOU KNOW?

People tend to remain attached to a certain choice they made in the past, even though it might no longer be a good choice anymore. The sunk cost effect is attributed to high-stakes decisions across a variety of contexts and often involves a wide range of costs that can be "sunk" – i.e., money, time, effort, emotion, and/or belief.

"We already put so much in, why not continue?"

More specifically, external vulnerability builds on the idea that no individual or company can operate in isolation nor control all variables. This means that we must recognise our dependencies on and influences from external stakeholders. Additionally, external vulnerability requires a certain openness to external input – consider the value you might derive from seeking feedback and insights from outside your organisation and, perhaps, industry. This could mean that you actively engage with experts, incorporate customer feedback into product development, or consciously collaborate with others, such as tech companies, startups, and academia in favour of new perspectives and capabilities. By doing so, you are more likely to better understand and be prepared for potential risks in the environment. By means of portraying external vulnerability, you can make a more realistic assessment of the external environment: it might help you identify risks and, more importantly, mitigate them by developing contingency plans to manage them effectively. For example, certain industry trends, competitor movements, or technological advancements might fly below your radar if your company's external vulnerability is not calibrated correctly.

In the context of external vulnerability, Voyager leaders start from a 360-degree introspection of themselves, their company and industry. This helps them in capturing blind spots and adapting accordingly. Because the Vigilant leader searches for external input, an active relationship appears between Voyager and Vigilant leaders. A Vigilant leader could suggest investing in advanced data analytics and market intelligence tools to gain real-time insights into market trends and customer behaviour. These tools, nowadays often empowered by big data and AI advancements, can help to provide predictive insights. A Voyager leader experiments with how these tools can be effectively put to good use. The combined power of these leaders improves decision-making as it is now based on a more comprehensive understanding of the company's internal capabilities and external realities.

EFFECTIVE AUTHENTICITY

Vulnerability invites authenticity. If people are not true to themselves, they end up playing a role. Vulnerability, in this regard, aids in being authentic – reducing the distance between who you are on the inside versus who you are on the outside. But authenticity – and vulnerability – does not always work. The notion of adhering to your "own true self" does not correspond with the idea that humans evolve with each experience. When you unearth new facets of who you are, what you can do, and where you can head to, your authenticity might change as well. Voyager leaders are aware of and create awareness of multiple landmines:

Authenticity has no borders. *False.* People often believe that being authentic gives them the latitude to be blunt. Opinions will still be perceived as attacks.

Authenticity is all about me. *False.* Authenticity without empathy creates selfishness. Some exclaim, "This is who I am" to excuse their behaviour. In most cases, toning down individualistic behaviour helps you master authenticity. Does this make you a fake? No. You are a team player who considers others.

Authenticity is where it all starts. *False.* People might believe that trust and credit come to them when they show authenticity. This is not the case. It is imperative that you have already shown competence and positioned yourself as relatable and credible – this is called the "idiosyncrasy credit", or your capacity to acceptably deviate from certain group expectations.

EXERCISE: AUTHENTICITY

What does authenticity mean in your life? And, in this case, where would you position yourself?

DISTANCE BETWEEN WHO YOU ARE ON THE INSIDE VERSUS WHO YOU ARE ON THE OUTSIDE

LOW ① ② ③ ④ ⑤ ⑥ ⑦ ⑧ ⑨ ⑩ HIGH

Can you think of specific situations at work where you feel you can be more authentic compared to other times? Are there situations where you feel you are less authentic? Do you fell less authentic entertaining digital transformation?

How does it feel when you are more authentic? And how does it feel when you are restricted in your authenticity? What are the moments when you say to yourself, "This is the real me"?

Do you feel like your colleagues can be authentic at work when discussing digital transformation, or does it feel like people are playing a role, trying to mirror the majority?

STORY CONTINUATION

Jonathan's preference for control inhibited creativity and the authenticity of his team. To ensure the success of the Digital Services Lab and the lighthouse project with GoWithCode, leadership has tasked Jonathan with relinquishing some of his controlling tendencies.

Addressing the burning platform at NexTalent

Firstly, Jonathan is addressing his **personal** vulnerability. Previously, his reluctance to admit he didn't have all the answers led him to maintain tight control, stifling ideation and experimentation. Now, by acknowledging and sharing his uncertainties, Jonathan no longer appears infallible. Previously, his lack of personal vulnerability inadvertently signalled that uncertainty and doubt were signs of weakness. Now, embracing personal vulnerability allows Jonathan to demonstrate that uncertainty is a natural part of digital transformation, encouraging his team to innovate and take risks without fear of failure.

Secondly, Jonathan is focusing on **relational** vulnerability. His previous micromanagement created relational barriers within the Lab, making it seem as though he lacked trust in his team to take ownership. By stepping back and allowing team members to make decisions, Jonathan is cultivating an environment where mistakes are viewed as learning opportunities, not failures met with reproach. This shift helps build stronger, trust-based relationships within the team, promoting open communication, and empowers team members.

Thirdly, Jonathan has begun to address **external** vulnerability. By unilaterally deciding to collaborate with GoWithCode, he limited NexTalent's exposure to new perspectives and innovations that could enhance the Lab or elevate the lighthouse project. Recognising this, embracing external vulnerability now allows Jonathan – and NexTalent – to be more adaptable to changing market forces and to seek out additional experts and vendors who can provide fresh insights and tools, enriching the company's transformation journey.

Adopting a more vulnerable leadership approach, Jonathan's shift in behaviour is clearly felt within his project team and the company. This shift significantly solidifies NexTalent's position in the rapidly evolving recruitment industry. By fostering a more vulnerable environment, Jonathan not only promotes a culture of innovation and authenticity, but simultaneously positions the company as more adaptive and collaborative. NexTalent stands to gain a competitive edge as it is now more likely to be considered a forward-thinking leader in the field.

Reflecting on NexTalent's situation, how would you rely upon **vulnerability and authenticity** to improve the lighthouse's chances of success?

BUILDING UPON DIVERSITY AND INCLUSION

THE INCLUSION IMPERATIVE FOR RUNNING DIGITAL TRANSFORMATION JOURNEYS

Introduction

Bram is project manager at Innovora, a mid-sized company specialised in the development and implementation of innovative healthcare technology solutions for enhanced patient care and healthcare workflows. Their current portfolio consists of tools that can be directly integrated in existing healthcare systems to provide seamless, patient-centred solutions. For example, their Electronic Health Record (EHR) Integration tool connects various EHR systems into one cohesive platform, allowing for easier data sharing between departments and external providers. More recently, they added an AI-powered diagnostics tool to their solutions to help healthcare providers in diagnosing medical conditions and offering insights and recommendations. Overall, Innovora has built a reputation for creating tools that support both the healthcare provider and the patient. The company is well-known for its mission of making healthcare more accessible, efficient, and patient-centric. As such, they have learned to focus on interoperability, user-friendly interfaces, and always meticulously checking regulatory compliances. They are approached by MediSana, the country's second largest consortium consisting of both large hospitals and small clinics.

The consortium strives to enhance their continuity of care and is asking for a telemedicine app. MediSana is already a long-time customer of Innovora, relying on various tools such as the company's EHR platform and various remote health monitoring devices. This app, however, has to enable patients to schedule consultations and consult with their healthcare providers remotely, receive personalised health advice, and track certain health metrics; for healthcare providers it is supposed to improve the speed and quality of pa-tient care. The consortium is confident that the data from the remote and online consultations will flow easily into the patient records and that health data tracked by wearables can be easily shared and accessed through the app as well.

The problem at Innovora

Excitement is high within the company but the stakes are high for Innovora as well. Not only is this a crucial project, the tool will be an unexpected addition to their product range, further helping them in their market reach and solidi-fying their position. Several departments (marketing, IT, etc.) eyed this project, eager to **collaborate**. Due to a gap in its internal development capacity, In-novora decided to bring in TechGears, a dynamic startup, **based abroad**, that is well-known for its technical expertise and innovative approach to product development. It has a reputation for delivering results rapidly and their in-volvement promised to add much-needed technical muscle and know-how to the project.

The **involvement of various stakeholders** initially seemed like a major as-set. All internal people brought different perspectives on how to build a us-er-friendly and effective app. Additionally, the inclusion of TechGears invited fresh ideas and new, more dynamic ways of working. Customers, too, were in-volved in the process through user testing, ensuring that the app would meet the real-world needs of patients and providers. Quite soon, however, Bram noticed **disconnections** on various levels. Internally, for example,the project team struggled to understand the different points of view. While marketing was concerned about how to make the app as customer friendly as possible, the IT person was focusing on how to make the app work.

Externally, TechGears' push for quick iterations and a remote-first approach **clashed** with Innovora's teams who were more accustomed to in-person meetings and pre-planned workflows. Innovora's IT staff, consequently, was **overwhelmed** by TechGears' fast pace and were unfamiliar with TechGears' digital collaboration tools. Feedback from patients and healthcare profession-als was left **unheard**.

The high levels of excitement and energy that had characterised the project's early days had dissipated. Deadlines were slipping. A **lack of harmonisation** fell upon the project, resulting in miscommunication and mounting frustration. People felt **excluded**, with trust eroding and morale disappearing. Innovora's leadership was questioning the viability of the project and MediSana's liaison had voiced concerns as well. Without a swift intervention, the once-promising telemedicine app would dive head-first over a cliff, with Innovora's reputation following suit.

With the forces of globalisation impacting companies relentlessly, we operate in an increasingly diverse tapestry of collaborations: companies are often engaged in sizeable partnership structures and ecosystems and find like-minded, yet also diverse partners to share ideas and prototypes with. On the employee level, 89% of employees occasionally complete projects in global virtual teams, and colleagues are from increasingly diverse and unique backgrounds.[100]

WORKING WITH DIVERSITY

Workplace diversity has the power to put companies ahead of the competition. Nancy McKinstry – who successfully managed to lead publishing company Wolters Kluwer[101] through a digital transformation – explains how increasing diversity raises a group's cognitive resources and ability to engage in more complex problem solving and thinking. As former IBM CEO Ginni Rometty said, "If you want to find new ideas, it can help to listen to different voices, to hear from people with different backgrounds and different experiences."[102] While diversity of thinking can enhance innovation performance by about 20%, this doesn't come for free.[103]

Kathleen Vangronsvelt, professor of organisational behaviour and human resource management, discusses how there are two opposite processes at work when it comes to diversity. When you collaborate in a team with diverse backgrounds, personalities, values, and so on, positive and negative processes are at play. Consider the positive: more diversity means more perspectives to approach a problem with, and, as such, more ideas and more knowledge. "Team members who differ a lot from one another bring in a wide variety of information,"[104] Vangronsvelt writes. Now consider the negative: more diversity causes less cohesion and weak group identity. "After all," she concludes, "we simply feel more attracted to people who are similar to us."[105] People with similar backgrounds share norms and assumptions on how to behave, set priorities, and so on.

Audre Lorde, famous 20th century civil rights activist, wrote that people often believe their differences divide them while it is actually the inability to recognise, accept, and celebrate those differences that causes the divide.[106] People's contrasting ideas and perspectives should be considered a bonus. They help you find new and innovative ways to understand challenges and deal with problems.

REFLECTION

It can be hard to shift our perspectives, especially when we are passionate about something. Do you often see things from other points of view? Or do you view alternative perspectives as a nuisance or even an inconvenience?

Where, in your job and related to digital transformation, could you benefit from multiple and diverse perspectives?

How will youacquire these perspectives?

TYPES OF DIVERSITY

In companies, diversity traditionally used to be about racial and ethnic diversity. Diversity in the workplace is more than that, however.[107] While people with a *neurodivergent* brain may display, for example, dyslexia and high sensitivity and are therefore often labeled as being "different", neurodivergence is also linked to several qualities such as creativity, pattern recognition, and hyper-focus. While they are often labelled as "different", neurodivergence is also linked to qualities such as creativity, pattern recognition, and hyperfocus. It's important for Voyager leaders to look broadly – to aspects such as background, education, life experience, identity, and neurodiversity.

What's more, employees differ in using technology, digital tools, and data. Consider *digital natives*, who grew up with digital tools; *digital immigrants,* open to learning and change; and *digital refugees*, who avoid digital tools. Digital transformation doesn't necessarily force employees to learn how to code nor to understand the underlying dynamics of advanced technologies, but still requires *immigrants* and *refugees* to grow in their understanding of and comfort in working with and alongside technology.

Voyager leaders build their awareness and map out the full latitude of diversity in their teams. Cambridge professor Brian Little said, "Each of us – each of you – is, in certain respects, like other people, like some other people, and like no other person."[108] Until you have a holistic view of someone and their team, your perspective remains flawed. Mapping out diversity helps you spot potential sources of strength and friction. But how broad can diversity really go? Three dimensions are identified that make up individuals and influence teams and projects.

— **Primary dimensions** (race, gender, age, and disability) are the immediately visible aspects of diversity that shape our basic self-image and influence how we perceive ourselves and interact with others. Including people from various backgrounds, might help a company in ensuring that a certain technological application is developed in a more inclusive manner and meet the needs of a broader user base. Furthermore, you are better positioned to avoid unintended biases in how the technology is designed.

— **Secondary dimensions** (religion, culture, sexual or political orientation, nationality, economic status, education, neurodiversity, etc.) provide a deeper layer of diversity that shapes thought processes and problem-solving approaches. These aspects are vital for a digital transformation, for example, as different educational backgrounds or cultural perspectives could help in inventing more innovative solutions and addressing challenges more creatively.

— **Tertiary dimensions** (beliefs, feelings, and values) are about the core of your identity and grow as a result of various experiences. During digital transformations, the Voyager leader can collaborate with the Visionary leader, who is well-versed in topics such as purpose, to better understand what drives each team member and how they relate to a certain vision. It's worth focusing on these dimensions as aligning deeper values can help you in fostering greater and more authentic teamwork.

WATCH OUT: RELATIVITY!

If one person, group, or culture experiences you like this or that, another person, group, or culture will not necessarily experience you the same way. In fact, their experience might contradict the first group's experiences. These are called opposite reactions. Erin Meyer states, for example, that someone from the UK can find a French co-worker imprecise and indeterminate, while a colleague from India can find the same French co-worker strict and rigid.[109]

While secondary and tertiary components are rarely visible, this doesn't mean that they are less powerful; on the contrary – their subtlety makes them extra challenging. The Voyager leader develops the awareness needed to notice and make sense of these silent interactions. By mapping out and integrating these three dimensions, Voyager leaders can create more inclusive environments for their entrepreneurial teams. Nonetheless, be aware that laying out all these aspects might be a threatening exercise that creates confusion and overloads you. Instead, try and focus on just a few of them rather than trying to address them all.

MYTHS OF DIVERSITY

When leaders wrongly understand diversity and how deeply ingrained some qualities within employees are – and the frustrations this could cause – an unhealthy atmosphere spreads throughout the company. As long as leaders do not evolve their understanding of diversity and inclusion, companies remain shackled by various myths.[110]

> **Myth 1:** The most effective approach to diversity hiring and diversity goals is to double down on the primary dimensions – i.e. visible aspects of diversity, such as race and gender.

> **Myth 2:** The best way to find your ideal candidate is by narrowing down the perfect profile as much as possible.

> **Myth 3:** If these diversity sourcing efforts are effective, everything else will be fine.

"Before you know it, you end up with an entire staff that looks, thinks, and – to a degree – acts almost exactly the same,"[111] concludes Naomi Wheeless, board member at Eventbrite. A narrow focus on diversity and predefined skills is the perfect recipe for overlooking people's broader, diverse qualities that could enrich the company. And even if you do succeed in avoiding myth 1 and myth 2, you may still struggle with making sure people feel included – i.e. myth 3.

Recruiters often hire candidates who mirror the existing workforce – the same educational background and skillsets; source candidates from the same talent pool; and search for similar personality traits during interviews. Companies that fall victim to these myths (and biases) risk stalling their internal ideation capacity. To prevent this, companies need to be aware of internal biases and understand the value of diversity of thought.

When you bring people from different backgrounds together, you have a much more complete way of seeing things. Your team might, as a result, spot more risks and come up with innovative solutions, but only if you manage these differences. How can you do this and what can Bram do at Innovora?

Respect diversity. It's dangerous to assume that you are identical to someone else in a certain way. For example, you and your new colleague have a history degree. You might conclude, "Awesome! We will be a great team!" But suddenly you find out this isn't the case. What happened? You forced one shared aspect onto the relationship and onto your colleague's identity.

In the project, Bram must be careful not to assume that certain shared roles or professional backgrounds will automatically lead to harmony or effective collaboration. For example, though both healthcare professionals and IT experts are working toward the same goal, their perspectives, work styles, and contributions to the project might still differ significantly. Bram should avoid generalising based on surface-level similarities.

Decode diversity. Colleagues' skills and qualities are assets to build upon. First visualise and map these skills to better understand them. You are also likely to map potential sources of friction, which can help you leverage diversity. This helps you in clarifying and promoting inclusive behaviours. Ideally, you do a similar exercise whenever you engage with an external partner.

Bram can map and visualise certain skills and perspectives within the stakeholder community, identifying strengths and weaknesses, which is likely to generate insights regarding potential sources of friction. For example, healthcare professionals could have valuable insights into patient needs, while TechGears brings technical expertise. On the other hand, diversity might create certain misunderstandings, such as the different work approaches between TechGears' agile sprint cycles and Innovora's more structured processes. In the context of TechGear, the diversity issue was two-fold: on the one hand, TechGear was a start-up, used to a culture of speed and rapid iterations; on the other hand, TechGear was based in another country and had a different cultural background than Innovora. Regarding this, it might be interesting for Bram to rely on Erin Meyer's Culture Map, which we discuss in more detail in the reflection below.

Get all the ideas out in the open. Try not to push your personal ideas but be open to different ideas – remember the importance of personal vulnerability and pulling feedback as a Voyager leader. When searching for new ideas, avoid the pitfall of wanting to reach consensus too quickly.

To foster innovation and collaboration, Bram might want to encourage an environment where all stakeholders can share their ideas openly without fear of judgment. Here, it's important not to push for quick consensus and instead allow space for different viewpoints – for example, healthcare providers are likely to provide relevant suggestions for patient care features, while IT professionals could provide insights into better system integration. By promoting vulnerability, Bram prevents the team from overlooking such valuable insights. Furthermore, sharing personal experiences might result in new, valuable insights.

Make things explicit. When you add colleagues and external parties to a project, the unwritten rules and understandings that acted as a common ground might transform into sources of conflict. You can move this implicit knowledge towards explicit knowledge through concrete rules of engagement. Define upfront how to take decisions, how time management is organised, how to disagree and give feedback, and so on. In countries like Sweden and the Netherlands, for example, decisions are made consensually, while this happens top-down in Italy and India. Germany has a very strict linear-time perspective, while China and Brazil prefer more flexible time-orientations. But two colleagues from the same country also differ[112].

The project was suffering from a lack of clear decision-making processes and task divisions. Bram might strive to address this by making explicit rules of engagement regarding feedback, time management, and more. This can help in avoiding conflicts that are rooted in different working norms and are thus particularly useful when dealing with diverse work cultures.

Be aware of the diversity paradox. Remember the two opposite processes of diversity: more diversity equals more perspectives, but also removes cohesion. Acknowledge the risk of difference. While diversity has various advantages – such as ideation and problem solving, humans are hardwired in their hostility towards "the other". This could result in enmity to outgroup members. When you invite diversity, tribalism often tags along. The Voyager leader builds teams that are diverse enough to be innovative, but also cohesive enough to work smoothly together.

Bram clearly faced a case of diversity paradox. His challenge is now to create a culture that balances innovation with cohesion. To this end, Bram can involve other leaders and, together, build shared values around the project's mission – improving healthcare accessibility. However, if the differences would be too big, Bram would be wise not to force this and instead search for another partner.

REFLECTION

Erin Meyer's Culture Map[113] is a framework to help teams navigate the complexities of working across different cultural backgrounds by breaking down communication and management styles into eight key dimensions:

— **Communicating:** high-context vs. low-context communication. In high-context cultures such as Japan or France much of the communication is implicit, while in low-context cultures such as the United States or Germany, messages are more direct and explicit.

— **Evaluating:** direct vs. indirect feedback. Some cultures are more comfortable with direct negative feedback, such the Netherlands and Germany, while others prefer a more indirect approach, such as Japan and India.

— **Persuading:** principles-first vs. applications-first Some cultures, such as the United States or France, emphasise principles first, while others focus on practical applications, such as in Brazil.

— **Leading:** egalitarian vs. hierarchical leadership. Some cultures such as Sweden and Denmark have flat(ter) structures and encourage egalitarian decision-making, while other cultures have a more hierarchical approach, as can be seen in China or Russia.

— **Deciding:** consensual vs. top-down decision-making. In cultures such as Japan or Sweden decisions are made by consensus, while in other cultures, such as in India or the United States, leaders make decisions more independently.

— **Trusting:** task-based vs. relationship-based trust. In the former, trust is built through business results and performance, while in the case of the latter, trust is established through personal connections and networks. In this regard, cultures such as the United States or Germany (task) differ strongly from cultures such as China and Brazil (relationship).

— **Disagreeing:** confrontational vs. non-confrontational approaches. Some cultures will be more comfortable with openly disagreeing, as can be seen in France and Israel, while others will avoid direct conflict, such as Japan and Indonesia.

— **Scheduling:** linear vs. flexible time. In linear-time cultures, punctuality and deadlines are critical, while in flexible-time cultures, schedules are seen as more fluid and adaptable. This is why cultures like Germany and Switzerland could sometimes be perceived as strict and punctual, while cultures like India or Saudi Arabia have a more flexible approach.

By understanding these cultural dimensions, people like Bram can ensure that their strategies for collaboration are considered inclusive and effective across different organisational context. Now,
— How would you map **your culture** on these dimensions? And, by having a look at your collaborations, how would you map **your international stakeholders** on these?
— Which **frictions and similarities** do you see appear?
— What kind of **agreements** could you install to make this collaboration work?

INCLUSION AS THE ROAD TO RETENTION

Diversity often invites additional complexity and will inevitably strain colleagues' abilities to understand each other. Voyager leaders forge teams where diversity is a strength – they do so by actively aiming for inclusion. A first solid basis is formed by understanding each other's way of working and background. But most of all, we must consider the nature of the tasks at hand: projects that require creativity benefit from diversity of thinking; projects that require completion or are more routine and task based often need less innovative thinking. In this case, less diversity could allow for more efficient completion of projects. In both settings, it's necessary to proactively assist colleagues, ensure more effective communication, foster strong interpersonal dynamics, and grow a collegial climate. However, this needs to come with a warning. Professor of Management Frederik Anseel perceives an evolution where companies cheer for more employee participation. Companies want a plentitude and diversity of voices. As such, Anseel says, "Leaders are trained to create a psychologically safe climate where people can voice their opinions without fearing backlashes. But if you invite people to speak up, don't be surprised when they actually have something to say and what they say is maybe not what you had envisioned."[114]

A diverse workforce can be important to customers and might give the business a cutting-edge advantage in globalising markets. The inclusion part of the story, however, plays hide-and-seek. Inclusion, within the context of DEI, is a practice where you strive for and create an environment where all individuals feel valued and supported, allowing them to fully participate in the organisation. It moves beyond more representation as it actively integrates diversity. While noninclusiveness is seen as one of the toxic five elements of company culture[115], diversity-and-inclusion initiatives frequently hit the brakes as "various subtle – and not so subtle – barriers are deeply ingrained in many organisations. These may go largely unnoticed in policies and practices," writes Marianna Fotaki, professor of business ethics.[116] Colleagues often cover identities – they hide important parts of themselves for fear of stigma, ridicule, and more. While inclusion is hard work, it's worth the effort.

— **Diversity** is about *the what* – it focuses on the makeup of your workforce.
— **Inclusion** is about *the how* – the creation of a work environment and culture that enables all employees to participate and thrive.

THE OUTCOMES OF INCLUSION

Employee engagement is an outcome of both diversity and inclusion: successful inclusion, for example, reduces levels of conflict and staff turnover. Josh Bersin, advisor on topics such as HR, leadership, and the work-life intersection, states that highly inclusive organisations have 1.8 times more likelihood of being change-ready[117] and research shows that teams with inclusive leaders are 17% more likely to report as high performing, 20% more likely to say they make high-quality decisions, and 29% more likely to report collaborative behaviour[118]. A diverse and inclusive environment also has a positive impact on innovation and creative problem-solving.[119]

According to Daisy Auger-Domínguez, CPO at Vice Media Group, "There is a very special energy in organisations when employees feel seen, heard, and valued and when they feel they can contribute, collaborate and perform without judgment or retaliation. It keeps organisations from feeling dark and heavy, it keeps the mistrust out of the air, and it keeps talented employees from leaving your organisations and worse."[120] Diversity and inclusion researcher Delia Mensitieri also considers it crucial to reduce identity threat if you want to promote and improve inclusion. She argues that,

> "Before diversity practices can work, there first needs to be an inclusive environment where everyone feels they can be their authentic self. If an employee feels that he/she cannot express who he/she is in their organisation, it can 1) trigger subtle and unintentional behaviours such as microaggressions (comments or actions that subtly and often unintentionally express prejudiced attitudes toward a member of a marginalised group), 2) negatively impact the way some employees perceive their organisation as inclusive, 3) which in turn impacts their performance, career aspirations, and employee satisfaction."[121]

A POSITIVE INCLUSION CLIMATE

Inclusive leadership ensures that everyone feels they are treated respectfully and fairly. A diversity-and-inclusion-rich company culture makes employees feel that their identities are valued and celebrated: it is the degree to which people are embraced and feel enabled to make meaningful contributions; it reflects a sense of belonging. People need this. Historian Rutger Bregman considers group feeling and group cohesion to be among the main characteristics that made homo sapiens the dominant species.[122] Inclusion and belonging are still principal drivers of survival for many of us. This also holds true at work: while colleagues who feel highly included in a workplace with a low commitment to diversity are more engaged compared to colleagues in a workplace with high diversity and low levels of inclusion, the combined focus on diversity and inclusion delivers the highest levels of engagement. Inclusion spans a variety of corporate dimensions, such as socialisation, training and education, and structural and informal integrations.

REFLECTION

What could the opposite of inclusion – exclusion – feel like? Perhaps you struggle with some of these feelings? Are you aware of colleagues who voiced struggling with this?
— The unease of walking into a meeting where no one else looks like me.
— The unease of leaving earlier to pick up your kids at school.
— The frustration of being ignored in meetings and not being asked for your opinion.
— The pressure of always trying to fit in.
— The anxiety to share and discuss personal stuff.
— The strain when conversing in my non-native language and hearing "how good you are at it".
— The exasperation of people assuming I don't have ambition because I am getting older.
— The indignation that my promotion is not celebrated.
— The anger that I was promoted just to fill a quota.

Successful inclusion creates a friendly, professional work environment that values employees' talents and unique perspectives, and makes them want to stay. You can start focusing on inclusion by making tweaks, whenever necessary. What can you do?

Fair and equitable treatment. Favouritism kills inclusion. By favouring certain stakeholders and assigning work to the same top performers, you often connect the wrong people to projects and risk disconnecting others. Treat everyone fairly and impartially. Provide new colleagues with opportunities to prove themselves.

Integrated differences and effective collaboration. Diversity of thought is important, but requires signals to show it is respected and valued. Engage in participative decision-making by encouraging and incorporating input. If you discount alternative views, people are likely to hold back their perspectives.

Humility and curiosity. Be modest and humble about your own capabilities, admit that you can make a mistake, and allow others to contribute – do you recognise the need for vulnerability? Be curious about your colleagues and try to understand who they are.

Decision-making. Make sure all team members consider each other's ideas and suggestions (without favouritism). If alternative views are stigmatised, colleagues won't bring forward challenging perspectives.

Safe space. Inclusion craves an environment where people feel safe and can be open. Do not fear an open-door policy, for example, and allow one-on-one conversations. Find out, together, what people care about. Vulnerability can be a start: share your own thoughts and feelings when you are tired, sad, or struggling. Perhaps take an interest in colleagues' families. It is hard to succeed at work when things at home are failing. We talk about work-life balance but forget the importance of work-life support – show appreciation of non-work responsibilities.

Belonging. People sometimes wonder whether the company truly cares about them. Simply addressing people by name is a strong gesture of recognition. Is a sense of camaraderie present? Create opportunities for employees to meet and develop interpersonal relationships.

MOR BARAK'S FOUR-STAGE PROCESS

Diversity expert Michelle Mor Barak[123] outlines a continuous four-stage process for companies to practise diversity and inclusion management.

1. "Where are we?"
   Start with introspective questions: what are you doing to enable inclusion? To what extent is a climate for diversity and inclusion present in your team or department, and what quality does this bring for your colleagues? Don't stop at

introspecting. Trace employee engagement via surveys and segment the data by gender, ethnicity, generation, geography, and more. If you only look at the total sum of the numbers, you get a misrepresentation of reality and miss out on a chance to identify simmering issues that cause frustrations. Nonetheless, even though you segment, some level of generalisation and stereotyping will remain: there is a need to zoom in further, to spot and meet people in their "uniqueness". Approach colleagues from a position of curiosity. Soon you will notice how you no longer talk to a segment (i.e. "a generation") but to an individual with their own experiences and history, dreams and fears, realities. In the reflection below, Bernardo Ferdman and colleagues formulated the Organisational-Level Inclusion Assessment Matrix[124] – which you can use to monitor inclusion, find out where to intervene, and better understand the multi-identity workplace.

2. "Where do we want to go?"
Discuss a strategic plan of action that aligns with your company's or team's specific goals. The Voyager leader communicates confidently about what these tangible goals mean, and do so together with other V-leaders. For example, the Visionary leader is skilled in goal setting and storytelling, and can provide extra guidance.

3. "What do we need to solve right now?"
Take actions that address conflicts, tensions, and dilemmas on the work floor. To motivate yourself and others to pay attention to inclusion, consider inclusion nudges. These are short, timely, insightful prompts that activate inclusive behaviours to create conditions for all colleagues to feel respected and to bring their best "self" to work. Focus on three pillars: behaviours, messaging, and audience. First, select the specific behaviours that you want to nudge. These behaviours are ideally supported by research and backed by employees' experiences. Find out how colleagues experience diversity and inclusion at work. Don't forget that these behaviours should be concrete and actionable. Second, your message should be concise, engaging, and fun to read. You want to elicit emotional responses. Third, build your audience upfront. Grow a network of colleague champions who are enthusiastic from the start and who help you to create buzz. The Vested leader, for example, is an expert in building a change coalition, comprised of employees that can help in sustaining change and managing the complexities and challenges that come with it.

4. "What did we do? And what can we do better?"
Collect data on diversity and inclusion to understand the effects of your proposed plans. Phase four, is key – you reflect on how to think about inclusion. The Voyager leader helps to track the impact.

Mor Barak's model is self-reinforcing. You go through phases one to four, then keep the flywheel spinning – do not stop, but re-evaluate and make changes to your plan of action. Diversity is an ever-changing concept, and so are the requirements for successful inclusion.

REFLECTION

— **Openness**: How much are variability, complexity, and ambiguity embraced? Can colleagues differ from "the system"?
— **Representation and voice**: Is there a critical mass of diversity, with a mix of dimensions, when you make decisions?
— **Climate**: How valued do colleagues feel? Can they openly express themselves? What does it feel like to be part of the company?
— **Fairness**: Does everyone receive what they need and deserve, or is favouritism present?
— **Leadership and commitment**: Are the company's vision and mission connected to inclusion? Are leaders made accountable for inclusive behaviours and are they committed to it?
— **Continuous improvement**: Is inclusion considered a one-off act or a never-ending flywheel?
— **Social responsibility**: What kind of contributions are made to community and societal needs outside the workplace?

STORY CONTINUATION

Bram faces a critical challenge as the telemedicine app developed by Innovora begins to falter. Bram understood how the *paradox of diversity* was at play – the different perspectives of internal and external stakeholders indeed brought various unique and contrasting ideas to the table, but also reduced the group cohesion when it was much-needed. The initial idea of, "the more diversity, the better" had spun out of control and Innovora understood how they had underestimated the intricacies at play here. Though people were eager to collaborate, various unaddressed differences in work styles, expectations, and decision-making processes hindered progress. To turn the project around, Bram must leverage the strengths of diversity while fostering an inclusive culture to improve the collaboration and communication in this digital transformation journey.

Addressing the burning platform at Innovora: Part One

Bram started by mapping the internal and external diversities he could see at play. First, he went for the internal differences at Innovora: he consciously mapped beyond the primary dimensions. He paid attention to people's professional backgrounds and related tasks, and their working styles. He even zoomed in on colleagues' communication preferences. As things had gone wrong on the decision-making level, Bram strived for in-company inclusion by focusing on the following:

— **Explicit rules of engagement:** together, the various stakeholders draft clear expectations about communication and decision-making strategies. For example, they agreed upon refraining from 'yes but' during brainstorm sessions and, instead, went for the 'yes and' strategy. It is furthermore a basic requirement now that everyone is provided the opportunity to voice their ideas and is actively listened to.

— **Transparent communication:** regular cross-functional meetings are installed to bring together the different perspectives in a cohesive and structured manner. In these meetings, Bram takes on a crucial role by encouraging open discussions about priorities, challenges, and opportunities. Rather than allowing one group to dominate the conversation, Bram facilitates dialogues that act as a platform for all to share concerns and ideas.

— **Mindset building:** while before people might have considered this diversity of perspectives sometimes to be somewhat of an hindrance, it is now being recognised as an asset. Marketing professionals don't shy away anymore from contributing sometimes to a more technical discussion; healthcare experts don't fear being overshadowed anymore by others.

Addressing the burning platform at Innovora: Part Two

As a second major tension had become visible – between Innovora's internal team and TechGears –, Bram repeated the mapping exercise on an organisational level. The startup is very young, he realised, and the people working there clearly resemble the fast-paced world of the startup ecosystem: digital-first, daily stand-ups and rapid iterations, and hot digital collaboration tools. These contrast sharply with Innovora's rather traditional approach to project management. These differences had clashed many times by now – TechGears perceives Innovora as slow and resistant; Innovora perceives TechGears as restless and unstructured. A clear cultural gap has established itself. The dissonance had eroded trust, making it difficult to achieve successful collaboration. By mapping these differences through, for example, Erin Meyer's Culture Map, but also noticing similarities, Bram was better positioned to manage the frictions.

He decides on the following approaches:

— **Building cultural empathy:** Bram recognises that friction stems from different expectations on how work should be conducted. He sets out to install a hybrid model that accommodates both companies' working styles. To get there, however, he first organises a series of team-building activities to foster a better understanding between the two companies.
— **Foster psychological safety:** TechGears brings innovative ideas but sometimes feels like an outsider in Innovora's more established corporate environment. To make sure that the startup's voice is heard, Bram includes them in key strategic discussions and ensures that any suggestions are taken seriously, fostering a climate of mutual respect and open dialogue.
— **Shared metrics for success:** TechGears and Innovora must rally around something tangible. Together, they decide to build in metrics that relate to the end-user experience, patient and MediSana's feedback, and technical performance. These shared metrics further break down the 'us vs. them' mentality that had installed itself in the collaboration.

By focusing on inclusion, Bram is gradually able to turn two significant sources of tension – internal stakeholder diversity and the cultural gap between TechGears and Innovora – into opportunities for collaboration once more.

Reflecting on Innovora's situation, how would you **leverage the power of diversity and inclusion** even further to improve the company's chances for more productive co-creative teamwork? How could technology help?

ENERGY SCAN FOR VOYAGER DIGITAL TRANSFORMATION LEADERSHIP

A Voyager leader is an entrepreneur who connects and teams people up to make ideas tangible. They bundle diversity and creativity to show opportunity at work and, in doing so, turn the abstract into something real. Voyager leaders invent new ways to propel the business forward. They look for digital technologies to boost the productivity of exploration teams. To make this succeed, Voyager leaders don't assume that the way things have always been done is the best way to do them. They place a high value on learning and capturing lessons from experimentation. The cycle of learning is important to guarantee rapid and lean iterations between thinking and acting. To stimulate the entrepreneurial mindset they combine the diverse strengths and creativity of people. Feedback of customers and other stakeholders is very important to them in order to reach results and develop new opportunities.

Do you want to find out which of the Voyager leader skills give you and your colleagues energy? Take this short test.

1 = never 2 = rarely 3 = sometimes 4 = very often 5 = always

Questions	Your response (1 – 5)
I like to brainstorm	
I enjoy exploring opportunities with a diverse group of people	
I am most creative when being challenged by others	
I like to build on other people's strengths to develop solutions	
I like to receive honest feedback from and give honest feedback to colleagues	
I like testing and revising solutions through fast feedback cycles	
I like to define clear criteria to evaluate different options	
I like to take responsibility when exploring new opportunities	

Total score:

CHECKLIST FOR VOYAGER DIGITAL TRANSFORMATION LEADERSHIP

If you now wonder whether signs of Voyager digital transformation leadership can be spotted within your company, you can reflect on the following set of statements:

At [your company name], we **co-create**, *as we...*

understand that our knowledge is incomplete.	
source and welcome input.	
identify (beyond) our (traditional) stakeholders.	
tap into collective creativity and innovate with others.	
engage in acts of shared value creation.	
allow others to express their creativity.	
dare to let go of (some) control.	
are restless experimenters.	
unlock creativity in the self, the other, and the organisation.	
balance openness with focus.	

... act through vulnerability and authenticity, as we...

embrace daring leadership.	
destigmatise failure, setbacks, and vulnerability.	
take emotions into consideration.	
can be personally vulnerable.	
can safely relate to others.	
are aware of external influences and changes.	
have a realistic view of the company.	
can be true to ourselves.	
feel that we are authentic.	
are self-aware.	

... include, as we...

understand the (dis)advantages of diversity.	
can accept and integrate our differences.	
have a holistic view of diversity's three layers.	
understand and respect each other.	
strive for inclusion.	
respect people's identities.	
address acts of exclusion.	
are aware of the diversity paradox.	
rely on the power of diverse perspectives.	
skilfully navigate the complexities of working globally.	

CHAPTER 3

Visionary Leadership

TRANSFORMATIONAL PURPOSE

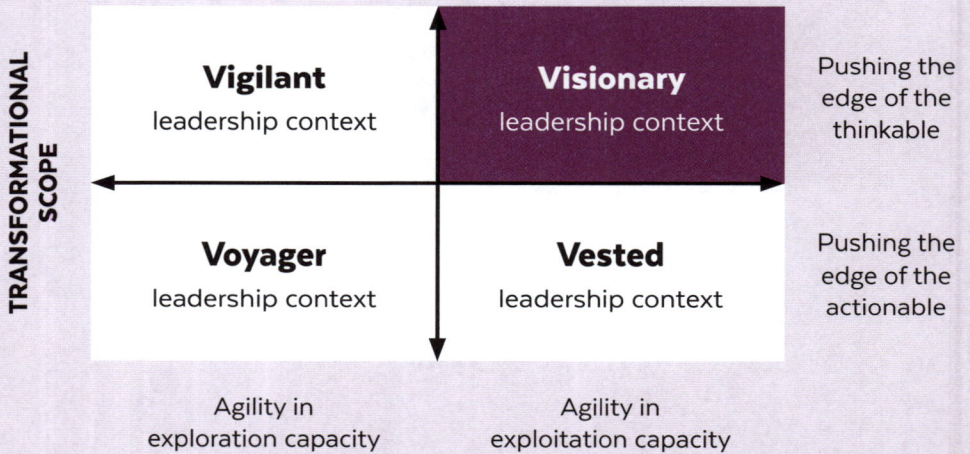

TRANSFORMATIONAL SCOPE

Vigilant leadership context	**Visionary** leadership context
Voyager leadership context	**Vested** leadership context

Pushing the edge of the thinkable

Pushing the edge of the actionable

Agility in exploration capacity

Agility in exploitation capacity

VISIONARY LEADERS

In the context of fostering and striving for a successful digital transformation journey, the Visionary leader focuses on a core set of tasks[125].

Visionary leaders...
— Tell a purposeful and inspirational transformative story of **competitive** advantage, advocating the empowering use of digital technologies
— Boldly rethink the organization's core **capabilities** and operating model for achieving digital-age customer-centricity
— Envision success by combining the organization's critical digital assets and those of ecosystem **partners**

To this end, Visionary leaders put various skills to good use in order to guide colleagues and the company through a *human-centric* process.

In the following chapter, we will introduce you to several digital transformation protagonists and how they build on these skills to foster a meaningful journey for themselves, colleagues and other stakeholders, and the organisation at large.
— Tom at Farbright School of Trade and Commerce who builds on the power of **purpose** to connect and inspire colleagues to foster greater **meaning;**
— Saim and Sophie at Family & Co Mart who discover how **storytelling** helps them in tailoring their message to their audience;
— Matthias at Müller & Sons Construction and how he shifted his mindset to become more appreciative of taking **risks;**
— Jürgen at AtlasNewspaper who approaches digital transformation **partnerships** from a fresh, new angle to move beyond standard collaboration practices.

CREATING A SENSE OF PURPOSE

TAKING THE LEAP IN THE DIGITAL AGE: THE POWER OF PURPOSE

Introduction

Farbright School of Trade and Commerce (FSTC), your business school alma mater and a prestigious institution with over a century of history, recently held its annual conclave. Having drinks with Tom, who is not only a long-term friend of yours, but also a fellow alumnus who had recently become business partner of the school, you hear that this year, the conclave focused on the school's digital **transformation narrative** and constructing an attractive vision aimed at preparing the institution for a future where the online and offline worlds of education seamlessly integrate. For the conclave, the school's corporate purpose was clear: to lead in the digital age by ensuring that its graduates are not just participants but leaders in a world where technology and human potential converge. "Overall," Tom says, "the discussions revolved around the question of what a business school could look like in five years' time."

The conclave kicked off with an inspirational keynote by a renowned digitalisation guru who highlighted the impact of digital disruptions worldwide. Attendees were then divided into small working groups to brainstorm ideas, with visual harvesters capturing the essence of each discussion. Among the numerous innovative and bold concepts, two ideas stood out that resonated with many: the **creation of a cognitive digital twin** for every student and building upon the **promise of digital twins for simulating learning** experiences. Both are expected to gamify the learning experience and provide the school with a modern image. The integration of digital twins in an educational setting holds immense potential for a personalised and adaptive learning experience, Tom tells you.

— By means of simulation, FSTC aims to vastly enhance students' levels of engagement by creating immersive learning experiences that simulate real-world settings. For example, students that want to strengthen their public speaking will be able to do so in various pre-modelled digital environments. Not only is this expected to help students hone their skills, capturing task-relevant data might help in effectively assessing and guiding the students' performance over time. Some stakeholders even suggested the introduction of certain active gaming elements such as rewards and challenges to encourage students to learn.

— In parallel, the school is brainstorming the idea of a cognitive digital twin. Together with an external provider, they are exploring the idea of developing a highly detailed, data-driven, virtual model of each student. The students' personalised *avatar* will evolve as the students' progress through their educational journey. The model behind the avatar would calculate growth and performance based on various data inputs, such as their scores, strengths and weaknesses, preferences, and overall progression. FSTC would be well-positioned to tailor each student's educational experience to match their needs.

The problem at Farbright School of Trade and Commerce
"The goal is clear," Tom concluded. "By means of this technology, we want to adapt the students' learning journey to maximise their potential." The introduction of digital twins for students is a bold first step towards realising and acting upon FSTC's corporate purpose. "However," Tom suddenly frowned whilst rubbing his temples, "we noticed that after presenting the conclave's outcomes and strategic agenda to our teachers and staff in a webinar, some **misalignment** started to appear. People are **uncertain** and **don't seem to connect** to our school's purpose." This is worrisome, Tom added, as the new academic year will soon start and they don't want the students' experience to be impacted by internal quarrelling.

PURPOSE AND MEANING

Shoei Yamana, CEO of Konica Minolta said, "My belief is that people don't work for numbers... they need to share the same belief that they are creating value in some way."[126] Richard Clark and Bror Saxberg, respectively professor of psychology and VP Learning at Chan Zuckerberg Initiative, furthermore write that "Managers are often at a loss as to how effectively motivate uninspired employees."[127] While the standard go-to solutions are often financial (higher salary and company car), highlighting the transactional nature of work, the rules have changed. Employees increasingly consider other aspects equally if not more important than traditional motivators.[128] For example, people who left their jobs cite how they didn't feel valued by their company (54%), didn't feel valued by the manager (52%), and desired to work with colleagues who care (46%).[129] Aaron De Smet and colleagues summarise this eloquently,

> "Employees crave investment in the human aspects of work. Employees are tired and many are grieving. They want a renewed and revised sense of purpose in their work. They want social and interpersonal connections with colleagues and managers. They want to feel a sense of shared identity. Yes, they want pay, benefits, and perks, but more than that they want to feel valued. They want meaningful – though not necessarily in-person – interactions, not just transactions."[130]

The positive effect of a signing bonus, for example, already fades after a couple of months. "People stay at a company because of developmental opportunities, challenges, a stimulating environment, purpose, or social awareness,"[131] HRM Professor Koen Dewettinck writes.

Considering this, *meaning* and *purpose* have become hot topics. They hold a core truth: people want to work for companies whose mission and philosophy resonates on an emotional and intellectual level. But what is the difference?

— **Vision** – the PICTURE: WHAT? Vision reflects a future-oriented, often aspirational statement that outlines where the organisation (or the individual) aims to be in the long term. By offering a shared picture, it strives to answer the question of "Where are we going?". This provides a clear direction and serves as a guide for decision-making and goal setting. **What do you want to see?**

For FTSC: "To transform education that empowers educators and inspires students"

— **Corporate purpose** – the FEELING: WHY? Purpose reflects the overarching reason for the existence of a company, its DNA beyond mere profit-making. It defines the company's reason for existence and is supposed to articulate how the company wants to have a positive impact on the world and its commitments to contribute to society, customers, and employees – which great problem are you solving? If you don't, what are the consequences or, who will do it instead? Why should people show up for your company? The corporate purpose digs into an organisation's morals, ethics, and beliefs. **What do you feel?**

For FTSC: "To foster an innovative world of education, where everyone has the opportunity to thrive in the 21st century"

— **Mission** – the JOB: HOW? A mission is aimed toward achieving a specific goal – often fulfilling the company's corporate purpose. A mission statement is the activity that you formulate to help realise immediate goals and provide focus to employees. **What do you do to create value?**

For FTSC: "To deliver cutting-edge digital tools, immersive content, and teacher training programmes that improve educational impact and meets the evolving needs of the modern classroom"

— It's important for organisations to formulate their corporate purpose. Not only does this provide clear directions and motivation for employees by means of, for example mission statements, it also provides customers with a certain clarity and certainty: "Why would I opt for this brand and not that brand?" Your purpose touches them in a certain way and convinces them that it's indeed your products that are the best option. Therefore, corporate purpose is often considered high priority for external branding efforts. But the importance of purpose doesn't end there – what about internal branding, for example? How strongly are your employees connected to your company and its reason for existence? The personal purpose of each employee remains often under appreciated in this story. Rather than merely focusing on building a strong corporate purpose, a Visionary leader understands how important it is to match corporate purpose with employees' individual purposes – ultimately striving for what is called *purpose congruence*.[132]

REFLECTION

— Deep down, what matters to me/you?
— What kind of relationships do I/you want to build?
— What do I/you want my/your life to be about?
— How can digital technologies play a role in what I/you want to achieve at work?
— How do I/you feel most of the time and which situations make me/you feel alive?
— What role do I/you want to play during digital transformation?
— Are there particular areas in which colleagues, and others, consistently seek my/your advice?
— What do I/you want people to observe when they see me/you?

INDIVIDUAL PURPOSE

At the same time, however, employees have their own personal purposes that motivate them. The **individual purpose** reflects the personal "why" behind an individual's actions and efforts. It reflects what drives someone, the values they live by, and the unique meaning they seek in their work and life. Individual purpose is often tied to a person's passions, talents, and sense of fulfilment. The COVID pandemic caused nearly two-thirds of employees to reflect on their personal purpose; and nearly half said the pandemic had them reconsider the type of work they did.[133]

Individual purpose is a difficult one; firstly, it cannot be mandated. The employee is the only one who can decide what their purpose is. Secondly, individual purpose is intensely personal, perhaps difficult to access for employers, and sometimes uncomfortable to discuss. Nonetheless, for 70% of employees, work defines their sense of purpose.[134] So why not assist them?

DID YOU KNOW?

Friedrich Schiller, German playwright, poet, and philosopher, wrote his famous poem "Sehnsucht" a Translation of 'Longing' by Friedrich Schiller, *The Society of Classical Poets*. in the 18th century. "Sehnsucht" can be translated as a combination of "longing", desire", "yearning", and "craving – a sense of incompleteness and imperfection in one's life, which might emerge when people reflect on and evaluate their lives.

According to researchers Susanne Scheibe, Alexandra Freund and Paul Baltes[135], sehnsucht "has important developmental functions, including giving directionality for life planning and helping to cope with loss and important yet unattainable wishes by pursuing them in one's imagination."

Purpose might sound like a pie in the sky. But it is more than a nice-to-have. The average employee works around 100,000 hours so it is important to look at how we can feel better about the time we spend earning a living. Everyone seeks profound reasons to get out of bed in the morning. Studs Terkel – author and historian – frames it as follows: "Work is about a search for daily meaning as well as daily bread, for recognition as well as cash, for astonishment rather than torpor, in short for a sort of life rather than a Monday to Friday sort of dying."[136] Purpose is a fundamental component of a fulfilling life.

Most people find it difficult to identify or articulate their purpose: approximately 85% believe they have a purpose, but only about 65% of them can really articulate it.[137] You may come across colleagues who know very well what motivates and energises them, and what their values are. Others might consider this a difficult, even confronting or confusing exercise. Most of the time, you plough ahead – autopilot on – and when your inner GPS no longer gives you a direction, you look left and right to see what others are doing. When you compare, you might be swallowed up, simply following the direction of the herd. We *go with the flow*. Unfortunately, going with the flow is a significant drain of purpose.

WALKING YOUR WHY

Interestingly, there is a *purpose hierarchy gap*, with executives nearly eight times more likely to say that work fulfils their purpose.[138] Visionary leaders can help people by, for example, asking them whether they are living their purpose and informing about the obstacles that prevent them from living it. To find your own purpose and help others find theirs, try the following exercises:

— **Keep a journal of activities.** Identify the projects and tasks that you find deeply satisfying. Which activities do you enjoy most, and which do you find energising? When do you feel fulfilled – when you can spend all day writing and reading, or when you're pitching new products to clients? What motivates your colleagues?

— **Share your "best-self" narratives with colleagues.** Daniel Cable, author of *Alive at Work*, proposes that colleagues share stories about seeing each other at their best. When was the last time you saw someone truly enthralled? Tell them. Encourage colleagues to do the same.

— **Build your five-year resume.** Who are you within five years' time? What has changed? Where do you live now? What courses have you taken? What industries and employers did you work for, and what have you learned from these experiences? Which technologies are you now able to use? What are your hobbies? And so on. Project an idealised form of yourself to help you uncover and better understand which steps you might need to take.

— **Write a love list.** Whilst building your five-year resume, it might be worthwhile to also start including things you would love to do (for example, "I want to learn more about street yoga," or "I want to read at least one fantasy trilogy every year," or "I want give learning to play the piano a try"). As you see, it doesn't have to be work or career related. By listing these, you might potentially uncover certain hidden passions. Allow yourself to be inspired by the power of, for example, images. The love list might grow or shrink as the years go on.

— **Build your Wheel of Life.** The Wheel of Life is a simple yet powerful tool to visualise all areas of your life at once: health, career, love, spirituality, family, money, fun, and friends. It is often used by life coaches and career coaches to give clients a bird's eye view of their lives. Visually representing this helps you to better understand which areas of your life are flourishing and which ones might need some extra attention.

— Over the course of 30 days, ask yourself the same two questions after closing your laptop or when returning home from work after a long and tiring shift: **when did I feel most alive today? When did I feel the most exhausted?** This could provide some interesting and possibly ground-breaking insights into how you feel about life and work. It might help you in identifying your values as well, which in turn, could help you filter out certain aspects of your life you may not want to focus on too much.

Ethan Hawke – actor, producer, and writer – mentions that "First we have to survive, and then we have to thrive. And to thrive and express ourselves, we must first understand ourselves. What do you enjoy doing? And when you get close to what you love, who you are is revealed to you."[139] To reflect further on this, consider the following statements and how this might link to Farbright School of Trade & Commerce.

— It is important to **act from a position of adaptability**, not absolute certainty. There is no such thing as sustained linearity in purpose, purpose comes and goes. Work and life are rarely consistently meaningful, and your purpose in your twenties could evolve into something else in your thirties, and so on. You can even pivot to new, different purposes to derive meaning from. You can lose sight of your purpose, but you can also discover new ones, and perhaps even resurrect old ones. You can even have more than one purpose. At Farbright School of Trade & Commerce, faculty members and staff can pivot and discover new ways to align their individual purposes with the school. By acting from a position of adaptability, they might be better equipped to re-engage with the school's new vision as their roles shift alongside technological advances.

— **Values are important** when you define individual purpose. They help you determine what is important to you. When your actions resonate with your values, you are more likely to find meaning. For example, if your values revolve around innovation and learning, making use of digital twins and being involved in their implementation could help you realise these values.

— **A relational approach is present** in the search for meaning. People can be moved by the "other" (i.e. a person or a company). In this case, your sense of purpose intensifies. You can be inspired by your manager, for example. When you notice that your work matters to others, you will perceive it as more meaningful. At FSTC, staff and faculty might benefit from understanding that their roles will also influence and shape students' digital twins and, as a result, they could even see their impact being visualised over time. Motivation theorist Abraham Maslow positioned self-transcendence at the apex of his human motivation pyramid[140] – people don't just talk about themselves when discussing meaningful work, they talk about its impact on others. In contrast, feelings of loneliness, disconnection, and marginalisation could appear if there is a lack of impact.

- **Meaningfulness and meaningful work don't always appear from a place of joy.** Often, people find purpose and motivation during difficult times, when painful experiences reveal causes they care deeply about. Consider how a personal hardship, whether experienced by yourself, a family member, or a colleague, inspires involvement in certain initiatives. For FSTC staff, the introduction of digital twins and the increased digitalisation of the teaching and learning process may initially be a disruptive or even uncomfortable change. However, this experience might very well help some employees discover new purpose in their roles, sparking a renewed sense of commitment and energy.
- **Purpose determines your attitude.** When you feel you act with purpose, you are more likely to feel at ease. Others will notice your inner peace.
- **Stories are crucial.** They provide direction and can open new possibilities from the past into the future. When people lack direction, motivation dwindles. At Farbright School of Trade & Commerce, storytelling can help to connect the past, present, and future, and help in motivating others.

REFLECTION

Purposefulness is rarely experienced "in the moment". Often, it only hits you when someone asks you to recount an event that you experienced as meaningful.

Which event in your organisational life of being a digital transformation traveler gave your life additional / a clear purpose? Don't stop there: ask your friends and colleagues the same question.

Purpose represents the "why" of our actions and efforts. It is something we do or create, not something we can buy, inherit, or pass on to others. Purpose is a "higher cause", a "raison d'être" – it answers why you are here on earth. Concepts such as goals and goal setting, on the other hand, can help people with the "what" and "how" to get there. Luckily, people have the power to imagine how their life can be different from the past and present. You set goals to get you to that future.

Why are goals so important? According to Edwin Locke[141], one of the founders of research on goals, they have multiple positive effects:

— Show you **the way**. Goals direct your attention and effort.
— Give you **energy**. Ambitious goals require you to exert more effort than goals that require very little effort.
— Increase your **perseverance**. When you have a clear, ambitious, attainable goal, you are more likely to continue your efforts.
— Stimulate your **creativity.** Whenever you face a goal, you look for different ways to overcome obstacles.
— Goals are less about the result and more about **the journey.** It might happen that you alter a goal along the way.

WATCH OUT: TWO TYPES OF GOALS

There are two types of goals: performance goals and learning goals.

Performance goals are phrased very strictly, and you have to adapt them repeatedly. For example, you might state, "We aim for a market share of 10%." It is clear, but people might feel little satisfaction while working towards it. Choose a **learning goal** on top: "We want to discover multiple ways to increase our market share."

Psychologist Arjan van Dam says it is perfectly fine to consider performance goals, but your immediate response should be to also reflect on what you want to learn, what knowledge you want to attain, and what skills you want to develop[142].

How you formulate your goals matters. Learning goals help you deal with change more effectively, according to psychologist Carol Dweck[143].

While you might have goals, you might act on them without feeling any purpose or deriving meaning from them. Purpose provides you with multiple goals, whereas goals don't lead to purpose per se. It's like what Antoine de Saint-Exupéry wrote in *The Little Prince*[144]. "If you want to build a ship, do not drum up your men to collect wood and give orders and distribute the work. Instead, teach them to yearn for the vast and endless sea." The drumming and task-formulation is nothing more than goal setting, while the yearning creates purpose.

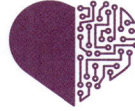

EXERCISE: LINKING GOALS AND PURPOSE

You are likely to be less motivated to do a task when it doesn't connect with or contribute to something you and/or your colleagues value. As such, it's necessary to find out what you and others care about and connect it to a task. The same, in principles, goes for any task related to digital transformation. Find the want to in the have to.

— **Interest** value. How intellectually compelling is a task? Find connections between the task and what someone finds intrinsically interesting. For instance, do I find it compelling to use AI for a specific task?
— **Identity** value. How central is someone's skillset to a task? Find out how a job/task draws on a capacity that they consider an important part of their identity and role. For instance, can I use my creativity skills to find digital solutions for our customers?
— **Importance** value. How important is a task? Identify what a task contributes to a team's or company's mission. For instance, is this task contributing to the digital transformation our company is going through?
— **Utility** value. What is the cost of achieving or avoiding a task versus the benefits of achieving it? Find out how task completion contributes to someone's larger goals.

In this exercise, be aware that what you are motivated by is not necessarily what colleagues are motivated by.

CORPORATE PURPOSE, OR "LET'S PUT A MAN ON THE MOON"

Alongside finding their individual purpose in life, it's important for employees to be able to relate their purpose(s) to the corporate purpose. During the early days of NASA, American president John F. Kennedy saw one of NASA's janitors sweeping the hallways. Kennedy struck up a conversation with him and asked, "What do you do?". The janitor replied, "Well, Mr President, I'm helping to put a man on the moon."[145]

It's a well-known management anecdote because it demonstrates how a strong sense of purpose acts as a *higher-order motivational goal,* linking internal sources of motivation with external sources. This purpose is the framework from which you organise your activities and projects. Ask yourself: why does my company exist beyond mere profit-making? What do we aim to contribute? Unfortunately, while 79% of business leaders believe that purpose is central to business success, 68% share that it is not used as a guide in decision making.[146]

A well-defined purpose not only clarifies what your company stands for; it also provides your employees with an aspirational sense of direction. In the absence of a strong corporate purpose, sometimes also called organisational meaningfulness, employee motivation dwindles exponentially. Two approaches can help you to clearly restore, redefine, and transform your purpose: the *retrospective approach* and the *prospective approach*.

DID YOU KNOW?

Sociologist Émile Durkheim coined the term "collective effervescence"[147] in the early 20th century. It describes how people who flock together around a shared purpose experience a unique sense of energy and harmony.

You've probably had your own experiences with this. Adam Grant[148] provides some examples: when you slide into rhythm with strangers on a dance floor; with teammates on the soccer field; or with colleagues during a surprisingly smooth brainstorming session. There is a sense of synchrony.

The reason for this collective effervescence is simple: emotion is a contagious disease – emotions spread from person to person, infecting the larger group without people realising it. Collective effervescence occurs naturally and can range from frivolous activities to group creations and problem solving.

RETROSPECTIVE APPROACH

The retrospective approach is an **inward-outward** tactic that builds on a company's existing reason for existence – you return to the founding origins. The salmon behaves similarly in the wild. During the salmon run, salmon always return to the stream where they were born. Once there, they spawn their offspring and die, allowing the salmon life cycle to begin again. Walmart is one such example.[149] The company was founded to assist low-income families by providing low-cost products. "Save people money so they can live better," was Sam Walton's purpose. When Sam passed away, the company gradually forgot the reason for its existence and became known for focusing on profit. With time, Walmart began to experience financial difficulties. The organisation opted for a retrospective approach and went back to the roots of the company – why was it founded in the first place? To assist people. To turn things around, multiple principles were included in Walmart: The sundown rule, where employees answer all customer and supplier questions on the same day; the 10-foot rule, where employees make eye contact, greet people, and offer help to customers who come within 10 feet; and more. Walmart worked hard to return to its core values of old (customer first, frontline focused, listening, and fairness) to exceed customers' expectations.

PROSPECTIVE APPROACH

The prospective approach is an **outward-inward** tactic that reshapes the reason for your company's existence. You assess your potential for impact in the larger ecosystem in which you (want to) operate. In contrast to the retrospective approach, you pose different questions: where can we go? What options do we have? Which external trends impact our business? What new opportunities do we see, and what challenges can and do we anticipate? More importantly, what differences do we make on behalf of our clients, the communities we are involved in, and society in general? Coming up with such questions and stretching the thinking in the process of answering them, ideally, is where Vigilant leaders come in to help out the Visionary leaders.

Tadataka Yamada, who became the chairman of research and development at GlaxoSmithKline in the year 2000, is a great example. During his first days, he discovered that the company was a defendant in a lawsuit concerning access to drug therapies for HIV/AIDS patients. GSK, along with 38 other pharmaceutical companies, accused Nelson Mandela of violating price protection and intellectual property rights. Antiretroviral therapies were around $1.000 per month in South Africa, or 30% of the average yearly salary. Treatment was out of reach for those who needed it most. Yamada understood that most employees were strongly opposed to the lawsuit – they didn't pursue a career in this field to support lawsuits and restrict healthcare on a global scale.[150]

Less than a year later, however, the 39 companies dropped the lawsuit and reduced the prices of antiretroviral drugs by more than 90%. With his team, Yamada had outlined a purpose of how GSK could become a leader in the fight against diseases such as tuberculosis and malaria. With the spread of this vision, top executives at GSK became leaders in global health issues; one of GSK's major laboratories in Spain was even converted into a profit-free laboratory focusing solely on diseases in developing countries;

and the company has since partnered with the Bill & Melinda Gates Foundation on global health initiatives. What did Yamada say about the lawsuit? "I felt it was really important for the company to make a commitment to make medicines for people where we might not make profit, but where we could have huge medical impact."

REFLECTION

What links your personal purpose to your company's corporate purpose? What links your personal purpose to the company's digital transformation purpose? You may want to start investigating these questions by revisiting the values of the company where you work.

TAKING STEPS FOR APPLYING THE RETROSPECTIVE AND PROSPECTIVE APPROACHES

You can consider both approaches so that the past and future can align and potentially even merge with one another. There are four steps you can take to determine your company's purpose and how it contributes to society as a whole:

— **Draw the map of your key stakeholders.** Who exactly are they? Define a purpose with your stakeholders rather than for them. This helps you deepen the ties. At FTSC, Tom could think in terms of students, staff, faculty, and many others.
— **Identify the relevant topics.** To do so, a company has to acquire the ability to read trends. By operating from a position of external vulnerability where the Voyager leader understands the company's inner reality and where the Vigilant leader scans the environment for external changes, the Visionary might be better equipped to incorporate new and relevant themes in society that the organisation can derive purpose from.
— **Promote reflection.** Don't impose purpose on colleagues. Instead, invite them to take a fresh look at their work. At FTSC, Tom could ask, "What do you do at Farbright?" and "What would your ideal role look like in a school that embraced digital twins?". People can submit their creative responses in any format. This helps in building an incredible "story bank". These mini stories, when combined, capture what is important to people and can be compiled to build a narrative that represents this. Also, encourage engagement by discussing topics like: what do we want to be, why do we have to be this way, and how can we become this way?

— **Articulate a purpose that is differentiated** and distill the corporate purpose into a single sentence. Use the insights that you gathered from stakeholders and reflection exercises. Five characteristics are important: conciseness, straightforwardness, authenticity, timelessness, and uniqueness. Consider the food company Kellogg ("nourishing families so they can flourish and thrive") or the insurance company IAG ("to help people manage risk and recover from the hardship of unexpected loss"). Both companies express their impact on customers while also providing employees with a clear direction.

The Visionary leader helps the company and its employees develop a sense of purpose. They accomplish this by, first, making the topic approachable within the company; and second, by connecting it to employees' personal goals and values. Consider how you can animate your company's slogan and purpose to ensure that the link between the corporate purpose and employees' personal purpose remains in place. Employees at KPMG,[151] for example, who had a boss who discussed higher purpose with them rated the company more highly as a great place to work, felt more pride, and were more likely to strive for continuous improvement. Employees who did not have such a boss were three times more likely to consider changing jobs. The latter group's year-to-date turnover was 9.1%, while the first group's turnover was 5.6%.

CORPORATE PURPOSE: DIMENSIONS AND TRAPS

A purpose statement is a good place to start. Your next step is to get your colleagues excited. When you launch your purpose statement it is critical to nurture it. Think of it as a plant that only sprouts if you water it and provide healthy soil.

REFLECTION:

Consider whether your company clearly links in the following three dimensions into its corporate and digital transformation purposes.
— **Knowledge:** do you have an explicit understanding of your company's purpose and how the company envisages reaching its digital transformation goals in that context? Do your colleagues?
— **Action:** to what extent is your company putting what it says into practice?
— **Motivation:** does the purpose touch your heart and that of colleagues?

As a Visionary leader, you can help internalise purpose. However, there are some purpose traps that may potentially suffocate meaning at work.

— **Mediocrity signals.** Hypocrisy, artificiality, and manipulation are common traps. To avoid them, consider whether the company buys into its own purpose, or whether it is just window-dressing? Do you put words into action? Think about the "action" dimension: 44% of employees believe their company purpose is not activated because decisions contrast with it.[152] When the company violates employees' beliefs, this causes such cognitive dissonance that they eventually leave.

— **Strategic Attention Deficit Disorders.** How frequently are initiatives launched and abandoned? Too much change erodes a shared understanding of why the company exists in the first place. In The Speed of Trust, Stephen Covey writes that you lose trustworthiness every time you make an appointment or launch an initiative only to cancel it. This can happen once or twice, but a habit of failing to fulfil commitments generates a trust-damaged culture. Commitment signals maturity; otherwise, employees will not believe that you really want to fulfil your corporate purpose.

— **Purpose remains "up there".** Companies must translate and connect the corporate purpose to smaller-scale individual and team-based missions. Consider your frontline employees who interact with customers every day. If one group is inspired and another group is not, which group is likely to provide customers with the most enjoyable experience? A company in the garbage collection industry places pictures of items made from recycled waste on the side of their trucks, to create a more tangible understanding of the value of the job and the company.

— **Purpose remains academic.** Rather than devoting months to the distinctions between a purpose, a vision, a mission, ethos, and culture, create the actual emotional connection. Actively demonstrate it to people, and have them demonstrate to you why their work matters.

— **Incorrect assumptions.** For example, a lack of discussion equals agreement; your company's purpose is good enough; your colleagues are emotionally invested in the company because they work there. It is critical to have difficult conversations to understand where the company stands on certain topics and how employees might experience these, particularly those that are rarely discussed.

Companies need to understand that corporate purpose is more than lofty intentions or a catchy slogan. While both are important, they are insufficient to motivate and inspire. Sally Blount, professor of strategy, and Paul Leinwand, global managing director at Strategy&, state that a powerful purpose achieves two objectives: first, clearly articulating strategic goals; and second, motivating the workforce. They conclude, "These objectives are important individually and synergistically. When your employees understand and embrace your organisation's purpose, they're inspired to do work that not only is good – and sometimes great – but also delivers on your stated aims."[153]

REFLECTION: THE SOURCES OF POWER

Employees unknowingly experience a constant flow of purpose from multiple sources:
— Outside of work (i.e. caring for family, hobbies, and volunteering).
— Purpose from work (i.e. engaging with and making progress on work-related activities).
— Purpose from the organisation (i.e. the corporate purpose, the company culture, and the overall experience of being an employee).

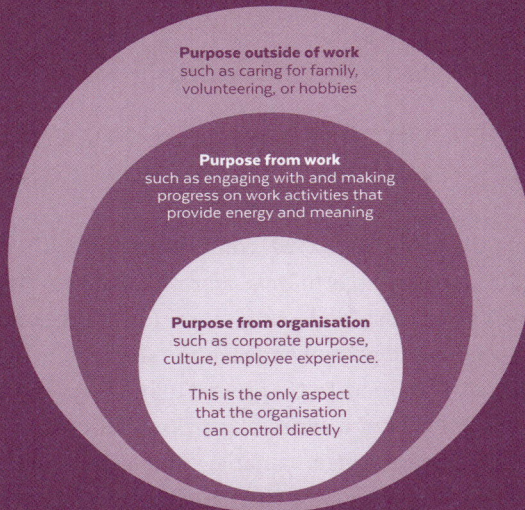

Purpose outside of work
such as caring for family,
volunteering, or hobbies

Purpose from work
such as engaging with and making
progress on work activities that
provide energy and meaning

Purpose from organisation
such as corporate purpose,
culture, employee experience.

This is the only aspect
that the organisation
can control directly

Reference: "Dhingra, N., Samo, A., Schaninger, B., and Schrimper, M. (2021),"Help your employees find purpose or watch them leave", *McKinsey.*

These three sources vary in proportion to one another and vary from person to person.

There is a certain amount of purpose that people give to work and derive from their work experiences. As a result, colleagues will almost always derive some purpose from experiences outside of work. What's more, there are sources of purpose that remain untouchable for companies.

But there are also work-related spheres where the Visionary leader can maximise the company's role. Ideally, you try to grow the size of the "Purpose from the organisation" to become as large as "Purpose from work". Employee engagement and motivation could rocket when colleagues regard their jobs as meaningful and contributing to the corporate goal. The Visionary leader considers this connection their target.

> To summarise, three potential scenarios exist:
> — The unaligned employee who is unfulfilled by the corporate purpose.
> — The aligned employee with little extra engagement and motivation.
> — The aligned employee who is fulfilled by the corporate purpose.
>
> We invite you to consider these three different sources of purpose for yourself: are they in sync? Do they perhaps match perfectly? And where do you see any differences?
>
> We suddenly have another way of using references.

WHEN A PURPOSEFUL WORKFORCE IS ALIGNED WITH A PURPOSE-DRIVEN ORGANISATION: PURPOSE CONGRUENCY

Purpose cannot remain a mere intellectual commitment though. The first step is to talk about values; the second step is to *walk your why*. For Ine – foodwaste warrior at too good to go, the app against food waste – working at the company is a perfect match with her own values and private endeavours: she prefers to fill bellies rather than bins.[154] Working at Too Good To Go proved to be the perfect place for her to kickstart her career and give her a sense of purpose. Her value is freely chosen, active and strong – she despises unsustainable companies – and she has acted on it, first privately and now professionally. This contributes to her sense of usefulness and encourages her to go the extra mile. She is surrounded by colleagues who share her thoughts and feelings. Social contagion results in a company brimming with energy, ideas, and passion.

People can find purpose*ful*ness themselves or by support of the Visionary leader, but businesses and leaders can also cause purpose*less*ness. Purpose is more easily destroyed than built – one bad experience or statement nullifies months of recognition and acknowledgement. Poor management is considered the top destroyer of meaning and purposefulness in business.[155]

It's worth paying attention to purpose, though, and give credit where credit is due. When colleagues lack purpose, boredom, anxiety, even depression might ensue. If colleagues experience purpose, on the other hand, they are likely to report higher levels of self-esteem, calmness, vitality, energy, and wellbeing. Furthermore, they report 1.7 times higher job satisfaction, 1.4 times higher engagement, and are three times as likely to stay with their employer. When their purpose is aligned with the corporate purpose, benefits are even more substantial: stronger engagement, increased loyalty, and a greater willingness to recommend the company. They are also likely to be more resilient and more resistant to the stresses of change and transformation, and are even 5.3 times more likely to stay.[156] Half of employees, however, do not find meaning and significance in their jobs and only 28% of employees feel fully connected to their company's purpose.[157]

The Visionary leader is purpose-enhancing, by aiming to connect corporate purpose with what should speak to personal purpose. According to Isaac Smith and Maryam Kouchaki, professors on topics such as morality and ethics of organisations, Visionary leaders can engage in various activities[158]:

— **Enable purpose discovery:** provide employees with sufficient time and resources to reflect on the individual purpose and how this links to the company purpose. During job interviews, for example, Visionary leaders could emphasise understanding what people want to get out of their job. During training, they can support people in reflecting how their particular job provides and perhaps supports their individual purpose.
— **Encourage purpose sharing:** when you allow people to talk about their purpose within the organisation, they might find likeminded colleagues – people with similar goals and motivations. You can also organise formal purpose sharing workshops where small groups engage with other colleagues to understand their perspectives on the corporate purpose and their personal purpose. Whatever you organise, Isaac Smith and Maryam Kouchaki do warn that you must be truly committed to helping employees.
— **Facilitate purpose integration:** work together with employees to co-design or co-refine their job in such a way that it personalises the corporate purpose to their specific tasks, and allows them to further expand on their personal purpose. Start from a simple conversation – for example, "How does this task align with your purpose?" – which helps you in identifying activities that have a high(er) impact on personal purpose. Focus on authentic connections rather than forcing them and, over time, you might come to notice how personal and corporate purposes gradually get integrated into people's daily job tasks.
— **Establish purpose reminders:** build certain reminders into performance reviews, team meetings, and so on. Purpose matters most when you maintain it as a priority and make sure that people can regularly reflect on it.

Still, it's important to remember that not all employees will derive the same motivation from your corporate purpose. People are diverse, and so is their personal purpose. Even if your company has well-defined values and purpose, it might very well be that some people might not enter that state of congruency. We might be inclined to believe that these colleagues are working at the wrong company, but this isn't necessarily true. The Visionary leader understands that someone's purpose and the meaning they derive from it, is a personal choice and experience. Respect and recognise these colleagues. After all, they can be very much committed to doing a great job.

STORY CONTINUATION

At lunch, Tom shared a table with Anja. She mentioned that the digital twin idea seems amazing. When she first heard about it, she was motivated to make this happen and was eager to see what FSTC would gravitate towards. She connected strongly with the school's future ambition – bold and daring, innovative, different. Exactly why she has always loved working here. "The webinar, however," Anja continued, "didn't seem to show that you reflected about our active roles as educators, mentors, and guides to students. Most of us, we commit to our jobs because of the direct interaction with students and the joy of seeing a student's "aha" moment. Introducing these digital twins, driven by algorithms and data, makes us wonder about **our place in this new vision**. We fear that you might take away this very reason." Tom had to conclude that the webinar had had the opposite effect of what they intended. Rather than energising people, the collective sense of enthusiasm and excitement had quickly vanished, leaving behind a growing group of people no longer connecting to FSTC's corporate purpose. The conclave had seemingly made some incorrect assumptions.

Addressing the burning platform at Farbright School of Trade and Commerce
For the business school to successfully navigate this digital transformation, it must find a way to align its corporate purpose with the individual purposes of its teachers and staff and, in doing so, ignite people's sense of mission once more. If Tom, and the entire conclave for that matter, want to act like Visionary leaders it will be crucial to make the topic approachable and actively connect it to people's personal goals and values. Considering this, Tom reflects on the corporate purpose according to the *prospective* and *retrospective* approach. On the one hand, he understands that one must think in terms of the **future** and assess how FSTC is operating in a new educational ecosystem where technologies play a key role; on the other hand, FSTC should not forget about

its **founding origins**. This is also what Anja's and other colleagues' feedback hinted at: the school's corporate purpose has to incorporate technological advancements, such as the digital twin concepts, but also remain true to the fundamental human elements that are central to education and people's individual purposes.

Additionally, Farbright now aims at developing Individual Purpose Plans. Just as students (will) have personalised learning plans, faculty and staff can also benefit from these. Each employee can now join a purpose alignment workshop that will allow two things:

— First, people will be able to **explore** their personal purposes and outline how their personal goals and values align with the school's corporate purpose. These plans will also be revisited during performance reviews and career development meetings.
— Second, the workshops will act as a fertile ground for **reflective** exercises, group discussions, and collaborative goal-settings. The insights that emerge here are treated as "purpose reflections" and the discussions that might ensue are expected to provide **clarity** regarding the success of developing and implementing digital twins. As such, these workshops have the added benefit of providing employees with a voice in decisions that will, either directly or indirectly, affect their work reality and, consequently, increase their sense of ownership.

FSTC's technological vision of digitalising students' learning journeys and staff's teaching journeys was now consciously being harmonised with people's individual purposes. The introduction of the IPPs and alignment workshops marks a vital step in this direction, allowing employees to reflect on their roles and engage in the school's future. By remembering the human element central to education, Farbright is now headed on a path that anchors innovation in purpose.

Reflecting on Farbright School of Trade and Commerce's situation, which actions would you take as Visionary digital transformation leader to **align the school's corporate purpose and employees' individual purpose** to improve the company's chances for a successful digital transformation journey?

HARNESSING THE POWER OF STORYTELLING

THE POWER OF VISIONCRAFTING: A STORIFIED BLUEPRINT FOR DIGITAL TRANSFORMATION

Introduction

Family & Co. Mart is a well-established retail business specialised in providing a wide range of high-quality, family-oriented products. Its main business revolves around offering everyday essentials, from locally sourced groceries and household items, to toys, apparel, and home goods, all curated to meet the needs of families. With a strong focus on creating a welcoming shopping experience, Family & Co. Mart is known for its commitment to supporting sustainable practices. The company prides itself on being a **community hub**, where generations of families have come to rely on their exceptional client service, diverse product offerings, and a warm, family-friendly atmosphere.

The company's IT director, Saim, and the CFO, Sophie, had long been the dynamic duo that steered the business through complex challenges. Their partnership is built on mutual respect, complementarity, and a shared belief in innovation. With the company **lagging in the digital age**, the board knew there was no better team to drive a much-anticipated digital transformation.

Saim and Sophie understood that this wasn't just about implementing new software or upgrading legacy systems; it was about **envisioning** the future. Both understood that for this transformation to succeed, it wasn't enough to simply deploy technology – while the nuts and bolts of technology matter dearly, so does the story that surrounds it. They needed to **craft a compelling narrative**, one that painted a future where the company wasn't just surviving but thriving. Saim and Sophie crafted "Digital Utopia", a blueprint designed to modernise Family & Co. Mart's operations and create new opportunities for innovation and growth.

The problem at Family & Co. Mart

In their excitement to drive the company forward, Saim and Sophie focused heavily on the technical advancements and potential business outcomes. They spoke passionately about the future, how the company would restore its position in the industry, and how innovation and tech would be at the core of everything they did. This included the proposal of a spin-off digital-only business. While the vision was bold, and the narrative they built around it was **meant to inspire and rally** the company behind a common goal, their focus on the endgame soon started to alienate employees. For many, the blueprint sounded more like a technical document than a relatable story. And while the roadmap was more comprehensive than expected, it **failed** to answer critical questions that were on the minds of many – questions arose about how this transformation would impact daily work routines; how it would improve customer service; which role people had to play to get to these desired results; and what would happen if things became difficult or failed?

This disconnect became evident when Vincent, a veteran employee from the marketing department, voiced a **concern that echoed** through the company. "Being here for almost two decades now," he said, "I trust that the company knows what it's doing, and the numbers in the blueprint seem to support that. But I must be honest. There's a very small section on customer service, and that's it. How will we create a better experience for our customers doing all this? I just do not see it." While the board and upper management were enthusiastic about "Digital Utopia", the broader employee base was less convinced. They **missed a clear, relatable and believable story** that connected the company's purpose, its core values, and vision to the day-to-day operations. Many felt out of the loop and were unsure about the roadmap's feasibility. Overall, the lack of practical clarity in the document created an atmosphere of uncertainty and scepticism, and soon, the grand narrative began to show cracks.

A Visionary leader shows colleagues a glimpse of the organisation aims for, by making bold choices and lays the foundation for understanding how they can actively participate in making that future a reality. When people share stories, they are likely to bond over them. Stories elicit emotions, inspire, and open possibilities.

WHY STORIES

Stories cannot be underestimated. They have an amazing power to drive your emotions. Your heart rate increases, and your brain produces chemicals that induce empathy. When you show colleagues a PowerPoint presentation, perhaps some graphs, two areas of the brain light up. But up to five times as much of the brain lights up when you tell them a story about the same facts. And these facts are more likely to become part of people's long-term memory. "Neurons that fire together, wire together", Hebbian theory says.[159]

In today's world, the power of the narrative helps us build organisational resilience in the face of constant change. Storytelling helps you portray *inspirational leadership,* and you don't have to be in the C-suite to seize vision-creation opportunities! As journalist and lecturer Rebecca Knight writes, "At some point in your career, if you're not a salesperson, you're going to have to sell something – whether it's your idea, your team, or yourself."[160]

A story is a means of transmitting information and has existed since the "human revolution" occurred between 40,000 and 50,000 years ago. Stories predate writing. "Where humans are is where stories are. Everywhere in the world at every time in human history in every known culture, humans have told stories,"[161] writes historian Clint Johnson. Stories are so fundamental to your humanity that Jonathan Adler,[162] professor of psychology at Olin College, considers the *narrative mode* the default mode of your human cognition. Stories shape how you see yourself, and they also empower you to shape others and effect change. The founder of positive psychotherapy, Nossrat Peseschkian, writes that,

> "Stories don't appeal to the rational, the pure logic [...], but on intuition and fantasy. For a long while it was a tradition to weave stories into education. They were vehicles with which certain values, moral views and behaviours were transmitted and anchored into people's consciousness [...] There are plenty of examples of how stories were used to handle problems."[163]

DID YOU KNOW?

Scientists can measure the amount of oxytocin released in our brains as a result of a story.[164] They can then use this measurement to forecast how much money people might donate to charity.

For example, the parable of the Good Samaritan teaches that we should show mercy and compassion to others; the story of Little Red Riding Hood can be considered a warning about trusting strangers; leadership trainings often rely on the Hero's Journey narrative that portrays employees as heroes who must overcome certain obstacles; and JFK's Moonshot story inspired an entire generation of scientists and engineers to innovate and push beyond boundaries.

Stories are more than just a source of idle entertainment; they help you find alternatives and solutions that were previously beyond your horizons. They help you confirm existing norms and values, but also help you relativise them. They promote a switch of perspectives and offer you examples of different ways of thinking, that might result in an *"aha!"* moment. Furthermore, stories help you win over people's hearts and minds: the emotional connection boosts energy levels, empowers, and spurs people into motion. As such, stories help you create identity, find purpose, and embrace new behaviours and even entirely new mindsets.

REFLECTION

— What is your experience with stories? Do you love them or hate them?

— What kind of stories did you like as a child? Why?

— Can you remember situations (i.e. at work, at a conference, or at a family dinner) in which stories were told to make sense of radical digital change? How did you feel?

— What story do you spontaneously think about when confronted with AI?

— Who is your favourite science-fiction author, director, ...?

— Which stories do you sometimes use (or could you use) to address important technology-related change?

THE IDEA IN THE GOLDEN CIRCLE

People sometimes believe that a story rises or falls with the narrator's speaking style or multimedia mastery. But this is just the cherry on top. The cake itself is the quality of your idea, your narrative, and how passionate you are about it.

In a digital transformation context, the Visionary leader tells the story of the transformation journey ahead. You invite colleagues to imagine how they can operate in this new environment. To accomplish this, you can craft a compelling story based on Simon Sinek's Golden Circle principle: people don't buy what you do, but why you do it – remember the importance of purpose. Here, as well, you concentrate on three aspects – the What, the How, and the Why.

— **Why.** Consider *Why* the company exists, *Why* employees should get out of bed in the morning, and *Why* customers should care at all. *Why* are your customers your customers, and *Why* are your employees your employees? And *Why* are you embarking on a digital transformation journey? As previously highlighted, a clear *Why* makes your customers and employees feel connected to something bigger.

— **How.** Reflect on *How* you will do something and *How* you will be different from and better than others.

— **What.** *What* exactly will you bring and offer?

In his book *Start with Why*, Sinek explains that the core of the circle – the starting point – is the *Why*: give a reason, provide a purpose. Humans have an innate desire to belong. Additionally, the *How* convinces and the *What* provides proof. Most often, companies overemphasise the outer circle, the *What*. While we believe the mind is our target when trying to persuade others, the heart is where the bull's eye is at. And you can achieve this by shifting your focus more towards the *Why*.

DIFFERENT KINDS OF STORIES FOR DIFFERENT KINDS OF SITUATIONS

When you launch a new project or embark on a large-scale digital transformation journey, it may be useful to divide it into five categories: dream, leap, fight, climb, arrive, (and maybe a sixth: "re-dream" as you move on to the next). If you want to know which type of story to go for, first understand where your colleagues are on the journey: are they struggling? Are they hesitating to commit? A Visionary leader first sees the journey through the eyes of colleagues – the story's heroes. Only then can they properly diagnose which type of narrative is most effective.

STAGES	DREAMING	LEAPING	FIGHTING	CLIMBING	ARRIVAL
	CALL TO ADVENTURE	THRESHOLD	CHALLENGES & TEMPTATIONS	TRANSFORMATION	RETURN
	THE 'KNOWN'		THE 'UNKNOWN'		THE 'KNOWN'

Dreaming and leaping. Make colleagues optimistic about the future. Prepare your colleagues to dare and take the leap during the dreaming stage.

Fighting and climbing. Your colleagues progress toward the desired goal, but they face setbacks. In the story, you communicate about overcoming obstacles and recommitting to the goals you have. Alternate between stories that pull people towards the desired goal and stories that push them away from an undesirable reality. It's tempting to focus on fairy tales with great endings, but few people ever crossed the finish line without any struggles. Rely on the combined power of both inspiring stories and cautionary tales to catapult colleagues forward.

Arrival. Focus on celebrating and even dare to (re-)dream. This can be your yearly New Year's reception to wrap up the year, but it can also be a party where you thank colleagues for their dedication, where you put some people in the spotlight, and much more. Do not always wait for large projects to be completed; instead, celebrate small victories too.

CHARACTERISTICS OF A GOOD STORY

People are easily captivated by other people's struggles and endeavours, and how they overcome challenging situations. When you hear or see a story unfold, your brain is heightened in anticipation and excitement. You unconsciously put yourself in the protagonist's shoes and you are more likely to experience empathy, as a result. If the hero is flawed, you are often even more drawn to them, because you can identify with them more easily. Consider Superman: despite being a *Super* man, Clark Kent also has weaknesses – kryptonite, a fictional radioactive ore, and a seemingly uninterested female journalist, Lois Lane. The story also requires an antagonist – someone to pit your hero against – and something that must be overcome by the triumphant hero. A good story arouses your emotions and triggers a "flight or fight" response in the amygdala.

Every memorable story includes a strong *call to action*. In the documentary *A Life on Our Planet*, David Attenborough narrates his life. In this witness statement, he takes you on a journey through his career and the devastating changes he has seen, ultimately inspiring us to act and turn the tide. Implement the call to action.

When you involve people and solicit their ideas for better ways of working, they are more likely to feel valued and believe they have a say in the outcome. Consistently feed your strategic narrative with new material to ensure that colleagues' levels of energy and commitment remain constant.

How you tell a story is critical, yet a trend in business is to communicate based on data and abstract information n dry and uninspiring, almost robotic, ways. PowerPoint presentations stand at the pinnacle of this. The issue consists of two parts:

— Data rarely influences behaviour; emotions do. Your story is the catalyst to compel action. The graphs and data are merely illustrations to support your findings. Data does not stick with us in the same way that stories do.

— Data never speaks for itself. Your brain fills in the gaps in what you see or hear, clouding the presented data. In other words, when people are not guided by a story, they reach their own interpretations. Data isn't always bad, and stories aren't always good, but a compelling story acts as a motivational magnet.

DID YOU KNOW?

The rumour mill is the process by which gossip originates and spreads among a group of people. Research suggests that up to 70% of all organisational communication occurs "through the grapevine" (or through rumours and gossip).[165] This informal communication network is present in every organisation but is especially prevalent in companies with a culture of silos and internal competition. Interestingly, rather than accepting a single version of the story, most people believe a combination of what they hear. The brain loves to connect, after all. Since the advent of social media, the grapevine is on steroids. It is impossible to outrun or kill the mill

COMING UP WITH A STORY

It isn't always easy to find a memorable story that captivates your audience. Ideally, you tell stories that you have personally experienced. This adds authenticity. To help us find these stories, author Nancy Duarte suggests the *notepad* to "conjure up deeper, dormant stories".[166] Let us take a closer look!

Create one-line summaries for each of these nouns. Some stories will be too personal or intimate to share, which is completely understandable. But you may have uncovered additional memories and anecdotes that can form the basis of an important story. This list of anecdotes and potential stories will grow over time, helping you create a personal story catalogue – it can be a journal, a spreadsheet with summaries, it can be whatever you want it to be. You can embed categories, themes, moods, and so on. Whatever makes most sense for you. When you build a story, various elements lead to effective storytelling:

Relatability. The *mere-exposure* effect states that people develop a preference for things they are familiar with. Because your brain is simultaneously afraid of and excited by the unknown, a dilemma arises: on the one hand, you do not want to introduce too many unknown elements. This could limit the relatability level of a story. On the other hand, you don't want a story to be a carbon copy. Some sense of novelty is recommended.

In the case of Family & Co. Mart, Sophie and Saim could start by drawing on certain familiar elements to create comfort (they might, for example, refer to a first major software update many years ago and how people adapted to it and how it made work flows smoother and provided better customer service).

This can be followed by introducing some novel aspects of the upcoming transformation (they can discuss how new technologies have appeared, presenting another opportunity – to take over certain repetitive tasks and improve customer service even further). Even though the brain is afraid of new things, it also enjoys the excitement that novelty brings. They can continue by balancing the new and the familiar. For example, highlight how AI and automation resemble the systems upgrade in the past, and how they are – just like then – not there to replace people.

End by grounding novelty into something familiar. They could state clearly how the company's purpose and mission don't change and how, in the case of Family & Co. Mart, you are still committed to delivering optimal customer service.

Tension. A great story, according to the Greek philosopher Aristotle, *consists of three elements*: "what is", "what is to become", and the gap in between. As the storyteller, it is your job to bridge the gap between what people have or where they are, and what they want to be or where they want to be. But creating tension is tricky – if the brain feels too much tension, colleagues could refuse to participate. In this case, Sophie and Saim could take turns:

What is: (Sophie) "Right now, we all know the challenges we face. Our systems are outdated, and the customer team is struggling, …"

What is to become: (Saim) "But imagine a different future – a future where your work is simplified, where instead of juggling between systems, you have everything you need at your fingertips. Imagine a customer service where queries are resolved faster, …"

The gap in between: (Sophie) "The reality is the path towards this will have its challenges. There will be moments of uncertainty. But we are in this together, …"

Keep the audience in mind. Before you decide which story to tell, consider who will hear the story. Think about the audience's values, goals, and interests. Be aware that some stories will be hilarious and may crack people up, while other stories could bring tears to the eyes. A story told in one group can elicit awe but can also incite rage in another. When you use analogies, consider how your audience interacts with the world. As such, determine beforehand which language your audience speaks – "What is their vocabulary"?

For example, Sophie and Saim could tailor their message differently, depending on whether they are speaking to the customer service team or a senior management team. The former would be more enticed by aspects of efficiency and ease of use, such as "speeding up customer response times" or "reducing the number of manual tasks", whereas the latter might prefer aspects of strategic positioning and long-term vision, such as "competitive advantage" and "sustainable growth".

Personal appeal. Assume you are overseeing a college campaign to help fund scholarships. How do you inspire the audience? Will you speak about the significant impact a scholarship can have? Or do you invite a current scholarship recipient to share a personal story and, in doing so, touch upon people's emotions?

Sophie and Saim invite another colleague to the stage, someone whose experience has been positively altered and who can provide insights into the improvements of the customer experience.

Simplicity. Translate the story to everyone's daily lives. Use simple references and analogies. The most powerful clichés are often understood the most easily. You can try to compare business realities to sports, movies, and so on. As we have a tendency to overuse complex words, and therefore make our stories too heavy, it's preferred to avoid making your stories sound great. *Concentrate on fluency* instead. You might even try to rely on some large language models, such as ChatGPT, to help you come up with simple analogies and make your story sound lighter.

Saim opts for an analogy that most employees can relate to, "Think of our digital transformation like upgrading your smartphone. You've been using your old phone for years – it's worked fine, but now it's starting to slow down. Apps take forever to load, and the battery doesn't last as long. Then you get a new phone – it's faster, more efficient, and you can do more with it. That's what this transformation is about. We're upgrading our systems so everything runs smoother, faster, and with fewer issues.

In the end, your story intends to hit the bull's eye – people's hearts. In their book *Made to Stick*, Dan and Chip Heath explain how "a credible idea makes people believe, an emotional idea makes people care, and the right stories make people act". But how can you hit the heart? Bill Gates' famous TED-talk on mosquitos and malaria is a wonderful example. In his talk, Gates corners the topic from the perspective of childhood mortality, something that touches on everyone's emotions. And even though the global figure has been steadily declining, malaria remains one of the world's deadliest diseases. Unexpectedly, Gates releases mosquitos in the room and says, "I brought some here just so you could experience this too." And off goes the lid, adding to the story's personal and emotional appeal.

EXERCISE: THE NOTEPAD

Sit down with a notepad/notebook (studies show that when you write, you are more likely to be creative than when you type). Inhale and exhale slowly. Think of places, people, and objects that have shaped your life.

— **People:** write your name in the centre and identify the various types of relationships: family, friends, colleagues, and so on. Think deeper whenever you draw a connective line between yourself and someone else – which story is hidden in the relational dynamics and emotions?

— **Places:** start broad, but gradually add specific details when you recall places. Don't just consider your holiday resort, for example, but also think of the hallways, the trees alongside the swimming pool, and more. Use spatial recollection and move through each location, whether it's your old neighbourhood or your teenage room. When you retrace your steps, scenes, sounds, and smells may be triggered, memories can be dislodged, and could reveal long forgotten events.

— **Things:** what objects or items have a strong symbolic meaning? Which books? Did you win any awards? Which gifts do you remember? Sketch these symbols on your paper/notepad and think about what made them so emotionally charged in the first place. Why do they hold meaning for you?

ARTICULATING AND GESTICULATING: TELLING A STORY

DID YOU KNOW?

When you listen to a lecture or attend a meeting, two small areas of your brain are activated: the Wernicke's and Broca's areas. This is where you process information, and it's also where you forget 50% of what you hear within seconds.[167]

When you hear a story, however, your entire brain lights up, and your senses and emotions engage. For example, if you mention a book falling on the ground with a loud smack, the listeners' occipital and temporal lobes light up as if they actually see and hear the book falling. Neural coupling occurs when the listener's brain lights up in the same way the storyteller's brain does. People unconsciously synchronise bodily functions (i.e. heartbeats and breathing) when they share experiences (i.e. a live performance or a personal conversation). People's heart rates even synchronise when they listen to a story.

What matters most is that the audience pays attention to the story. Research found that listeners experienced increases and decreases in their heart rate at the same points in the narrative; that a lack of attention dropped the synchronisation of heart rates; and that fluctuations in heart rate were predictive of how well participants could answer questions about the story.

Thus, storytelling creates an artificial reality in which people feel the story and develop empathy for the storyteller. And the more empathy people experience, the more oxytocin (the feel-good chemical) they have and the more trustworthy they consider the speaker. Stories affect our hearts and bind us together.

Even if your written ordeal is strong and impressive, the nonverbal aspects of your storytelling can still make or break it. Especially for inexperienced speakers, having to be physically on stage invites some challenges to tell a story. What should you be mindful of?

— **Take note** of your tone of voice, facial expressions, how you move, and the gestures you employ. People often move their bodies too much – swaying from left to right or shifting their weight from one leg to the other – because they are nervous. But it distracts the audience. Move with purpose. If you prefer not to, it's simply better to stand still and rely on the power of your hand gestures. Similarly, a warm smile is more likely to build a connection when greeting the audience or consider a raised eyebrow when gunning for excitement. Regarding tone of voice, practise the power of the pause, which adds weight to an important point when it's well-timed – for example, "This transformation is not just about technology – it's about empowering all of you to succeed."

— **Make eye contact.** It's not easy, we know. Try to spot five friendly faces evenly spread across the room and look them in the eye when you speak.

— **Make your audience feel as if they are part of the story.** This necessitates a willingness to relinquish some ownership of the story – drop the "I" and replace it with "we".

— **Stop thinking about yourself.** Many people)dread the many eyes gazing at them. This is in our DNA. In prehistoric times, humans perceived eyes watching them as an existential threat – they were probably predators' eyes. Rather than fearing the eyes, remind yourself that you are there to help the audience. Make eye contact, but don't try to look at everyone at once; focus on one person at a time, or alternate between the various corners in the room or the audience.

— **Talk to the little cortex man.** Did you know that there are more neurons connecting your brain to your eyes and hands than to any other body part? The cortical homunculus, also known as the little cortex man, exemplifies this. This is a scientific model of your body and depicts the proportion of neurons assigned to each of your body parts. While the hands are more tactile and the eyes are more visual, both are important in how you process information. You can trigger the audience by "talking" to their eyes – making things clear and visual – and by "talking" to their hands – by having them experience and touch things. If your company manufactures gloves, for example, bring several pairs to the next meeting. If your company wants to introduce virtual reality, don't just talk about it, but let people experience the technology firsthand.

— "What about **multimedia**?", you might think. The little cortex man is not easily satisfied. Let's assume you rely on a PowerPoint. What is the worst thing your audience could experience? Someone who seems to repeat what's on the slides, right? While it's a universal advice not to do so, people violate this every single day. "Information is interesting only once and hearing and seeing the same words feels repetitive,"[168] Chris Anderson, curator of TED, writes. Does that mean that you cannot use slides, for example? Of course, you can. Use photographs and illustrations that really make the topic come alive. Refrain from using too many words if you really want people to listen to you.

WATCH OUT: THE BURNING PLATFORM

Change experts associate the "burning platform" with a sense of urgency, in which you create the impression that something must happen. Now!

Creating a sense of urgency is frequently a prerequisite for people to start moving. When the pain of not-moving outweighs the pain of moving, we act. This sense of urgency should extend beyond management in companies because a corporate sense of urgency will be felt most strongly when it is shared by all employees.

When you contemplate digital transformation, consider not only the benefits of the change, but also consider the dangers of the status quo. What will happen if we do not change?

Many people however, believe that creating a shock effect (through drama, horror stories, and even threats) spurs movement. This is frequently counter-productive though. If the sense of urgency is too strong and feels too threat-ening, people will want to flee rather than stay and fight. Consider it like a cup of coffee: one cup wakes you up and makes you alert, five cups give you the shivers, make you sweat, and make you restless.

STORY CONTINUATION

The initial approach to storifying Family & Co. Mart's digital transformation was missing a human-centred message. To overcome this, Sophie and Saim set to crafting and delivering a compelling story that connects the strategic vision with people's minds and heart. Storytelling principles helped them turn the odds. Three challenges are identified.

Addressing the burning platform at Family & Co. Mart

1. Build a compelling story with the Golden Circle: make it **relatable** and **inclusive**.

Saim and Sophie highlight **why** the journey is necessary. Avoiding a tech-nology-centred narrative, they stress the importance of competitiveness and the need to further enhance customer loyalty and satisfaction. They do not avoid the important role of technology but instead blend it into the storyline. Next, they focus on **how** this will be achieved. They outline the steps to be taken, making it clear that it will be a collaborative effort that leverages each employee's competencies. Part of providing this clarity is about **what** needs to be done, and pinpointing the expected changes and outcomes, such as new technologies, processes, and expected new business models. Instead of presenting these as technical upgrades they make sure to frame them as enablers of a better future for the company and its customers. However, and this had been the biggest hurdle for them, Saim and Sophie had to make the story as relatable and inclusive as possible to avoid alienating people. They focused on three elements: first, they went for personal appeal and authenticity, sharing anecdotes that connect on an emotional level. Both had faced challenges in their careers and personal growth had come for them by embracing change. Second, they opted for interactive storytelling, involving others in the narrative and have them share ideas, concerns, and experiences. Town hall meetings, workshops, and small group discussions acted as platforms to contribute to the story. Third, they asked employees to provide everyday examples that illustrated how technology had helped, for example, in solving customer issues, resulting in happier customers. This reduced the risk for abstract storytelling.

2. Address any concerns: **build alignment**.
   Voices such as Vincent's had made it clear that some uncertainties had to be addressed and that difficulties and obstacles were ahead. In response, they clarified that these could be overcome. Furthermore, Sophie and Saim asked various internal stakeholders to collect the small wins that were happening within the business so that these could be celebrated. Celebrating these wins and recognising those teams and individuals that contributed would help in keeping people engaged and motivated. Equally important, Sophie and Saim will incorporate data on customer satisfaction, employee engagement, and other key metrics that show the positive impact of the transformation. However, they remain aware that these metrics should, preferably, be tied back to the emotional core of the story – how is it making a difference in people's lives?

3. Go for continuous storytelling: **sustain story momentum**.
   Storytelling is not a one-time effort, both understand. To sustain energy throughout the transformation, they continually feed the strategic narrative with new stories and insights, including regular updates regarding challenges and opportunities (and the small wins), engaging multiple storytellers to broaden the narrative's reach, and evolving the story based on

the feedback employees provide. This makes the story more relevant and demonstrates that leadership values and acts on employee contributions. Experience with digital transformation over time allows for a strong technology-infused story to emerge rather than being imposed or assumed to be ready from the outset.

By shifting their focus to storytelling, Saim and Sophie act as Visionary leaders that evolve the digital transformation journey from a top-down initiative into a shared journey that energises and aligns Family & Co. Mart. By adhering to these solutions, they refrain from succumbing to alienation and misalignment and, instead, foster an engaged and motivated workforce.

Reflecting on Family & Co. Mart's situation, how would you **craft an engaging vision and construct an attractive story** to improve the company's chances for a successful digital transformation journey? Also think about how digital technology can help to make you do this better or differently.

EMBRACING RISK WITH CONFIDENCE

BUILT ON TRADITION: PRUDENT RISK-TAKING FOR SUCCESSFUL DIGITAL TRANSFORMATION

Introduction

Matthias Müller is the founder and CEO of Müller & Sons Construction (MSC), a thriving mid-sized construction company. Over the past two decades MSC has built a solid reputation for delivering high-quality residential and commercial projects across what country. The company's success has largely been driven by Matthias' strategic vision of bold regional expansion and his **commitment** to sound traditional construction methods. The landscape of the industry changes, however, as new technological innovations enter the picture. Matthias, although successful, is not well-versed in these emerging technologies. Competitors, on the other hand, already incorporate a variety of them to meet the heightened demands of the modern customer:

— 3D-printed modular designs significantly reduce construction time and costs while allowing for greater customisation and precision.
— Building information modelling (BIM) creates a shared knowledge resource and provides reliable information throughout a project's life cycle. Competitors rely on BIM to plan, manage, and execute projects.
— Virtual reality (VR) offers immersive experiences to customers, which allows them to visualise and walk through projects before the first brick is laid. Customer satisfaction increases and costly revisions can be avoided.

Recently, MSC noticed a slight decline in market share and despite recognising the underlying trends for this, Matthias remains **sceptical**. In response to growing pressure, not only from his sons, Lukas and Ralf, but also from other stakeholders, Matthias agrees to have a small team of employees investigate these technologies and compile a report on their potential use cases within

MSC. This team is composed of some of the company's best project managers, engineers, and IT staff, who spent several weeks researching construction technologies, visiting other companies, and consulting with technology vendors. Matthias's sons are also part of the team. They hope to convince their father of a new, digital-proof vision for the company.

The team's report is thorough and detailed. It didn't just highlight the theoretical benefits but laid out some clear use cases specifically tailored to MSC. Unsurprisingly, the document discusses the 3D printing, BIM, and VR – as seen at competitors – but also zooms in on several other technologies that most competitors have not adopted, yet. Some of the proposals are:

— 3D-printed materials are likely to help the company significantly reduce waste, lower labour costs, and shorten construction timelines. Furthermore, these 3D-printed components might provide greater design flexibility.
— BIM is likely to help in integrating project phases whilst also allowing for real-time collaboration among different stakeholders, such as architects, engineers, and contractors. This might reduce miscommunications and errors that often lead to costly reworks.
— VR and augmented reality (AR) provide a better client experience resulting in higher satisfaction and less changes in orders. AR could additionally assist workers as it overlays 3D models onto physical construction sites, ensuring high accuracy.
— Drones could be deployed to survey construction sites, monitor progress, and inspect hard-to-reach areas, significantly reducing time and risks involved in manual inspections.
— Leveraging IoT sensors to monitor construction equipment and building materials in real time could allow MSC to predict equipment failures more easily and track material usage overall.

The problem at Müller & Sons Construction

Considering all this, the report laid out a clear path for how MSC could leverage these technologies to remain competitive and increase the company's profitability, enhance its operational efficiency, and improve customer satisfaction. However, despite all this exemplary work and the compelling data, Matthias remained **unconvinced**. He acknowledges the potential of these technologies but is **hesitant to disrupt** his well-oiled machine of old, **fearful** of the overall cost and complexity of implementation and the disruption to the status quo. Matthias still focuses excessively on the organisation itself; he does not dare to look beyond it. Also, his cautious nature prevents him from taking enough risks. The complexity of the outside world and its impact on his organisation are currently impeding him.

By continuing to operate the way it always had, MSC risks positioning itself for potential irrelevance in a digitally driven industry. The construction sector's shift toward technology accelerates and the pace of change is unforgiving. Matthias' decision to stick to traditional methods puts MSC on a collision course with destruction.

New ideas are always fraught with uncertainty and unlike in academia or in medicine, where hypotheses can be stress tested and rigorously validated, control trials are nearly impossible in most businesses. "You must typically repair the ship while it's sailing on open waters in weather conditions that you do not control,"[169] Frank Cespedes and Neil Hoyne, respectively senior lecturer at Harvard Business School and chief measurement strategist at Google, conclude. A paradox is present in the corporate world. While small ideas, aggregated, often have a bigger impact with less risk, companies prefer to allocate tons of testing time and money to large-scale initiatives to limit the risks taken. A need for perfection and control emerges to avoid loss of money and reputation. As a result, they restrict the process of innovation and experimentation – the act of trial-and-error, progress, and listening to the small ideas out there – and primarily invest in those ideas that, seemingly, carry little or no risk. However, our filters for risk are biased.[170]

RISK PROPENSITY

Innovation has become unavoidable, and no innovation lasts forever. Nickelodeon's former creative director Anne Kreamer says that "In today's marketplace, where jobs and job categories are being destroyed and invented at an accelerated rate, I'd argue that the riskiest move one can make is to assume that your industry or job is secure."[171] Companies must improve and grow if they want to survive. And this means to bet and take risks, large and small. Leaders should thus foster a culture where a suitable level of risk-taking is allowed; where the company disrupts itself before somebody else does; and where Thomas Edison's adage is accepted – "I have not failed. I've just found 10.000 ways that won't work."

OUR PREFERENCE FOR RISK

People differ in their risk assessment, their willingness to commit to risks, and their innate levels of risk tolerance. Furthermore, the higher you are in the company, the more influence your risk-taking attitude has on the development of new business activities and on its risk-taking climate. *Risk propensity* describes people's willingness to take risks, and two profiles can be identified.[172]

— People with a **higher preference** for risk. You believe chance favours you and add risk. You lean more towards a positivity bias and are more likely to consider the potential gains from risky decisions – but you may also overestimate the probability of gain. When you are excessively overconfident, a toxic positivity enters the picture, and people suffer from the overconfidence bias that might have them double down on investments and risks.

— People with a **lower preference** for risk. You believe chance disfavours you and reduce risk. You lean more towards a negativity bias and loss aversion. You are more likely to consider the potential losses from risky decisions – but you may also overestimate this probability of loss.

REFLECTION

Do you have examples of when you took a risk – big or small – in your life? Did you, for example, switch to a career in a totally different industry? Did you make a risky investment or ask for a promotion? Maybe you took out a loan to pursue a management degree abroad?
— How did it feel? Which emotions and thoughts did you experience? What were the reactions of people close to you – colleagues, family and friends, your partner – before and after?

Do you have examples of risks that you didn't take and opportunities that you let pass by? Perhaps asking your crush out on a date, maybe opting not to start your own company?
— Why didn't you? How do you feel, looking back at it? Why did you stop and which barriers did you experience?

THE LESSONS FROM (REFLECTING UPON) EXPERIENCE

Overall, excessive risk aversion is built into an individual's cognition and aggregates on the organisational level. For example, most managers are overly risk averse, states Justin Berg at Stanford Business School.[173] Their attention is frequently drawn to the costs of investing in bad ideas rather than the benefits of piloting good ones; where they favour marginal improvements, cost-cutting, and safe investments.

Employees are often discouraged by a culture where multiple layers of sign-offs are present. When signatures are constantly escalated, progress slows down or is even parked completely. While your colleagues might still try to promote an idea, they will feel more and more disheartened the longer it takes to get a signature. After a while, people won't even make the effort to try and kickstart something anymore. Ralph Swalm, professor at Syracuse University, studied risk attitudes among 100 executives. While companies are supposed to create new value and risky invest- ments have long since been seen as central in this, the findings "do not portray the risk-takers we hear so much of in industrial folklore. They portray decision-makers quite unwilling to take what, for the company, would seem to be rather attractive risks."[174] Not only is value left on the table, inconsistency in risk preferences across decision-making is a costly mistake for both individuals and organisations.[175]

The corporate innovation archives overflow with tales of managers who instructed employees to stop working on projects that turned out to be some of the biggest hits ever: Microsoft's Xbox, Xerox's laser printer, and Pontiac's Fiero. It might be that a company has corporate incentives and control processes installed that ac- tively discourage people from taking risks. If you reject a great idea, people will never know, but if you approve a bad idea, you're the one that will be blamed. As such, when they are faced with uncertainty, the instinct is to reject novelty and vet new ideas from an evaluative mindset. They compare new ideas to successful, but often outdated ones.

They look for reasons why unfamiliar concepts might fail and ignore the reasons why they might succeed. "Too many people," says Ginni Rometty, former CEO of IBM, "abandon a good idea when it pushes them or others outside of their comfort zone, when that idea may actually be the best thing to help the person or organ- isation grow [...]. One sign an idea is a good one is if it makes people a little bit uncomfortable. And that's because growth and comfort never coexist."[176]

Levels of expertise and experience play a huge role in this: the more knowledge someone gains in one field, the more entrenched their world view becomes, and the more hubris they are likely to develop. Experts, as a result, struggle to reject the default and often take longer to adapt than a novice. Adam Grant even states that experts become prisoners of their own prototypes.[177] In 1982, Steve Jobs went as far as to say that if you are going to make connections that are innovative, you cannot have the same bag of experience as everyone else.[178] This calls for diversity in ideation teams. Also, people are also most open to radically creative ideas when they have low to moderate expertise in a domain. Why is that?

Unlike people with a higher or lower preference for risk, *risk neutrality* has you consider the size of an investment and how relative the risk is to your resources. Taking what is called a portfolio approach, people understand that the overall risk of, for example, a diversified portfolio is lower than the average risk of individual projects.[179] Matthew Rabin and Max Bazerman, Harvard Business School, write that people shouldn't necessarily change their risk perception, but that they might want to be wary of making intuitive decisions based on those feelings.[180]

Experts frequently rely on their intuition to make decisions – a gut feeling bolstered by years of experience. At Müller & Sons Construction, Matthias remains convinced that the old way of approaching things is the most solid way of moving forward. However, according to Daniel Kahneman and Gary Klein,[181] people's intuition can only be trusted if they gain experience making judgments and decisions in predictable environments. Predictability, in this regard, rests on robust relationships between the patterns you see today and those in the past. This is useful for doctors or firefighters, for example, when they diagnose a patient or enter a burning building. In other trades, however, the past is rarely identical to the present, and cannot be a reliable guide to the future. As technology speeds up, organizations have to change faster too, causing the trustworthiness of our experience and intuition to decline in tandem.

WATCH OUT: THE POWER OF LOSS AND LOSS AVERSION

Daniel Kahneman writes that the motivational power of loss will always be greater than the motivational power of profit. As a result, people who suffer minor setbacks during times of change will oppose change more strongly than those who don't.[182]

This "asymmetry", as Kahneman puts it, "makes large-scale reforms and changes exceptionally difficult. And, because of that, more expensive than you would expect. Because, in one way or the other, you will have to please the losers."

HOW TO APPROACH RISK

We must distinguish between two realities: taking more risk in an irrational way; and taking more risk in a rational way through better risk management. If people understand the difference, they might feel more at ease with pursuing a higher level of rational risk-taking. However, when the company culture is not aligned with better risk management, employees' aversion to risk keeps the company stationary.

You could approach risk in the same way that you (hopefully) approach your stock portfolio. If you are going to make a risky investment in the stock market, you should protect yourself by investing conservatively in other areas. You're hedging your bets. People can be seen doing the same in their daily lives; when you take risks – or embrace danger – in one area, you reduce your overall level of risk by exercising caution in another area. You probably know someone who has taken a course in their spare time, and is considering starting their own business. For example, you may have a colleague who has been taking yoga courses for years, obtained her instructor's certification and is now permitted to teach yoga. She could quit her job and devote all her time and resources to her passion. But she can also start working on her new venture on weekends, build a solid client base, and then start nibbling away at the full-time job. Anne Kreamer says, "Perhaps the biggest impediment to change in our working lives is the sense that any significant change has to be all or nothing."[183]

People frequently perceive risk-taking from a very black-and-white perspective – "go big or go home". Risk-taking, however, is not synonymous with risk-maximisation or big bets, but rather with prudent risk-hedging and mitigation:

— Risk hedging involves diversifying investments or actions to minimise potential losses. You balance your exposure across multiple projects.
— Risk mitigation involves identifying and implementing strategies to reduce the likelihood or impact of potential risks.

In sum, the combination of risk hedging and mitigation helps you maintain a healthy balance in your financial, professional, or personal portfolios. Having a sense of security in one domain allows you to grow in another. *Security* is where the true value and benefit of a well-balanced risk portfolio can be found because it helps you benefit from an informed mind at peace instead of going for intuitive decision-making.

THE THREE HORIZONS OF GROWTH

There is clearly rationality to be found in thoughtful risk-taking. You can, for example, make a list of your company's internal capabilities and external market opportunities. When you pay special attention to overlaps and gaps, you can reach clarity on where you stand with the organization, which then helps you decide whether the risks (that is, expanding on the overlaps or closing the gaps) are a "must do", a :worthy experiment", or a "no-go". This allows you to identify and capitalise on opportunities by exploiting existing assets and exploring new resources. McKinsey's Three Horizons of Growth model encourages companies to simultaneously focus on the past, present, and future. It bases itself on the assumption that companies face a clear tension: on one hand, they must run their existing businesses and make them more digital over time; on the other hand, they must build something completely new and digital by nature. You can rely on these three horizons to organise and structure your thoughts:

— **Horizon 1:** "Defend and expand your current core business" (low-risk exploration; short-term time frame): this stage respects what made you great and focuses on optimising your current operations by integrating digital technologies that either enhance or complement the current business model. The goal is to optimise and leverage known strengths to generate consistent revenue and growth without disrupting the core business.

At Müller & Sons Construction, they might think in terms of automating certain back-office operations by deploying software solutions for accounting, payroll, and compliance management to reduce employees' administrative workload. This can be considered a relatively low-risk investment that improves business productivity. Furthermore, the company could consider using certain project management platforms to improve communication, visibility, and work flow among teams.

— **Horizon 2:** "Foster emerging new businesses" (medium-risk exploration; medium-term time frame): you are less concerned with short-term returns and instead explore new opportunities, technologies, and adjacent businesses that have the potential to significantly boost the business in the future. These ideas require more time and resources and might not be immediately profitable.

At Müller & Sons Construction, they might explore establishing Virtual Reality (VR) showrooms where clients can take a virtual tour of a building before deciding to buy it. This would likely enhance the client experience, although it requires more investment and could come with the risk that customers don't really see the added value. Furthermore, the company could think about partnering with or acquiring a smaller company with certain digital capabilities and growth potential. Perhaps there is an interesting drone provider to collaborate with or a startup showing impressive data analytics through Internet of Things (IoT).

— **Horizon 3:** "Seed future businesses and disruptive innovations" (high-risk exploration; long-term time frame): you participate in pilot projects, (thought) experiments, or minority stakes that are highly speculative in nature. You are less concerned with returns or profits; instead, you strive to learn by planting seeds.

At Müller & Sons Construction, they might reflect on exploring autonomous construction robots to handle tasks such as bricklaying, painting, or plastering. Furthermore, it might be potentially interesting to invest in the development of smart materials that self-regulate based on environmental conditions, such as concrete that self-heals. The construction industry is teeming with technological innovations that could (or perhaps not) transform the industry.

FOSTERING A CULTURE OF RISK-TAKING

While Visionary leaders are active on all levels of the organisation, they might still struggle to promote a risk-taking culture. Taking the kind of risks that Visionary leaders stand for, may, from the perspective of the employee, be perceived as carrying too many negative consequences if things go wrong. Even though your colleagues might have various ideas to improve the workplace, they hesitate to bring them out into the open. Your perception of risk and voicing opportunities is influenced by your surroundings. INSEAD professor Herminia Ibarra writes that often our networks don't help us to reinvent ourself, nor lead us to something new, different, and potentially better.[184]

You can invite colleagues to come up with completely new ideas. Remember the innovation paradox of small ideas and large-scale initiatives.[185] Small ideas sometimes have the power to introduce a new business model and propel a company forward. One such example is the case of Dick Brams,[186] St. Louis regional manager at McDonald's in 1977. Dick wanted to trial a meal designed specifically for children and pitched his idea to management. Two years later, McDonald's sold its very first Happy Meal. And let's be honest, who hasn't had a Happy Meal as a child (or as an adult...)?

REFLECTION

When was the last time you had an interesting idea regarding the use of digital technology? Did you share it with others or did you decide to keep it to yourself? Why didn't you share it?

TAPPING INTO THE WISDOM OF THE CROWDS

In the autumn of 1906, British scientist Francis Galton left his home in Plymouth and headed for the annual West of England Fat Stock and Poultry Exhibition. Galton was known for his work on statistics and the science of heredity. Despite his age – 85 at the time – he still exuded curiosity. This time, livestock caught his eye. Local farmers and townspeople gathered at the fair to appraise the quality of one another's cattle, sheep, chickens, and more. Even though Galton didn't fit into that group, there was a logic to him being there: he was obsessed with measuring physical and mental qualities, and with breeding. He believed that very few people had the characteristics necessary to keep society healthy. In fact, Galton had devoted most of his career to measuring those characteristics and wanted to prove that the vast majority was "not fit for breeding". Because of his experiments in the decades before, Galton had lost faith in the intelligence of the average person.

But on that day, he had to revise his opinion. What happened? Galton had stumbled upon a weight-judging competition. An ox had been selected, and the gathering crowd was placing wagers on its weight. The best guesses would receive a price. A diverse group of about 800 people tried their luck. While some were butchers and farmers who were presumably experts, there were also a lot of people with barely any knowledge. Later on, Galton wrote up his scientific article, stating that "The average competitors were probably as well fitted for making the just estimate of the dressed weight of the ox as an average voter is of judging the merits of most political issues on which he votes."[187] When the contest was over and the prizes had been awarded, Galton borrowed the tickets and ran a series of statistical tests on them. He added all the contestants' estimates and calculated the mean of the group's guesses. The number represented the wisdom of the crowd. The result was astounding. While Galton believed that the average guess would be way off the mark, that wasn't the case. The crowd's guess was that the ox would weigh 1,197 pounds and, in fact, the ox weighed 1,198 pounds. The crowd's democratic judgment was more accurate than expected.

While it's of course always worthwhile to source experts' knowledge on their respective fields of expertise, it doesn't necessarily mean that you should not tap into the many brains of your diverse stakeholder pool. This helps you build on *the Wisdom of* Crowds, as author and journalist James Surowiecki called it.[188]

DID YOU KNOW?

Danish politician and social worker Uffe Elbæk took out a $100,000 personal loan in the early 1990s to establish Kaospilot, an unusual business school. Chaos pilots are individuals who drive results and create transformation.[189] They can be described as changemakers who can creatively lead a project through uncertainty. They can extract structure from chaos and use it to their advantage. They motivate their colleagues even when the environment is changing.

Most of the time, chaos pilots receive mixed performance reviews. Not because they are bad employees, but because they make those around them somewhat uncomfortable by questioning the status quo. Still, they succeed and perform admirably.

TOWARDS RISK-TAKING

A digital transformation requires you to engage with the future with a forward-oriented mindset and a hunger for experimentation and innovation. But fostering such a mindset is not easy. It asks companies to be introspective, evaluate, and frequently reconsider their existing success formulae. This could create resistance at all layers of the company. Matthias Müller wondered, as many people would, if his company should change its formula if it didn't seem broken. We must dare to consider whether previous winning ways are still valid. What can you do to stimulate a culture where risk-taking is welcomed?[190]

— **Bring risk out in the open and deploy premortem sessions.** When you approach a new idea from a best-case scenario perspective, you overlook the numerous ways a plan can fail. Psychologist Gary Klein is known for his prospective hindsight research – you imagine an event has already occurred – and found that it increases your ability to correctly identify reasons for future outcomes by 30%. Klein recommends premortem sessions to identify potential roadblocks. You explicitly identify the critical risk factors that might influence certain outcomes.[191] Think in terms of product price risk, environmental risk, execution risk, and so on. For example, you might conclude that resistance to change is expected with employees being hesitant to adopt new technologies; it might be that you identify a potential integration issue with existing systems due to incompatible software or data migration issues, or it could be that you stumble upon certain cybersecurity risks. Next time, try to hold a premortem session and invite various stakeholders to reflect on potential risks beforehand. When you specify these risks in advance and have people agree with them, you strengthen your position as an organisation to identify what might lead to the success of a new project.

— **Create awareness of the "success trap" and the "failure trap".** These have a common pitfall: losing yourself in your commitment. In the "failure trap" (or, the escalation of commitment) you commit more resources than expected to something that isn't working. As a result, you take on more risk. In the "success trap", on the other hand, you are primarily focused on the aspects of your business that have always guaranteed you success. You are less likely to seek out new adventures and one-of-a-kind opportunities. Both jeopardise a company's long-term viability. To create awareness, it's worth regularly reviewing certain strategic assumptions within the organisation. You can, for example, hold quarterly reviews, training sessions, or workshops where you challenge these assumptions, and where people can express concerns about sticking to outdated methods or doubling down on failing projects.

— **Make risk less personal.** People might refrain from sharing bold and daring ideas as they fear they will be held accountable in the end if the project doesn't work out as expected. To resolve this, it might be worthwhile to separate the idea, the decision, and the execution from each other. If necessary, you can choose to assign accountability to different people in the decision and execution phases and tailor certain incentives as you deem fit.

— **Think like peers.** Before you judge other people's ideas, give yourself the opportunity to brainstorm for five minutes about your own ideas and thought processes. Usually, we tend to look for reasons to say "no" and we have rejected an idea from the get-go. By first allowing ourselves to enter a brainstorming mindset, we are less likely to think evaluatively and, instead, more creatively. For example, refrain from asking "why?" and ask "why not?" instead. The traditional response to a new idea is always "Why would we do this?", unwittingly rejecting it from the start. Instead, aim for an "Indeed, why wouldn't we do this?"mentality.

— **Celebrate the inevitability of failure.** Failure will happen. Not all projects or investments are meant to be a resounding success. Dozens of experiments and trials are sometimes necessary to achieve results. Iterations are necessary to build and improve. Each project will help you learn and give you insights that might benefit you in future endeavours.

— **Stretch your colleagues.** They are a source of inspiration. In the next round of evaluation talks or feedback, focus on what they have learnt and ask where they would like to take a risk. Perhaps combine this with pitching competitions and space for your experimentation – you give the winners the freedom to pursue their winning idea within the company and provide budget and mentoring.

— **Battle the adaptability paradox.** People prefer to stick with what they know. This is especially the case when they need to learn and change. Unless the brain learns something completely new, it forecasts based on previous experiences. And while adaptability is not a natural skill, it can be nurtured. Adaptability takes you from being resilient and enduring a challenge to thriving beyond the challenge. Rather than bouncing back, adaptability has you bounce forward. It helps you remain calm and display curiosity in the face of turbulence. Adopting shoshin, or the beginner's mind, is one way to battle the non-adaptive mindset. In contrast to the expert's mind, the beginner's mind stimulates thinking in terms of possibilities. To (sometimes) detach from experience, the expert could learn to embrace curiosity. Both the Vigilant and Voyager leaders can help you explore new possibilities.

In settings like these, it's important that the Visionary leader actively collaborates with the other leader types. The Voyager leader, for example, takes the lead making sure the company can rely on acts of experimentation, while the Vigilant leader makes sure that alternatives to the current focus get enough consideration. The Visionary leader bundles everything together and constructs an attractive story and vision, embodying bold choices at the highest level carrying a certain overall risk-reward balance.

STORY CONTINUATION

Matthias's decision to stick with traditional methods has placed him in what is known as the **success trap** – he is only willing to commit to what has led to success in the past. At the same time, he is a victim of the adaptability paradox, where his very expertise and years of experience make it harder for him to adapt to a rapidly changing landscape. While these approaches worked for Matthias in the past, his **risk aversion** crystallises as a liability. It's of course understandable, colleagues know. Matthias is emotionally attached to the business he built and he is very proud of the baby he raised. It's his life's work. But his fear and resulting unwillingness to take measured risks now threatens MSC.

Addressing the burning platform at Müller & Sons Construction

Benjamin, who took the leading role in the team, stops Matthias in the hallway: "Matthias, do you have time today for a meeting with us? There's something we must discuss.". Matthias pauses, knowing Benjamin's reputation for avoiding small talk. People know that when Benjamin asks for a meeting, it's worth agreeing to. Later that day, everyone sits down around the table. Benjamin begins cautiously, "Matthias, we feel that during our recent meeting, our approach was off. We'd like to reformulate the business proposal as we have been asking the wrong question. Instead of 'why change', let's ask, '**why wouldn't we** do this?'". Matthias, intrigued but cautious, tilts his head slightly. Benjamin continues, explaining the rationale behind thoughtful risk-taking and how it's not about jumping into risk maximisation or betting everything on some pie-in-the-sky unproven idea. "This isn't about excessive risks or making reckless bets," Benjamin says, "but we want to suggest that this is about prudent **risk-hedging** and **risk-mitigation**. Our proposal is specifically designed with the company's financial and professional portfolio in mind. The core business is strong. It's the foundation that got MSC to where it is today. We're not new to technology either. We've already made great strides in increasing back-office efficiencies in the past with digital technologies. This is our Horizon 1 – the foundation is robust and there's room for further expansion and growth."

Matthias acknowledges that the team isn't asking him to abandon previous successes. Benjamin continues, "Yet, we shouldn't ignore what is happening in the market. Currently we are still in a luxury position where we can start exploring new opportunities – this would be our Horizon 2 where we identify new ventures that might result in significant returns in the future. As you've read before in the document, 3D printing and BIM are quite low-hanging fruits that might get us back in line with our direct competitors, solidifying our comfortable position. They won't disrupt our current operations at all." At this point, Matthias looked thoughtful, no longer defensive. Listening. Benjamin continues, "On these slides we also clearly included our cost-benefit analysis, timelines for implementation, and even some suggestions for smaller-scale pilot projects. Some Horizon 3 projects might be interesting to explore with other parties. We can learn from them, collaborate, and who knows, perhaps one day implement them and gradually scale from there. And this doesn't need to happen overnight. If we take thoughtful, measured steps, we aren't putting the company in jeopardy and we are more likely to strengthen our position and reputation.".

The room falls silent, with people eyeing Matthias, waiting for his response. Then he speaks, "This sounds... reasonable. Thank you for putting it this way. I understand that these things, these Horizons, can run in parallel to each other." People smile, recognising a first minor **shift** in Matthias' **perspective**. While this conversation was just the first step, Benjamin and the team know how critical this was for MSC. By reframing the discussion around rational risk-taking and focusing on prudent exploration, they helped Matthias see that digital transformation isn't something to fear – it's an **opportunity to build** on the company's existing **strengths** and **leverage** the power of a well-balanced portfolio.

Reflecting on Müller & Sons Construction's situation, how would you **reframe the story around risk-taking** to improve the company's chances for a successful digital transformation journey?

DEVELOPING PARTNERSHIPS

BEYOND THE HEADLINES: TRANSFORMING MEDIA THROUGH ACTIVE BUSINESS RELATIONSHIPS

Introduction

The media industry is experiencing strong digital disruption. Content is now produced, distributed, and consumed in an entirely different manner. For example, AI empowered journalism aims to bring quality, societal relevance, and the entire business model to a new level. Traditional media companies, as a result, are forced to rethink established routines. To stay relevant, however, it's not simply about adopting some digital tools and companies need to fundamentally innovate how they operate and engage with their audience. This is difficult to achieve in isolation and business collaborations are deemed essential in such a new digital landscape: no single organisation possesses all the necessary resources, expertise, and technologies to achieve success.

Heritage Broadcasting Network (HBN), a leading national multimedia player, and Atlas Newspaper (Atlas), an important regional player, understood this. HBN is well-versed in video content, online platforms, and engaging with their audience through digital channels, while Atlas has a long-standing reputation for investigative journalism, credibility, and reader trust. These companies want to invest more time and resources to their already **ongoing partnerships** aimed at creating a seamless digital customer experience. Together, these companies have weathered the industry's transition to digital platforms and embraced the era of free media. In the last decade, both players emerged and positioned themselves as digital media **trailblazers who adapted** their operational methods while respecting the core principles of independence, expertise, and journalistic integrity. Again, the stakes are high, though. Despite previous successes, they face significant **external pressures** from digital-native competitors, including tech giants and independent content creators. The advent of Generative AI poses another crisis moment. Everything combined, these players are siphoning off audiences and advertising revenue. With consumers increasingly gravitating towards other sources, HBN and Atlas notice their market shares dwindling, growing ever fearful of becoming irrelevant. They sound the alarm.

The problem at Heritage Broadcasting Network and Atlas Newspaper
Jürgen, well-known and respected at HBN and Atlas, is appointed director of cross-organisational digital transformation and oversees four teams that are tasked with driving digital innovation. Roughly six months later, however, three out of four project teams have **disbanded**, and the fourth team is currently headed in the same direction. Jürgen **struggles to align** both companies under a common agreed-upon vision for digital success. Both companies say they want to be digital pioneers but have **differing ideas** of what this could look like. Communication between the teams was too **fragmented** and ineffective, pulling stakeholders in different directions. As a result of misunderstandings and unclear expectations, trust was broken.

Meanwhile, both HBN and Atlas see their market share dropping further and their brand value is eaten away by declining revenues and financial instability. What's more, the companies' HR departments signalled a talent drain was taking place with top employees relocating their careers to more innovative competitors. The impact of **failing to collaborate** effectively and tap into opportunities for innovation is felt all over. If nothing changes soon, both companies will miss out on the chance to shape the future of media and create new revenue streams.

Jürgen and his teams - or rather, one remaining team - are at a critical juncture. The recent collapse of the third team and the **impending collapse** of the fourth one is a symptom of deeper, systematic issues threatening the success of the digital transformation initiative. To salvage the initiative and secure the future of HBN and Atlas, Jürgen needs to **tie the business relationship** more strongly again.

TRUST AND COMMITMENT

Future success no longer belongs to a single firm, but to networks, where a win-win arrangement is possible for all involved. Boundary-spanning partnerships are now pivotal to build products, attract and retain customers, and offer a winning proposition. Nonetheless, research on startups found that only 28% were satisfied with their corporate partners.[192] Companies strive to increase their agility and innovation speed, satisfy their hunger for creativity and curiosity, and improve their product development; they might do so by gaining insights into experimental technologies or by accessing new, untapped markets. Most businesses, however, lack the complete set of organizational capabilities and skills to tackle this solo. As such, Linda Hill and colleagues write how you need to "encourage an outside-in and collaborative ecosystem perspective [and] forge new partnerships with key players in the ecosystems."[193] These might even be your competitors. Considering this, *partnership management* has become a critical pillar of of digital transformation.

Companies sometimes relied on "hard power" tactics that revolved around confrontation and negation. This is analogous to flexing your muscles to impress the other party and obtain the most competitive terms and conditions. Though the relationship will probably last – with one party gaining quality at a reduced cost – you set up a win-lose situation. The relationship might persevere, but it's unlikely to be a healthy one. An adversarial atmosphere and confrontational mindset spreads. The potential of partnerships is typically restricted when companies engage from a control mindset. Stakeholders are less likely to fully explore what the partnership could truly offer.

Instead of neglecting the human aspects of partnerships and collaborations, a new paradigm advocates for fostering *trust* and *commitment*, where each party has mutual confidence in the capabilities and actions of the other.

Trust: our willingness to be vulnerable to the actions of another party and, when present, it can be observed as risk-taking behaviour.[194] It is often considered the lubricant and glue of most collaborations.

Commitment: will only be present when trust is actually there. If it is, stakeholders are much more likely to work at preserving the relationship and resist short-term gains that could be harmful.

Trust and commitment interrelate strongly. When trust is high (resulting from drivers such as respectfulness, sharing values, and the perceived value of the relationship), stakeholders' commitment will be influenced positively as well. When both trust and commitment soar, you might see your partnership benefiting from more cooperation, less uncertainty, less propensity to drop out and leave, and higher levels of agreement.

CREATING A PARTNERSHIP

During the launch phase, concentrate on developing a strong value proposition for all stakeholders. You begin from and maintain a broad and holistic perspective where you incorporate customer feedback. Try to build and strive for consensus as much as possible, ranging from the purpose of the collaboration to key initiatives, even to stakeholders' behaviours and values. You might want to call in the help of the Voyager leader to benefit from his prowess in making diversity and inclusion productive in co-creative teams. This helps you create consensus in a way that brings out stakeholders' differences and growing tensions – and opportunities to solve them.

Collaborative excellence in this regard requires a strong alignment of people, technology, and processes. The non-profit association ECLIC, founded in 2018, is a co-creation community that strives for interoperable chemical logistics industry solutions. Individual members (such as shippers, carriers, and storage operators), or a group of members, can fund and launch solutions. The overarching mission revolves around creating shared benefits, offering a smart company network, whilst being mindful about our planet. By using certain technologies and services, these actors aim for trusted data sharing to enhance their operational safety, efficiency, sustainability, and compliancy. From this, various solutions have been developed and installed, such as a hybrid solution that merges paper and digital documentation.

Furthermore, the net value derived includes lower costs and greater synergies. Companies at ECLIC join forces for mutually beneficial reasons that are based less on power play and more on value exchange. Of course, it is fallacious to assume that a trusting relationship would emerge naturally. From the start, you might stumble upon certain frustrations that, ideally, had been identified upfront. As such, a Visionary leader approaches and vets new partnerships by means of, for example, premortem sessions. These help you in identifying and preparing for potential hurdles to come. In this case, Jürgen could first pay attention to various critical factors.[195]

— **History.** What is the candidate's history and reputation when it comes to partnerships and collaborations? What can other players tell you about them? Companies with a bad partnership reputation are more meticulously surveyed and trust is missing. Here you can find out about their reliability and ethics; you can also ask customers about their experiences.

— **Motivation.** How motivated and dedicated is the candidate to truly nurture and commit to this partnership? Do they seem rather hesitant? Are they willing to jump? Their overall attitude towards collaboration matters. If they seem sceptical, it's likely you'll have to put in more effort to build trust.

— **Values.** Which corporate values and culture do you see? Do you speak a similar language and have similar work standards? When similarities are identified, it's more likely you will trust one another.

— **Willingness.** Is the candidate willing to proactively exchange information and accept vulnerability as a result? Will they treat your data and information as confidential and with respect? Or, are they, instead, data and information hoarders?

— **Competence.** Is this the right candidate to engage with – do they have the right kind of expertise and intelligence for this project?

— **Liaison.** Who is your contact person? Do you consider this person to be the right fit for supporting the project? Is this person likely to boost or harm trust in the future? Be mindful that having only one liaison is considered a risk. When that person disappears, the impact on your partnership and collaboration might turn out to be a big issue.

POSSIBLE PITFALLS IN A PARTNERSHIP

It is worth fostering mutual awareness about various common pitfalls when you are starting a new collaboration:

— **You over-rely on interpersonal relationships.** Partnerships sometimes survive solely because of the relationship between two key stakeholders – this can be CEOs, managers, and so on. These people have a strong personal bond, feel connected, and see eye-to-eye on most matters. However, people might not stay in the same company or position and it often happens that a partnership fails when one of these people leaves the company or switches responsibilities.

— **You underestimate the turbulence and uncertainty of partnerships.** Companies often enter a partnership with overly optimistic expectations, believing that everything will go smoothly. However, as the partnership progresses, the reality of differing priorities, market shifts, communication breakdowns, and more become apparent, often causing unanticipated friction. The initial optimism fades and companies are suddenly forced to confront the complexities they initially overlooked.

— **You engage in opportunistic behaviour.** Engaging in a win-loss act, where you gain advantage at the expense of your partner – without their explicit agreement – causes trust to collapse. This could include predatory or copycat behaviour, the unauthorised sharing of proprietary and sensitive information, withholding crucial information such as market insights or technological development, manipulating contract terms, poaching key employees from your partner, and more. These reasons could end a collaboration immediately as they usually erode trust in such a way that it causes irreparable damage.

— **You lack an established governance process.** Trust doesn't imply that you should allow or welcome lack of clarity. There are still rules of engagement to be agreed upon and followed, deadlines to be defined and met, and communication methods to be outlined. Create a clear framework.

Adapted from Sloan & Oliver (2013)

Trust grows in a gradual S-shaped curve, like a meandering river. It does not travel in a straight line to its destination; it twists through the landscape, swirling slowly in some places and quickly in others. And like a river, trust starts as a small spring, while the banks gradually widen as the river flows to the ocean. Because of the ebb and flow of trust, partnerships will face difficulties. These issues are known as *critical emotional incidents* – intense emotions that are triggered by certain stimuli and that warrant attention.[196] For example, it might be that your partner repeatedly doesn't show up in meetings or cancels last minute; it might be that they share sensitive information that wasn't supposed to be shared. Considering this, *various practices* can help in preventing a total collapse of trust and help repair and strengthen it instead:

1. **Ask provocative questions.** These questions can bring up sensitive issues and negative emotions. For example, ask "Where exactly is the value in this partnership?". While perhaps a seemingly easy question, it's also one that is rarely voiced. Asking about and expressing negative emotions can be beneficial. Not only do they serve as a litmus test for commitment and sincerity, they will also provide you with an opportunity for reflection and alignment. This helps in uncovering underlying tensions or unspoken concerns that might hinder future progress. By addressing these head-on and early, a stronger foundation for collaboration can be created.

2. **Offer sensitive disclosures.** When confronted with provocative questions, it's crucial that your responses are open, honest, and transparent. Sharing concerns, doubts, and mistakes, demonstrates your sincerity and willingness to show vulnerability. By sharing these vulnerabilities, you build emotional bridges that strengthen the relationship, showing that you are willing to take risks to foster trust. Your openness might also prompt the other to be more transparent in return, leading to a partnership based on mutual trust.

3. **Open the agenda.** It's important to allow room for spontaneous ideas and discussions that weren't originally part of the agenda. Encouraging open discussions and reflection on new or unanticipated ideas might potentially lead to breakthrough moments. Such agenda flexibility allows fresh thinking and creativity to flow. However, it's important that you strike a balance between spontaneity and maintaining control of the main objectives. Losing control in this sense could derail progress. Aim for joint planning and decision-making, and do so by consulting each other. Align and communicate whenever necessary.

4. **Value the other.** By acknowledging the other and their contributions, albeit large or small, you instil a sense of pride and ownership in the partnership. It's essential to exhibit equality, respect, and inclusivity if you want enthusiasm and commitment to follow. Furthermore, if you collaborate with smaller players, such as startups, it's critical to not treat them as side projects. Instead, approach each partnership as an opportunity for mutual learning and recognise the unique strengths each brings to the table.

At Atlas and HBN, emotional incidents kept happening on a team level as well. Team members soon dropped out and project teams got disbanded after a while. In any cross-company collaboration, you will interact with individuals – people with different habits, who might speak a different cultural language, and so on. Decades of research led Paul Zak, founding director of the Center for Neuroeconomics Studies, to define various tools that might help Jürgen with the situation at Atlas and HBN.[197] Jürgen could...

- **Listen.** People rarely send explicit signals about their thoughts and feelings. As such, it's important for Jürgen to monitor and spot signals that might be weak at first but are likely to fester. Listening in helps to get into people's minds and moods, and will allow Jürgen to respond adequately.
- **Recognise excellence.** Immediately after a goal is met, Jürgen could celebrate the achievement in a personal and open manner, where other team members can see it and be part of the celebration.
- **Establish achievability** in goal setting. Jürgen could set difficult, but achievable, goals. This is likely to increase people's focus and strengthen social connections between team members.
- **Share information.** Jürgen might want to be more transparent about certain goals, strategies, and tactics HBN and Atlas agreed upon. Here, he could help in creating and communicating a compelling vision in which all parties have a clear stake. When there is uncertainty about a direction, chronic stress emerges, and teamwork is undermined. To prevent this, Jürgen could voice clear expectations and be transparent about any additional responsibilities. "Openness is the antidote," writes Paul Zak.[198]
- **Show vulnerability** and allow vulnerability to be shown. For Paul Zak, asking for help is the ultimate sign of a secure leader. People worry about upholding a positive image and feel the incessant urge to attend to the obligations and demands that come with it. If the team members see Jürgen as more *human*, someone who dares to ask for help and insights at times, people might be more inclined to voice their needs and feelings. Furthermore, their willingness to cooperate is likely to grow.

WATCH OUT

Partnerships are dynamic and include more than just the written agreement. They should be regarded as living systems that evolve in their capabilities. In other words, the partnership of today is not the same as tomorrow's partnership. If you nurture it properly, it could open new doors and provide both sides with unexpected opportunities.

A business partnership goes beyond an exchange of assets. When you engage in activities in which all participants create new value together, you can be considered successful.

Formal systems to control partnerships are a last resort. You want to build on interpersonal connections and collaborative behaviour across all layers of the participating companies.

REFLECTION

Think back to a moment where you professionally collaborated with another company on a digital transformation journey and where tensions rose. Do you have such example in mind? Let's try to fill out the following reflections:

Incident: what happened?
Context: When/where did it happen?
Impact: What was your initial reaction? Which emotions did you feel?
Solution: What did you do (to solve this)?
Impact: How did you feel? Did your emotions change?
Evolution: How did your trust evolve throughout this experience?

STORY CONTINUATION

"These business relationships," Jürgen muttered to himself, "aren't as easy as we thought". Conducting a postmortem made it clear to him that HBN and Atlas had entered this with rose-tinted glasses, overlooking potential risks that should have been addressed from the very start. Jürgen decided to tackle the problem on three fronts. First, he aimed to create a more **unified vision** and establish clear rules of engagement; second, he sought to strengthen **emotional engagement** and commitment among team members; and third, he brought in **other key players**.

Addressing the burning platform at Heritage Broadcasting Network and Atlas Newspaper

Idea 1
To address the high-level issues, Jürgen organised a **joint leadership summit** where key stakeholders from HBN and Atlas worked together to outline a shared vision for digital innovation. This involved crafting a detailed roadmap of goals, timelines, and metrics that both companies agreed on. As part of this effort - and as a soft power tactic - Jürgen encouraged the stakeholders to share market intelligence, data insights, and best practices. For example, HBN **contributed** insights on digital broadcasting trends, while Atlas offered their expertise in journalism ethics and audience engagement. However, recognising the sensitivity of this information, confidentiality protocols were put

in place. Jürgen knew this approach didn't necessarily signal full trust between the companies - both parties were somewhat concerned about potential exploitation and theft of proprietary data – but it was a necessary step toward **building deeper collaboration**. Leadership also agreed to work on setting new industry standards for digital content distribution and data usage.

Idea 2

At the team level, Jürgen gathered all team members for a discussion not only about the new shared digital transformation vision but also to encourage **open dialogue** and **mutual vulnerability**. Various emotional engagement practices were used: Jürgen started by asking provocative questions - uncomfortable but necessary to bring sensitive issues to the surface. For example, people from HBN felt that they were shouldering the bulk of the workload, believing that their company was putting in more resources. Meanwhile, colleagues from Atlas felt disrespected when their ideas on customer-oriented digital innovation were ridiculed, leading them to feel their expertise was not trusted. Minor issues like differing work schedules, missed deadlines, and sometimes personal tensions had also exacerbated frustrations. As team members from both sides chimed in, opening up and sharing personal vulnerability, it became clear that the absence of an established governance structure had left many feeling confused, uncomfortable, and disengaged. Rather than trying to fix things, people had simply dropped out. By the end of the roundtable, a **formal framework** was put in place, defining roles, decision-making protocols, and agreed-upon communication channels. Jürgen also suggested drafting an agreement on expected behaviours and mutual respect, helping teams to operate from a foundation of trust.

Idea 3

While both organisations had a lot to offer, innovating together was not enough. They decided to **leverage the external ecosystem**. This involved partnering with other players in the media industry to introduce fresh perspectives and enhance digital capabilities in a more agile and creative way. Both companies had recently signed a deal with EtnAI - a Southern European artificial intelligence company – specialised in training large language models, allowing for a deeper integration of journalism in AI technologies. Atlas and HBN would benefit themselves from seeing their information being accessed and appreciated by a broader and more diverse audience, which would safeguard certain revenue streams.

These efforts transformed the struggling partnership between HBN and Atlas into a more effective collaboration, allowing both companies to regain their positions as major players and innovation frontrunners in the digital media landscape. The combination of trust, improved governance, and strategic external partnerships resulted in more agile innovation initiatives that, over time, led to a resurgence in market share and new revenue streams.

Reflecting on the situation of Heritage Broadcasting Network and Atlas Newspapers, which actions would you take as a Visionary leader to **better the business relationship** and the story around risk-taking to improve the company's chances for a successful digital transformation journey?

ENERGY SCAN FOR VISIONARY DIGITAL TRANSFORMATION LEADERSHIP

Turn the "what is" and "what could be" into a vision of "what should be", advocating the use of digital technologies to create competitive advantage. They combine signals, ideas, and experiments into a winning business aspiration. Great visionaries tell engaging and energising stories of the organisation in the digital age. They create a shared purpose and stimulate colleagues to realise this. They also believe that assisting others in finding meaning in their job is crucial to realise digital transformation. Through their stories, they help others see why they matter to the organisation. They choose to compete with an ecosystem lens as they understand the innovation potential is associated with digital partnerships and collaborations.

Do you want to find out which of the Visionary leader skills give you and your colleagues energy? Take this short test.

1 = never 2 = rarely 3 = sometimes 4 = very often 5 = always

Questions	Your response (1 – 5)
I like to participate in creating shared purpose	
I like to stimulate colleagues to realise our shared purpose	
I like helping others see why they matter to the company	
I enjoy some risk-taking	
I enjoy forging successful relationships with external parties	
I enjoy testing strategic choices and giving feedback	
I like to clarify strategic choices	
I enjoy helping people find meaning in their job	

Total score:

CHECKLIST FOR VISIONARY DIGITAL TRANSFORMATION LEADERSHIP

If you now wonder whether signs of Visionary digital transformation leadership can be spotted within your company, you can reflect on the following set of statements:

At [your company name], we **foster purpose**, *as we...*

know our corporate purpose.	
feel connected to our company.	
are offered space to reflect on our individual purpose.	
avoid suffocating meaning at work.	
talk about our values.	
avoid signals of hypocrisy and artificiality.	
see purpose and meaning as fundamental.	
close the purpose hierarchy gap.	
understand why we are doing something.	
have clear goals to act upon.	

... *tell stories, *as we...*

inspire.	
use the power of the narrative.	
are passionate about our ideas.	
aim for the heart.	
prepare colleagues for the future.	
motivate colleagues to overcome obstacles.	
celebrate.	
rely on more than data.	
engage others.	

*... **riskcomfortable**, as we...*

assess our risks appropriately.	
understand our risk propensity and tolerance.	
can deal with uncertainty.	
hedge our bets by balancing risk with caution.	
identify and capitalise on opportunities.	
question the status quo.	
dare to experiment and embrace failure.	
avoid over-commitment success and failure trap.	
foster a culture of risk-taking.	
dare to embrace some discomfort.	

*... **collaborate**, as we...*

commit to our partners.	
trust our partners.	
are confident in our ongoing partnerships.	
are alert to the uncertainties of collaborations.	
dare to ask (uncomfortable) questions.	
dare to respond to (uncomfortable) questions.	
strive for excellence.	
build on consensus.	
put in the necessary hard work to make this a success.	
refrain from opportunistic behaviour.	

CHAPTER 4

Vested Leadership

TRANSFORMATIONAL PURPOSE

TRANSFORMATIONAL SCOPE

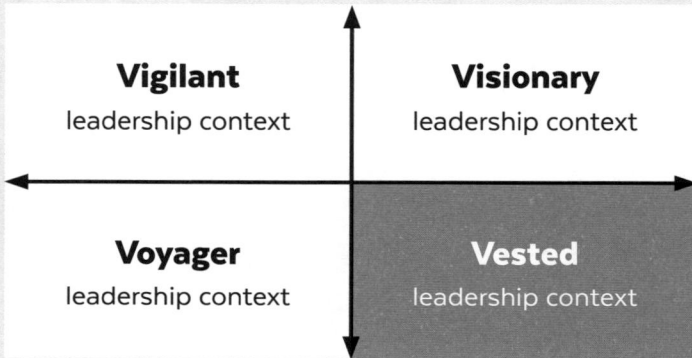

Vigilant leadership context	**Visionary** leadership context
Voyager leadership context	**Vested** leadership context

Pushing the edge of the thinkable

Pushing the edge of the actionable

Agility in exploration capacity

Agility in exploitation capacity

VESTED LEADERS

In the context of fostering and striving for a successful digital transformation journey, the Vested leader focuses on a core set of tasks.[199]

Vested leaders...

— Keep the **entire** organization, rather than individual elements, on a roadmap to successful digital transformation
— **Mobilise** the right skills and resources for timely exploration and exploitation
— Facilitate the **learning** and adoption of digital technologies, work and organizing practices at scale for an empowered workforce

To this end, Vested leaders put various skills to good use in order to guide colleagues and the company through a *human-centric* process.

In the following chapter, we will introduce you to several digital transformation protagonists and how they build on these skills to foster a meaningful journey for themselves, colleagues and other stakeholders, and the organisation at large.

— Will at Fortura who connects to other internal stakeholders to build on the promises of a **change coalition** to help guide the digital journey;
— Maria at EcoGoods and how her understanding of **change fatigue** and people's **absorptive capacity** helps her maintain a steady pace of transformation;
— Adil at InnovTech who learns to **break silos** in his ambition to reconnect people in favour of true, organic collaboration;
— Arthur at GreenFuture Labs who deploys a **bi-directional feedback strategy** to ensure people are empowered and engaged.

BUILDING A CHANGE COALITION

THE PERILS OF ACCOMMODATION

Introduction

Fortura operates in the consumer goods industry. Various competitors started leveraging artificial intelligence, supply chain automation, and e-commerce platforms, gaining a competitive edge by increasing their operational efficiency, reducing time to market, and creating more personalised customer experiences through advanced data analytics. Noticing these changes, Fortura's board formulated an ambitious five-year digital strategy roadmap to catapult the company ahead. The goal is mostly to optimise internal operations and the plan touches on nearly every aspect of the business. Will, the newly appointed digital transformation lead, has been tasked with overseeing this transformation. The board entrusted him with executing the roadmap, aligning departments, and ensuring that Fortura achieves its ambitious objectives.

As soon as Will began his role, he prioritised building **strong relationships** with each department head. His goal was clear: to ensure that every stakeholder feels **heard and included.** However, this eagerness to get everyone on board quickly evolved into a **double-edged sword.** Each department manager, seeing the opportunity to modernise their own unit, started approaching Will with several ideas for digital solutions. For instance, the marketing department proposed implementing an AI-based tool for personalised customer targeting, arguing that this would enhance the company's brand image and increase customer retention. Meanwhile, the sales department pushed for a complete overhaul of the existing CRM system to integrate more advanced analytics and AI-driven sales forecasting; furthermore, they were eyeing some experimentations with Generative AI. The finance team, on the other hand, wanted to adopt blockchain technology to improve the security and transparency of financial transactions. Similarly, the supply chain department suggested a radical shift to IoT-enabled smart logistics to track shipments in real-time, enhancing visibility. Whereas some people were proactively pushing for their new ideas, others were stuck in a state of shock and disbelief over the news of such digital transformation. People, long accustomed to their stable routines, struggled to grasp the shift and could not picture their place in such digitally redefined workplace.

The problem at Fortura

Will, eager to foster a culture of **inclusivity** at Fortura, adapted the initial roadmap to **accommodate** these demands. Each time, he altered the strategic plan to fit in new suggestions, which required him to revisit timelines, budgets, and the scope of initiatives. He felt that making these adjustments would help boost stakeholder buy-in and contribute to the long-term success of digital transformation. This approach, however, kickstarted a **snowball effect.** Once employees realised that Will was willing to adjust the roadmap to meet their specific needs, more stakeholders came forward. The HR department, for example, now wanted to develop and include VR-driven employee trainings. The legal team proposed digital solutions to automate compliance tracking and risk management. What Will didn't anticipate was that each addition came with new complexities, dependencies, and costs. While the suggestions were definitely valuable, forward-thinking, and technologically sound, implementing them meant constantly **deviating** from the roadmap.

The more Will tried to accommodate, the more **fragmented** the board's initial strategy became. Instead of following a cohesive, company-wide plan, the transformation now resembled a patchwork of small, **disconnected** initiatives. Three months into the project, Will's attempts to satisfy every department brought consequences. Progress had become sluggish and the longer Will followed this way of working, the more strain was put on resources and the more complex the roadmap became. For example, with so many different departments pushing for differing solutions, integration issues and inefficiencies can be expected. Additionally, conflict had appeared between teams, with each pushing harder for their own ideas, resulting in severe pushbacks from the other teams who now saw their own initiatives being threatened.

Meanwhile, the company was operating at two speeds. On the one hand, there were indeed those colleagues who voiced their ideas and saw this transformation as an opportunity to bolster their own department's efficiency. On the other hand, people were left behind. They felt vulnerable and unsure about the future of their work, resulting in a somewhat depressing climate.

Will's **eagerness to entertain** everyone's suggestions, adapt to each department's individual demands, and misunderstanding that people experienced this news of change quite differently, was causing significant problems for the company. When Will is asked to present his progress to the board, he suddenly feels like he is in very tight shoes as leadership starts to doubt his capacity to manage this crucial initiative.

CHANGE COALITION

Successful organisations recognise that change is inevitable and essential for an organisation's growth and development. However, implementing and sustaining a healthy dose of change within any organisation is easier said than done. It requires careful planning and strategic execution. As such, it becomes crucial to build a well-positioned team that helps in gaining buy-in and support from other employees – the guiding change coalition.

> "A change coalition is a group of influential and diverse stakeholders within the organisation who share a common vision and goal for the change, and who can help communicate, motivate, and empower others to adopt the change. A change coalition can include leaders, managers, employees, customers, suppliers, or any other relevant parties who have a stake in the outcome of the change. A change coalition is not a fixed or formal structure, but rather a dynamic and flexible network that can adapt to the changing needs and challenges of the change initiative."[200]

Surrounding yourself with the power of the many is considered a powerful tool, particularly in times of change. Consider the learnings and insights you could derive from a wide range of perspectives, experiences, and skills that not only compliment but also amplify yours. Together with people from different departments, levels of hierarchy, you form the *guiding change coalition*, consisting of multiple *influencers* – people, who despite their diverse backgrounds and expertise, might also possess and share several characteristics.[201]

— **Credibility.** Influencers are respected by their peers and have earned the trust of others, making them effective advocates for change.
— **Coaching.** They possess the ability to guide, mentor, and support colleagues in a supportive and empathetic manner. They are good at motivating and energising others, helping them navigate the complexities of transformation.

— **Linking.** They act as connectors, linking pins, who facilitate communication and collaboration across teams and departments, often operating quietly but effectively below the radar.
— **Position power.** Influencers hold positions that enable them in making decisions or influencing others, which helps in driving transformation forward.
— **Expertise.** They have a deep knowledge in their respective fields, which allows them to provide valuable insights and solutions during the transformation journey. These can be skills related to project management, change management, or specific technical skills.
— **Plan.** Influencers know how to plan, execute, and manage well.

These abilities help influencers in engaging other people, having colleagues ask questions, and expressing their opinions and concerns. Vested leaders identify and recruit these influencers in time and, together, the coalition plays two key roles:

— **Assisting** others in understanding the *why*, *where*, and *how* of the digital transformation journey.
— **Unfreezing** old attitudes, values, and beliefs, and **freezing** new ones. They help to avoid that people revert back to the old ways.

Prior to creating such a change coalition, the active change agent – that is, the Vested leader – assesses and maps potential support and resistance within the organisation. During a period of digital transformation, a workforce typically consists of four groups: 20% resisters, 60% bystanders, 10% helpers, and 10% champions.[202] Whereas the Vested, Voyager, Visionary, and Vigilant leaders are most likely to play active champion roles, making up (part of) the core change team, it might sometimes be difficult to properly identify some influential others. When they do manifest as resisters – becoming rebels, raising their fists to the change at hand –

the Vested leader may want to respond by involving (some of) them in the change coalition, on the condition that their presence remains minimal. If they are too dominant in your coalition, they may come to feel empowered to stymie progress. Resisters who join the coalition will see the preparation and implementation of change firsthand and as they are likely to feel heard and listened to, their negative attitude towards the change might evolve into a change-supporting one. They are now more aligned with the company's vision. You never know if they will end up in a helping role, turning other resisters to the side of change. Overall, the strength of the change coalition revolves around *shared ownership*, where people consider digital transformation a shared responsibility.

FULL INCLUSION: COLLABORATING EQUALS ACCOMMODATING?

It may be tempting to collaborate with all your colleagues to maintain the peace and status quo. You might be lured into incorporating every idea they bring to the table. But this would kick off the digital transformation process from the assumption that full inclusion is the only way forward. At Fortura, Will strives to do exactly that; unaware that by trying to include everyone and everything in the roadmap, he is stalling progress. What's more, Will has fallen victim to four dangerous assumptions.

1. Striving for full inclusion does not necessitate meeting all individual expectations. Active participation, through gathering and listening to feedback from colleagues, matters most.

2. A roadmap is not synonymous with a wish list. Instead, it is a high-level plan that outlines which steps are needed to connect the company's vision to specific transformation goals. A roadmap, as such, makes the digital transformation journey (and the strategy behind it), clear, focused, and potentially even measurable. Considering this, it's important to select your feedback and input wisely.

3. A preoccupation with being liked tends to harm rather than help the digital transformation process. Decisions are still to be made. Unfortunately, they will not always be in line with others' wishes. But people who feel heard are more likely to accept decisions that do not necessarily correspond with their own input.

4. The Vested leader is a people- and change-oriented leader, which is not the same as being an accommodator. A preoccupation with consensus and conformity clashes sharply with the pressing need for progress, change, and digital transformation. Considering this, Will might want to eliminate the assumption that he cannot go against other people's advice as that would jeopardise consensus and tranquility. Nor is it necessary for him to get all colleagues on board from the start. The critical mass can grow over time.

The sufficient change coalition

Vested leaders face the considerable task of creating a critical mass – a group large enough to *collectively* influence and transform the change effort from something necessary or desirable to something that actually takes place. If this critical mass is not achieved, complacency, fear, and anger might undermine and sink your change initiative. It is of course tempting to know which specific percentage to aim for (some say, for example, 75%[203]), but change management experts Linda Anderson and Dean Anderson write that, "There is no exact formula for determining the numbers needed. It is more like creating a snowball of support that grows as it rolls, regardless of the amount of snow in your initial ball."[204] The ball gathers mass and speed and moves with increasing ease. The main task is to ensure that the initial number in your collective becomes powerful enough to overcome past inertia and future resistance. But how do you get there? How do you make the change coalition work?

— **Scan the people in your company and beyond.** Determine which stakeholders currently enjoy a higher level of trust, influence, and authority. They could be thought leaders, covert or overt opinion leaders, employees with a large personal network, but also external stakeholders, such as customers and suppliers with a vested interest in the success of your organisation.

— **Rate the influencers.** The reason for classifying them champions, helpers, bystanders, or resisters is straightforward. Those who are "for" the change will be part of your critical mass, while those who are "against" will need to be approached differently to reduce their power in blocking progress. What matters most is that you have enough weight to get that snowball rolling. Hence the importance of recruiting colleagues with influence.

— **Figure out how to reach and work with your influencers.** Decide how you will communicate and which media channels you will use; how you will listen to feedback and input and how you will collect it; and clarify people's roles in achieving critical mass (i.e. communicators, feedback collectors, trouble-shooters, change advocates, rumour- and barrier-busters, and new behaviour models).

— **Keep the change coalition informal.** If you make it too formal, employees could feel manipulated and directed, and your influencers' potential for impact is reduced. Rather than holding scheduled meetings, you could opt for casual gatherings such as a coffee chat or a lunch meeting. Furthermore, it might be best to avoid giving formal titles or roles (such as "change officers") as this could impact how they are seen by others. It's also preferred to not install a clear hierarchy. In this case, Will might for example want to opt for a guidance role rather than asserting authority.

— **Pay extra attention to the primary resistors.** Don't try to persuade the entire group of resistors; but concentrate on those with the most negative influence. Inquire about their opinions – "What needs to change for you to support this transformation?" While you cannot guarantee that their needs will be met, the fact that you asked and listened already reduces resistance. Consider their resistance a strong source of feedback.

DID YOU KNOW?

The term "critical mass" originated in nuclear physics. When applied to digital transformation, it identifies the appropriate number of helpers and champions required to mobilise and sustain change.

It's crucial that your influencers and coalition are in place – particularly in those parts of the company that are most likely to be impacted by the change. For Will, establishing a solid change coalition might help him increase his credibility and legitimacy as a change leader, and could also help him leverage the skills of others to broaden his reach and impact. Together, these influencers can then respond to employees' emotions and concerns, which is likely to reduce resistance and increase employee buy-in. Influencers, however, must be mindful of four roles.

The communicator: communicate the change vision and reinforce the importance of the planned change. Influencers serve as role models and put words into action.

Broes, a respected manager in the marketing department, holds a casual team coffee session to explain the company's digital transformation goals, emphasising how adopting certain AI-powered tools will improve the team's campaign targeting. He shares specific examples of how the application has been successfully implemented in other companies in their industry, which currently provides them with some competitive advantage.

The translator: translate the change story to a more personal, almost individual level. Colleagues will ask and wonder, "What does this mean for me?". Influencers help to formulate an answer.

Zophia, sales team leader and part of the change coalition, sits down with a colleague who is concerned about how a new CRM system will affect their daily work. Zophia takes time listen to the concerns and tries to explain how it will streamline certain sales operations, making tasks easier for people rather than more complicated. She tells the colleague, "This means that you'll spend less time on data entry and more time building relationships with clients. And that's what you always liked most about your job, right?".

The message-bearer: Sometimes you will have to bring a message that not everyone likes to hear.

Gregory, active in the finance department, communicated that the implementation of a blockchain application would require a strong restructuring of certain processes, resulting in roles being redefined. While difficult, he focuses the messages on the opportunities for colleagues to retrain and acquire new skills that will strengthen their profile attractiveness in a changing industry. He acknowledges the disruption but also emphasises how Fortura is committed to supporting people during the transformation and preparing them for future success.

The listener: Influencers are sufficiently available and take the time to listen to their colleagues – what keeps them awake at night? Some may be concerned that their job will be drastically altered; others may believe that they will be out of work in a matter of months. In-depth conversations help you spot unexpected resistances. Resistance is valuable feedback.

Davy, IT veteran, is often available during lunchtime to answer people's questions and respond to their concerns. One colleague, for example, is worried that a certain automation process will make their job redundant. As Davy listens patiently, validating the concerns, he provides reassurance that the automation will actually allow the colleague to focus on more strategic tasks. After the lunch, Davy circles the feedback into the change coalition, suggesting it might be worthwhile to adjust certain aspects of the communication strategy.

RESISTANCE TO CHANGE AND THE KÜBLER-ROSS CHANGE CURVE

Throughout a digital transformation process, you will be confronted with colleagues' *commitment* (which should increase) and *resistance to change* (which should decrease). The change coalition's ambition is to grow the overall *change acceptance* that accompanies digital transformation. In doing so, however, they are likely to encounter a paradox. Neesha Malik and colleagues write,

> "Human mind thrives on distraction for a change. Yet, counterintuitively, any alteration from the regular or routine baffles mankind and is perceived by default as a problem that automates resistance. [In fact], the association of change with the loss of one's routine is cited as one of the main motives for resisting change."[205]

How do people cope with change?

The different stages of grief were first discussed by psychiatrist Elisabeth Kü-bler-Ross in her best-selling book *Death and Dying*. This was later applied to the business world, giving rise to the Kübler-Ross Change Curve,[206] which visualises how people experience and process change in their own way and at their own pace. Instead of treating employees and their emotions as a group – ultimately increasing the chances for trauma and resistance –, the Vested leader understands that it's sometimes necessary to have patience and accept the differences between people. Overall, the Kübler-Ross Change Curve consists of four phases, and seven stages.

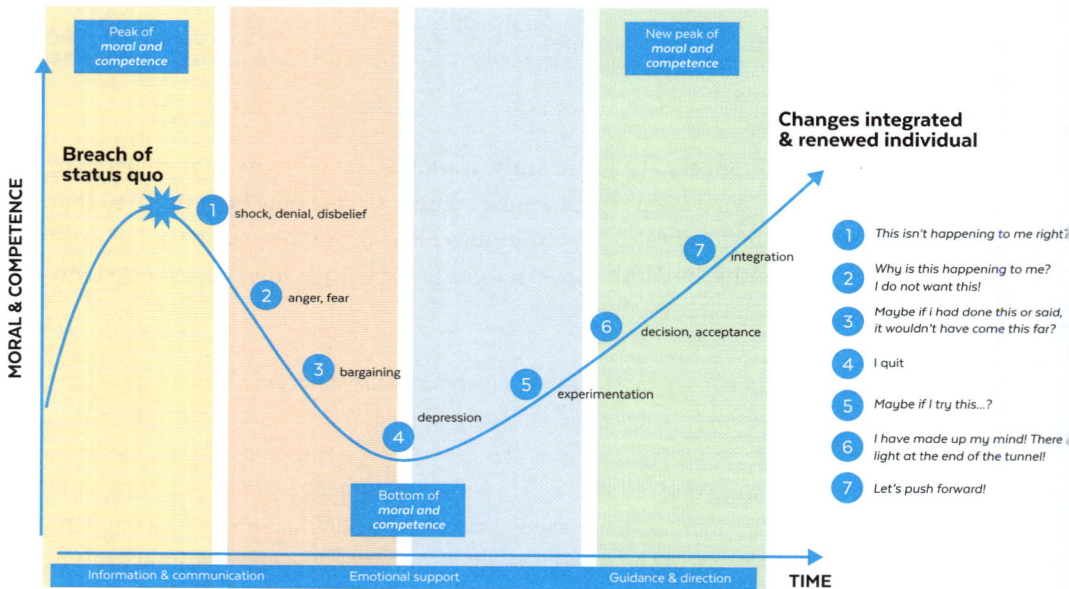

Figure. The change curve

Phase One: the *status quo*. There is no talk of change echoing in the hallways. Employees at Fortura are comfortable and accustomed to familiar routines. Operations have been stable for years. People's morale and competence steadily improved as people grew into their roles. However, this comfort is disrupted when the board introduces a high-level digital roadmap that aims to integrate various advanced technologies across departments. The announcement sends a shockwave through the company – people are suddenly faced with the reality of impending change. The initial reaction is denial as many employees cannot grasp how this new direction will impact their daily work, ultimately sparking a sense of disbelief and apprehension.

Phase Two: *disruption*. As the details of the digital roadmap unfold, employees begin to grapple with what this transformation means for them personally. Anger and fear become prominent at Fortura, especially among resisters who are vocal in their objections: "Why is this happening to us? We don't want this change!" Bargaining follows, with some employees questioning whether different actions in the past could have prevented this shift. Morale drops as old systems and practices – loved by many – are suddenly seen as outdated. Competence is questioned and people feel overwhelmed by the skills they will need to adapt to new technologies, leading to a sense of depression and self-doubt about their future roles in the company. It's important for Vested leaders to listen to people – what do they fear? –, show some understanding, and in doing so, provide emotional support as people near the bottom of the curve. Emphasise effective communication and provide information about the upcoming journey: what are the changes about? Consider the soundness of your reasoning and the overall change vision.

Phase Three: *exploration*. Eventually, after an initial struggle at the bottom of this emotional curve, some employees start to see opportunities within the change. Curiosity is triggered, and people try to reclaim control. They begin experimenting – exploring how digitalisation can improve their workflow or how new technologies could add value to their work. For instance, a sales representative was taking the initiative to explore how the new CRM system could help her in closing deals faster; a finance colleague started looking into blockchain and how it could provide additional transaction transparency. While Fortura's employees are still finding their footing and didn't yet fully commit to the change, they are in a phase of *fertile emptiness* where self-reflection and learning can occur. They learn new things about themselves.

Phase Four: *rebuilding*. Finally, as the change coalition continues to support and guide the transformation journey, more employees start to see the benefits and embrace the new direction. People make up their minds, saying, "This is indeed the way forward!", aligning themselves with the overall roadmap. Gradually they gain confidence in using new technologies and adopting new processes, and regain their morale and competence. Over time, their enthusiasm and capability reaches a new peak. People now feel renewed and equipped to contribute to Fortura's evolving vision, ready to drive the company towards a digitally enabled future. Vested leaders play a crucial role in this phase as they can consciously guide people, provide them with direction, and help them develop the necessary skills.

The COVID-19 pandemic

Consider COVID-19's impact on people's habits, behaviour, and overall mood. People underwent a sudden and abrupt shift that was completely at odds with what they were used to. It wasn't easy.

Some people were in denial and disbelief and while many believed that the situation wouldn't last for long, months and months had soon passed. People feared redistribution of work and were wary of being replaced by technology; they got angry over reduced working hours and, in turn, income. Resistance rocketed: people became reluctant to learn and adapt. They loathed quarantines and restrictions, the digitalisation of work and the non-stop integration of technology in their professional life. People hit rock bottom, burned out because of uncertainty. Some wondered whether this was truly the job they wanted to do for the rest of their lives. But the human species has made it this far because of its ability to change and progress; to evolve. People adapted – some earlier than others. We asked ourselves, "How can we do business in a way that's better than the ways of old?" Companies started experimenting. We can't have job interviews face-to-face? Okay, let's do video interviews. We can't organise in-person meetings? All right, let's add some digital spice to the mix. Gradually, we accepted this new reality. Companies and employees together explored new opportunities and rebuilt the way the company operated.

DID YOU KNOW?

Isomorphism in business is sometimes seen as the inertia that pushes companies to return to how things were before.[207] People believe that the pandemic was an exceptional situation. All we have to do now is leave it behind and go back to "business as usual". But what if business is no longer "as usual"?

STORY CONTINUATION

Will realised that his initial mistake was trying to satisfy every stakeholder's demands, leading to a loss of focus and increased fragmentation in the digital transformation effort. While inclusivity is important, he recognised the need for balance – he can accommodate key needs but should not compromise the integrity of the original roadmap. He understood that digital transformation cannot succeed through fragmented initiatives, which prompted him to shift his approach from attempting full inclusion to building a strong coalition of champions.

This **change coalition** – influential colleagues who guide the process, rally support, and break down resistance – would become the driving force behind the transformation. By focusing on a core group of champions, Will aimed to create momentum, leveraging their skills and enthusiasm to influence others and achieve the critical mass necessary to avoid inertia. Furthermore, Will made sure that everyone knew which roles they had to play.

Addressing the burning platform at Fortura

To build this coalition, Will identified key **influencers** at Fortura - employees who are respected by their peers, have coaching abilities, and serve as natural connectors across teams: Davy, Gregory, Zophia, Broes, Anaïs, Toby, Gerben, These influencers would play a vital role in communicating the vision for change, translating it into practical terms for their colleagues, and being available to listen to concerns. Will saw this as essential for "unfreezing" outdated mindsets and encouraging the adoption of new behaviours. Together, the coalition would guide employees through phases of disruption, exploration, and ultimately, rebuilding.

Will also took a more strategic approach in selecting individuals from different departments, even considering including some resisters. While initially hesitant about this, he recognised that involving a few resisters early in the process could potentially convert them into supporters. By addressing their concerns and including people in planning and implementation phases, Will limited delays and reduced resistance. However, he remained mindful of the risks of over-inclusion, also understanding that the coalition would evolve as new challenges emerged.

Another major shift in Will's approach was to **filter feedback more strategically.** Rather than treating every suggestion as equally important, he focused on gathering input selectively, homing in on projects that would deliver the most significant value to Fortura. He accepted that not every decision would please everyone. Still, by ensuring that employees felt heard, he increased the likelihood of their support – even if their ideas weren't (fully) incorporated. Through the change coalition, influencers acted as **ambassadors**, who explained the "why" behind decisions and who helped colleagues understand the rationale for strategic choices. Will no longer treated the digital roadmap as a wish list, but as a strategic plan to drive the company forward, reducing the risks of chaos and delays.

Taking on the role as a **Vested leader**, who listens to feedback without being beholden to every suggestion, Will makes it possible for himself to make decisive, strategic choices that align with Fortura's overall goals. Leveraging influencers who can help him manage resistance carefully and who take on a shared ownership of the process and the progress, Will could regain control of the transformation roadmap, steering Fortura's digital journey back on track.

Reflecting on Fortura's situation case, which actions would you take as a Vested digital transformation leader in **this balancing exercise** to increase the company's chances for a successful digital transformation journey? Can you think of ways to use digital technology to help you?

COPING WITH CHANGE FATIGUE

LEADING THE ELEPHANT: TURNING CORPORATE BURNOUT INTO INNOVATION POWER

Introduction

EcoGoods is a mid-sized regional retail leader with a strong focus on the urban and suburban areas. EcoGoods has always prided itself in its deep commitment to sustainability and circularity principles, even before it became a widespread phenomenon. The company offers eco-friendly and sustainable sourced products. In recent years, the retail industry has experienced additional pressures from both customers and governments to adapt to technological advancement and align with Environmental, Social, and Governance (ESG) principles. The company's leadership is committed to a future of responsible consumption and pledged to reduce its carbon footprint, minimise waste, and support the circular economy by encouraging customers and partners to recycle and reuse products. To succeed in this, EcoGoods understands that digital transformation can support in scaling these initiatives.

One of EcoGoods' key competitors recently integrated several advanced digital solutions to better their sustainability initiatives. Maria, head of strategy, found out that they introduced AI-powered demand forecasting, machine learning for dynamic pricing, and additional layers of automation in their supply chain. These efforts caught the eye of EcoGoods' partners who are now complaining about the company's slow technology adoption and their lower efficiency compared to other market players. The competitor's success and the indirect threats from partners has created a **sense of urgency** for EcoGoods to digitally **accelerate.**

Maria, alongside other key stakeholders, outlined **a two-year, four-wave digital transformation journey** to position the company as a leader in sustainable retail with optimised product life cycles. The plan aimed to integrate new technologies:

— **First Wave:** (i) new customer relationship management (CRM) system for personalised, sustainable product recommendations; (ii) introduce AI-driven customer service solutions, with a strong preference for virtual assistants.

— **Second Wave:** (iii) predictive analytics for eco-friendly inventory forecasting to prevent surplus, shortages, and waste; (**iv**) robotic process automation (RPA) to improve supply chain efficiency and reduce carbon output.

— **Third Wave:** (v) **digital** product lifecycle management (PLM) system to track the environmental impact of each product from production to disposal; (vi) launch an innovation hub that will act as a dedicated space for employees to experiment, share knowledge, and maintain progress.

— **Fourth Wave:** (vii) explore blockchain technology to provide transparency on product origins and help customers make more **informed** choices; (viii) explore new modes of transport for more efficient, on-demand deliveries.

The problem at EcoGoods

At this moment, EcoGoods found itself nearing the end of Wave 2. The fast pace of the transformation, however, created stress among employees. People reported feeling **overwhelmed** and **struggled** to absorb the new technology at the requested speed. Many were at a risk of **burn-out.** Employees were mostly busy trying to manage the fast pace of change. Employees, furthermore, lacked the time, training, and resources to fully understand how they could leverage predictive analysis or automation tools in their roles. Eyeing the Third and Fourth Wave, **fear** had set in. One manager echoed the sentiment of many employees, "We are not going through a digital transformation process, Maria. We are stuck on a high-speed **collision** course."

CHANGE FATIGUE AND SURGE CAPACITY

Digital transformation is the current apex of change. Under normal circumstances, most people can deal with a certain amount of change – your *surge capacity* – "a collection of adaptive systems, mental and physical, that humans draw on for short-term survival in acutely stressful situations".[208] However, people's surge capacity only allows employees to adapt to short-term pressures, such as the initial stages of a digital transformation, and is unlikely to suffice for prolonged periods of time. When organisations rely extensively on people's surge capacity without sufficient time for recovery, this will eventually lead to change fatigue, which compounds the challenges of implementing any further transformation efforts. At the Center for Creative Leadership, they use the following analogy:

"Think of your team as having a bank account. At any point, each team member only has so many resources saved — energy, attention, and interest that can be put toward the current projects and efforts your organisation faces.

Handling every workplace change, large or small, requires a withdrawal from the account. The problem comes when your people never have a chance to build up their reserves. Even the smallest change or challenge will be felt as overwhelming, or unnecessary, when your team's capacity feels so limited."[209]

Consider a pandemic with an unprecedented level of uncertainty. It impacts job security, financial assurance, health and loved ones' health. The disaster stretches out indefinitely and the damage is situated on an invisible level. People feel overwhelmed and drained. As such, the COVID-19 pandemic perfectly illustrates surge capacity. Professor of child development Ann Masten says, "The pandemic has demonstrated both what we can do with surge capacity and the limits of surge capacity."[210] In the context of business life in general, this holds true as well. Smaller changes that impact colleagues' day-to-day life (i.e. moving to a new team or getting a new manager) impact employees 2.5 times more than larger structural changes (i.e. a merger).[211] Gartner VP Jessica Knight says leaders must take responsibility for more than just the Big Bang type of transformations; the small ripples of change take the greatest toll.[212] Employees need support when change is announced and even more so when they experience the impact of this change.

At some point, companies and employees are expected to be burdened by *change fatigue* – "a resistance or passive resignation to organisational changes on the part of the employee".[213] It refers to the emotional and physical exhaustion that employees experience when they are constantly surrounded by a stream or streams of changes. During a digital transformation, employees must learn new technologies, adapt to different workflows, and reframe their roles within the company. When these changes occur too quickly or too frequently without sufficient support, people will struggle with compounded obligations (investments of time and energy) and might reach a breaking point. This will cause quite significant organisational challenges:

— **Burn-out and apathy:** EcoGoods employees are already showing clear signs of burnout and apathy due to the rapid implementation of predictive analytics and automated inventory systems in the first wave. The fast-paced transformation left little time for people to adapt, leading to emotional exhaustion and an inability to keep up. Some employees have reached a breaking point, which increased the risk of absenteeism, reduced motivation, and potential turnover. This presents a significant threat to EcoGoods transformation journey as it could result in the departure of skills staff who are vital to maintain change momentum and continuity.

— **Decreased engagement and productivity:** Additionally, EcoGoods' employees experience change fatigue and lose their willingness to engage with new technologies and any change efforts in general. The CRM system, amongst other things, is not used effectively and fails to realise its full potential. This decreasing engagement enthusiasm slows down the transformation process which further impacts EcoGoods' position in the market.

— **Resistance to change and frustration:** Many employees feel frustrated by the constant upheaval in their day-to-day work and the feeling of not being properly supported. Resistance to change has appeared, further fuelled by the fact that employees are not provided sufficient time to absorb and learn new skills. Some, by now, openly resist technology, whereas others resigned passively, appearing disengaged. Maria struggles to maintain momentum and keep up people's spirits.

To overcome these challenges, Maria – in her role as Vested leader – must recognise the impact of surge capacity and change fatigue on EcoGoods and take deliberate action to address burnout, improve engagement, and reduce resistance. If not, progress will stall further, bringing the journey to a complete stop. What can Maria do? [214]

— *Colleagues' trust levels* and *beliefs*. Companies have entertained various ways to motivate and engage employees for many years. While numerous approaches exist (i.e. external and internal motivations, aligning values and purpose), employees in high-trust environments are more productive, energised, and experience less chronic stress. Employees who believe they can rely on their leaders demonstrate greater trust and openness to change. They are also more likely to believe what leaders say. In this context, it's important to understand how people have experienced previous implementations and, linked to that, how well management performed in their eyes. Such perception is often negatively related to people's stress levels and scepticism. At EcoGoods, Maria might first want to recruit a change coalition to consult colleagues and hear their stories. Second, the coalition can also investigate the relationship quality in the groups: how strongly do colleagues trust their peers? Identify and recruit the covert and overt key opinion leaders in these groups.

— *Change perception.* Consider whether everyone sees *"change"* in the same way – some might think in terms of managerial change; others, in terms of technological change. This could cause strategic misalignment from the start. Feedback rounds are essential at all levels. They reduce the likelihood of employees being defensive or retaliating against changes.

— *Convince colleagues.* Employees might be put off by the term *digital transformation* – it's a heavy and loaded term. This comes down to individuals' appetite for change – are they more prone to flexibility and adaptability; do they have a certain tolerance for uncertainty; and do they believe they have some control over change? When people are confronted with change, or even the possibility of change, they instinctively weigh *the gains versus the losses*. Most people prefer a certain level of stability in their lives, and because change disrupts that status quo, they often consider change to be harmful. You can change this initial negative perception of change in two ways. You can adjust the perceived favourableness of the change – how do colleagues weigh the gains versus the losses? Maybe they overestimate the losses? Help them see the bigger picture. You can also call in the help of the Visionary leader to create a "change-supporting" vision and identity. Some people are more likely to be assured by clear facts and figures, whereas others want a comprehensive and transparent roadmap to position themselves on.

— *Monitor and adjust.* It's important to continuously gauge people's morale and engagement levels. If you can see clear signs of change fatigue and/or a depleted surge capacity, Vested leaders need to understand that the pace of change might be too high. They can adjust the pace or offer additional support such as offering consistent training, clear communication, and any other resource that could help colleagues.

— *Pace and build recovery time.* Instead of launching a full-scale overhaul of the organisation, roll out smaller manageable updates to ensure that employees have the time to absorb each one before introducing more. Acceptance is likely to increase if changes are presented incrementally rather than as a whole package. It's, however, crucial for Vested leaders to allow people time to recover and to allow periods of stability where no major changes are introduced. While smaller bites of change might not sound as dreadful, they become overwhelming when you introduce these at a too rapid pace, risking change fatigue once more.

EXERCISE

You might now wonder how trustworthy you are. Let's find out!

Which factors influence your perception of someone's trustworthiness? As it stands, we judge people on two dimensions: **competence** – *"Does this person know what they are talking about?"* – and **warmth** – *"Do I have a connection with this person and do they care about my wellbeing?"* When you answer these questions, you are better able to determine someone's trustworthiness.[215] The axes of competence and warmth yield four outcomes:

A disclaimer: It's not necessary to score highly on both dimensions per se, but it is preferable. For example, if you have a higher level of competence but a lower level of warmth, you can still be considered trustworthy for colleagues who find competence more important than warmth.

— Think about someone with whom you work(ed) on a digital innovation.
— Think about your team as it undergoes a digital transformation journey.
— Think about a colleague or a customer with whom you have a more difficult time collaborating on a digital innovation project.
— Where would you position yourself? What do you do to be perceived as a trustworthy person?

When you want to increase your trustworthiness, you have three options: increase your warmth, your competence, or both. We compiled various tools for each of the options below:

Warmth

— *Show empathy.* Ask open-ended questions and get to know colleagues better. Share some personal experiences. Identify and acknowledge colleagues' concerns and emotions.

— *Pay attention.* Make eye-contact, nod during conversation, and smile. Nonverbal communication is just as important as verbal communication. Remember *social contagion*? People are heavily influenced by the emotions and behaviours they observe in their surroundings. The emotions on your face are contagious.

— *Show vulnerability.* Dare to seek assistance from colleagues. When you ask for help, you engage others to reach goals together. Being open about what you don't know contributes to your credibility.

— *Trust them first.* Share information, listen to problems and ideas, and offer advice. Be the first to demonstrate trustworthy behaviour, and your colleagues will likely follow suit.

— *Put the "why" before the "what".* Don't just focus on the things that need to be done, but also pay attention to the story behind it to help people identify with the bigger picture.

Competence
— *Demonstrate willpower.* Fight back when you are faced with setbacks. Don't let your emotions get the better of you; instead, keep them under control.
— *Be aware of overconfidence.* Don't succumb to optimism bias. This might have you exhibit overconfidence and set unattainable goals that are not reached. This impacts how others view your competence.
— *Adopt a "power posture".* A power posture is an open posture: look at people, stand up straight (no slouching!), and maximise the physical space that your body occupies.
— *Emphasise* potential. Don't focus on the past and brag about what you have accomplished; rather talk about the future and how you plan to solve problems. People are more interested in the future than they are about your past (which they were probably not a part of).
— *Share your knowledge.* Which insights do you already have on certain technologies, change processes, and so on? Dare to openly disclose (some of) this information.

Can you think of other ways to boost trust?
What could help to increase trustworthiness in your team and/or organisation?

THE ELEPHANT AND THE RIDER

Even when your company embarks on the path of digital transformation with zeal, and you and your change coalition are considered trustworthy, the hunger for change tends to fade.

To keep colleagues engaged, consider the "elephant and the rider", a powerful metaphor used by Dan and Chip Heath in *Switch*.[216]

Three elements are intertwined in this metaphor: the rider (you and your change coalition), the elephant (your colleagues), and the path (the digital transformation process). Dan and Chip Heath devised three tips and tricks for each of these aspects, which we applied to the situation of EcoGoods.

— **Find the bright spots.** In difficult times, people often tend to see problems everywhere which results in a case of analysis paralysis. It is, however, crucial for the ride to provide a clear direction, and prevent the elephant from walking in circles. At EcoGoods, various examples exist of successful digital transformation initiatives, such as a department or a team that has smoothly implemented a new technology like an automated inventory system.

Concrete action for EcoGoods: Maria can highlight such previous successes, understand why they worked, and use these bright spots as examples for other teams and initiatives. She can conduct a review of a team that successfully adopted a certain technology and ask stakeholders to share best practices. This case study can serve as a model for others and simultaneously help Maria in shifting the focus towards positive change results.

— **Script the critical moves.** Employees are often overwhelmed by the rapid pace of change and the ambiguity it creates. Change brings uncertainty, and this uncertainty makes it difficult for people to understand which road to take. When we are confronted with a lack of clarity or change overload, we tend to opt for the most obvious and familiar path. It is preferred to break down the journey into specific, clear actions that employees can follow.

Concrete action for EcoGoods: Maria can create a step-by-step guide for integrating, for example, predictive analytics into the supply chain process. Here, she can focus on one or two critical tasks that employees should start with, rather than simply expecting them "to use the new system". This makes the expected adoption less intimidating.

— **Point to the destination.** It's important for people to know where they are going and to understand why the journey should be undertaken – why do these changes matter for EcoGoods' sustainability mission?

Concrete action for EcoGoods: Maria could launch a company-wide communication campaign that ties the success of the journey to EcoGoods' broader sustainability mission. For example, she could inform people about how "successfully implementing certain technologies into our procedures, such as AI and automation, could help us further reduce our waste by 15 to 30%, helping us to fulfil our commitment to a more sustainable future".

MOTIVATE THE ELEPHANT – ECOGOODS EMPLOYEES

— **Shrink the change.** The size of digital transformation journeys could feel daunting to many, ultimately leading to resistance. To counter this, it's worthwhile to break the transformation into smaller, achievable goals. Furthermore, these can act as small milestones that can be celebrated as victories. In doing so, you engineer early success and hope, both valuable commodities.

Concrete action for EcoGoods: When 50% of the workforce completed its first training round, Maria called for a small celebration; similarly, when the first successful predictive inventory forecast is made, the team heading this throws a small after-work drink. By publicly recognising these achievements and showing that, indeed, progress is made, people at EcoGoods feel more motivated.

— **Grow your people.** Employees need to feel that they are learning and growing throughout this transformation. Considering this, companies do well to stimulate and cultivate a mindset where employees see mistakes as learning opportunities rather than failures. This can help in alleviating people's fear of adopting technologies and new ways of working.

Concrete action for EcoGoods: The change coalition decides to introduce regular feedback sessions where colleagues can openly discuss challenges they face with new systems. Furthermore, the company decides to install regular training opportunities for employees to get acquainted with new technologies in practical, hands-on sessions.

SHAPE THE PATH – THE TRANSFORMATION PROCESS AT ECOGOODS

— **Tweak the environment.** Friction ought to be removed wherever possible. The fundamental attribution error is considered a tendency of people to attribute people's behaviours to how they are, rather than the situation they are in. For instance, if people at EcoGoods struggle with a new tool, it might not necessarily have to do with them resisting the tool, but it might have to do with a user-unfriendly interface or a lack of support.

Concrete action for EcoGoods: The company can set up a "digital help desk" where employees can quickly get answers or assistance with the new systems. This reduces frustration and smooths the adoption process.

— **Build habits.** Creating an environment that nurtures the development of positive, change-oriented habits is essential for sustaining transformation journeys where new ways of working become natural extensions of existing practices. Can you see, for example, how certain new habits might link to existing ones?

Concrete action for EcoGoods: Maria can implement checklists or team meetings that focus, for example, on using the new CRM system or other tools. This would help in reinforcing the necessary behaviours. The company could install certain reminders to unburden employees and help them more easily remember new practices.

— **Rally the herd.** Pay close attention to social signals and cues. The reason is simple: a herd feeling is strong. It can either guarantee or derail a change effort.

Concrete action for EcoGoods: The change coalition helps in identifying respected opinion leaders or early technology adopters at EcoGoods. These people can, for example, publicly endorse certain changes, promote a specific tool, and answer any pending questions. This helps people to feel more confident in adopting technology and adapting to change.

WATCH OUT: SELECTION REGIMES

When you eagerly eye digital transformation, your company is likely to weigh multiple investments, interventions, technologies, and more. The final decision often depends on the processes in place to select them. These are internal selection regimes. However, don't just rely upon senior management and the C-suite in the selection of transformational efforts or activities. Involve front-line staff and managers. This is crucial to create support for change and adoption of the new practice. It is also a great way to expand the coalition of Vested leaders. Including the voice of the customers is also integral to the success of a new initiative. Don't be blind to the turbulence outside either; it is best to involve your Vigilant leaders, too, for inspiration and challenge. Find out about the benefits of participative internal selection regimes firsthand!

CASE CONTINUATION

The competitive landscape is unforgiving. While EcoGoods is struggling, its primary competitor has already moved into the next phase of its digital efforts. EcoGoods cannot afford to slow down, but it must balance speed with the wellbeing and capacity of its employees – currently, employees experience change fatigue because of these continuous transformations. Their surge capacity is at an all-time low.

Maria wonders: is the company currently able to absorb change and innovation? Do people **understand** what this digital transformation is about? And **how quickly** can we introduce different change processes? To get more transparency on this, Maria decides to recruit different opinion leaders and influencers. She asks these key players to venture into their respective teams and departments to gather feedback and play a coaching role.

Addressing the burning platform at EcoGoods: Part One

First, she finds out that **time for reflection and iteration** is needed to help people better absorb new technologies. The relentless speed has harmed people's perceptions of leadership competency and their trust has severely dwindled. A colleague introduced Maria to the bank account principle: employees only have so many resources (energy, attention, interest) to handle multiple changes. With each change, they make withdrawals from this account, and without time to recharge they risk emotional and mental bankruptcy. A **recovery period** in between waves of transformation is much needed, not only to allow time for training and reflection, but also to savour the successes of the wave.

Second, the complexity of the journey and the intensity of the four waves had created confusion. To address people's low absorptive capacity further, Maria draws inspiration from the Rider and Elephant metaphor. In this setting, the rider represents Maria and the change coalition that Maria has gathered. The elephant is representative of employees and their capacities for innovation and absorption. The path represents the processes and the transformation journey. To start, Maria is expected to provide a clear direction to people:

— **Find the bright spots:** Maria analyses the areas where transformation has already worked well. For example, the automated inventory management system was successfully implemented and adopted – She wondered what conditions had enabled this success and can we replicate them?

— **Script the critical moves:** Maria comes with clear instructions that are broken down into simple, actionable steps. She understands that ambiguity will only increase anxiety and lower motivation. Together with her change coalition, she outlines concrete behaviours such as weekly targets.

— **Point to the destination:** Maria recruits Tarik, a Visionary leader, to communicate about the long-term benefits of the transformation for clients, employees, and the company. She furthermore suggests that employees can think along about what the final destination can be like. This feedback is used by Tarik.

Addressing the burning platform at EcoGoods: Part Two

Furthermore, the change coalition gathered to reflect on how they can "motivate the elephant". Together with Maria, they discussed how to "shrink the change" and "grow people". First, employees at EcoGoods were overwhelmed. As such, the coalition decided to break the transformation into more **manageable chunks** to make the journey feel achievable. Small victories are to be celebrated to add optimism and momentum. Secondly, Maria emphasised that setbacks are normal and might even be beneficial. That's also why they initially had decided to launch the innovation hub in the Third Wave. Additional **training programmes** are installed.

Finally, the path must be reshaped to make the journey feel smoother. To "tweak the environment", Maria and her team decided to remove unnecessary barriers such as unclear communication; to "build habits", they decided that employees can set aside weekly time to engage with a new technological system. Furthermore, Maria understood that her change coalition would play a crucial role as champions that "rally the herd" and visibly support and explain the changes.

By enlisting the insights from the Rider and Elephant metaphor, Maria and the change coalition could successfully tackle certain operational shortcomings and re-energise employees. However, Maria kept reminding herself that the pace of the change would have to be manageable if they wanted to keep moving forward in the Third and Fourth Wave.

Reflecting on EcoGoods' case, which actions would you additionally take to **strengthen colleagues' (and the company's) surge capacity** to better the organisation's chances for a successful digital transformation? How can technology help?

BREAKING DOWN SILOS

SILO-BUSTING: MOVING FROM FRAGMENTATION TO AUGMENTATION

InnovTech is market leader in B2B technology solutions, specialising in providing innovative software platforms to large enterprises. Founded 37 years ago, InnovTech has built a reputation on cutting-edge solutions and superior customer service. Its global footprint spans multiple markets, and the company has thrived on its ability to innovate in response to rapid technology advancements. The industry is now surfing on a new wave of technologies such as blockchain, 5G networks, generative AI, and cloud computing. While customers move quickly to integrate digital-first business models, InnovTech also embarked on its own digital transformation journey. The company has successfully completed the first phases – automating certain internal processes. Now, it faces the next and most crucial phase: aligning departments to leverage these technologies for consumer-centric growth.

Adil, the head of the direct sales department and a proven go-getter, was selected to draft a **company-wide strategy** for this next stage. His reputation as someone with an assertive personality seemed to make him the ideal candidate. Determined to drive change, Adil assured colleagues that their interests would be heard, feedback incorporated, and he would stand by them through any turbulence.

The problem at InnovTech

Today, however, Adil finds himself **at odds** with other departments. They call him a 'loner', a leader to a department that approaches this digital transformation solo. In response, departments like Marketing, Customer Success, and Product Development each began to approach digital transformation as isolated projects rather than part of a unified vision. Every department has its own set of KPIs and ideas on how to adapt to digital disruption. **Misalign-**

ment has led to redundancy, conflicting priorities, and resource waste, as no one wants to share any information or insights. Direct Sales is moving ahead with its own CRM overhaul, Marketing is developing a **separate** engagement platform, and Customer Success is rolling out a chatbot system that conflicts with Sales' initiatives. Product Development pushes new AI features that haven't been communicated to Sales or Marketing. Instead of synergy, InnovTech finds itself with a **multitude of visions** that don't align, leading to confusion, inefficiency, and mounting frustrations.

This **fragmented** approach has begun to bleed into the customer experience. For the first time since InnovTech's founding, its quarterly customer satisfaction numbers have dropped. While always more or less stagnant, it has now dropped with a whopping 28%, a steep decline that people had not anticipated, but even more so a significant red flag in an industry where customer loyalty is considered the key differentiator. The written customer feedback revealed the core of the issue – departments were **failing to deliver a seamless customer experience.** Marketing's digital campaigns were promising features that the Sales team wasn't even aware of and that the Product Development team could not deliver on time. A new AI-driven product was rolled out without the support and training required to make people feel confident in using them. Customer Success was overwhelmed by technical issues they hadn't been briefed on and were unable to handle support queries effectively. InnovTech struggles with internal chaos where **no one is speaking the same language** and makes their own plans. A culture of **egocentrism** festers.

Humans evolved as a social species that relied on community for survival, where being part of "the pack" was essential. Feeling cut off from that very pack often feels terrifying. According to Simon Sinek, humans are wired to thrive on the support of their communities, much like our ancestors did in small, tightly knit tribes. Today, in our hypermodern world, this fundamental need for connection persists, yet the digital age has introduced new complexities that challenge these social connections and reshape how we experience the opposite of belonging: loneliness and isolation.

— **Loneliness** is the emotional response to feeling disconnected from others. In the context of technology, loneliness can be amplified despite constant digital communication. Hyperconnectivity – through social media, for example – creates the illusion of connection while deepening feelings of loneliness. In the office, employees can feel overwhelmed by digital interactions yet deprived of genuine human contact. For example, instead of having meaningful face-to-face interactions, we might spend hours on virtual calls or collaborate via on-line project management tools. Loneliness might be especially ardent during times of rapid change, where employees risk feeling left behind or are unable to relate to new technologies and processes.[217]

— **Isolation**, on the other hand, refers to a more structural issue – lacking access to the resources, information, and opportunities necessary to feel integrated in the organisation. In the era of constant digital transformation, employees may feel isolated if they don't have the skills or don't have access to technology and/or information to succeed. For instance, employees that lack training on new digital tools or that are excluded from discussions because they work remote-ly are more likely to feel structurally cut off. Isolation in this sense is not just about a physical divide, but also about a deeper disconnect from the knowledge that is critical for success.[218]

DID YOU KNOW?

Loneliness is an emotionally painfully sensation that registers as physical pain in the brain. A neuroimaging study looked at the neural correlates of social exclusion and tested the hypothesis that the brain's response to social pain and physical pain are similar.[219]

Loneliness is an emotional state, whereas isolation is a technical, structural state. In the modern digital workplace, loneliness and isolation often reinforce one an-other. The more structurally isolated employees feel – lacking access to informa-tion and resources – the more likely they are to experience emotional loneliness, believing they are cut off from the "pack". Similarly, loneliness can result in iso-lation, as disengaged employees withdraw from collaborative efforts or avoid en-gagement altogether. When positive social relationships are present at work, lower rates of burnout and higher levels of job satisfaction can be seen.

Overall, buildings are restructured to reflect contemporary trends: the action office became the cubicle, which, in turn, was demolished for open floor plans. Surprising-ly, open floor plans rarely lead to collaboration because most colleagues take actions to muffle the increase in noise and distractions. Anette Timmer writes, "With noise a top concern [...] many counteract this by wearing headphones for example. And while this may seem to be supporting productivity, it's also cited as a contributing factor in the workplace loneliness issue."[220] Open floor plans even result in a 70% decrease in employee interaction and an increase in electronic communication between those very colleagues who share the same open office.[221] Employees withdraw socially as a response. Some companies introduced rotating desk assignments, clean desk policies, and comfortable seating areas to resolve this.

The dynamic between loneliness and isolation becomes even more pronounced in a digital transformation journey. People struggle to adapt and feel both isolated from certain tools and feel lonely as their work environment shifts around them. Entire departments can even harbour feelings of isolation, developing their own silos that create additional barriers to collaboration.

ABOUT LONELINESS

Neuroscientist Kay Tye says that some people can spend their entire day alone and feel incredibly energised, whereas others slowly stew in feelings of alienation despite being surrounded by large crowds, friends and family, or colleagues.[222]

Loneliness tricks the brain into believing that you are the only one out there who experiences this. But is this truly the case? Let's visualise it: take four identically sized glasses. Fill three glasses with white rice and the fourth one with wild rice. Take two white sheets of paper. Place one in front of you and pour the three glasses with white rice onto it. Pour the wild rice on top of the white rice and mix it. What do you see? The wild rice is very visible and abundant. On the second sheet of paper, draw three identical circles. Label the first one "family", the second "friends", and the third one "colleagues". Take a pinch of rice from the first sheet and drop the rice in the first circle. Do the same for the second and third circle. The white rice represents people around you who do not feel lonely; the wild rice represents those who do feel lonely. What do you notice?

Even if you don't feel lonely yourself, chances are you brush shoulders with someone who does, even in those groups closest to you. 33 percent of people feel lonely "often", "sometimes", or "all of the time"[223], with almost 4 in 10 people mentioning how feelings of loneliness have led them to experience a low mood.[224] Even more striking is that 25% of adults feel ashamed about being lonely, with 35% saying that they would never admit to being lonely.[225] It is especially crucial that digital transformations are not lonely activities. These efforts require widespread collaboration, engagement, and alignment across the organisation. Vested leaders such as Adil at InnovTech should remain mindful of this and can pursue several activities that foster deeper connections.

— **Give your undivided attention.** Our mind often dares to wander during a conversation and we try to multitask by checking our phone, email, and other devices. Nothing worse than trying to have a meeting with a colleague or your boss when they are constantly checking the messages that pop up on their new fancy smartwatch, right? Instead, Vested leaders tune their awareness toward the other person so people will feel heard and, as a result, remain willing to hear you.

— **Dare to be vulnerable.** Vested leaders learn from the Voyager leader, who is an active practitioner of vulnerability and authenticity. At InnovTech, Adil can model openness by sharing about some of his own challenges, signalling that it is okay to discuss how you feel.

— **Foster genuine human connection.** Together with the change coalition, Vested leaders can strive to create mentorship and peer programmes that help colleagues build long-term meaningful relationships within and across departments. Furthermore, the change coalition ought to encourage opportunities for in-person meetings to rebuild the trust and connection that is often lost in email chains or chat messages.

— **Recognise the signs of loneliness.** We might not always see the physical, mental, or social struggles that employees are going through. Vested leaders, as such, are attentive for signs of disengagement, withdrawal, or decreased morale. They try to meet over genuine conversations and do so with compassion.

— **Cultivate inclusivity.** It's important for Vested leaders to understand that employees sometimes want to feel included in decision-making processes, rather than always being told what to do and where to go. Additionally, this also allows the organisation to benefit from people's diverse perspectives and insights.

EXERCISE: THE PULSE-CHECK AND THE LONELINESS SCALE

Have an honest **pulse-check** with colleagues to determine how connected they feel. During a digital transformation journey in particular, people can feel lonely. They sometimes believe that they do not have the skills to cope with digital innovation, they are afraid their job will be completely different, ... As a Vested leader, it is important to connect with these colleagues and let them know that they are not alone in this journey. Always try to ask open-ended questions. If you believe that someone is lonely, there are several ways to reconnect with them.

— Make statements that leave very little room for somebody to divert the conversation. People often ask, "How are you?", and it seems like everyone is "fine". But are they really? Instead, add, "Something's different" or "You're not the person I know", and do so with empathy.

— Each Monday, have people share their three "small moments of happiness" of the previous week (e.g. did you find €20 alongside the road or did you see a triple rainbow?)

— Don't send another email, but (video) call colleagues or visit them in their office.

Do you have any additional ideas, examples, or experiences? Which actions will you try? Which questions are you going to ask? What matters most here is the *act of service* – you help others, also by listening

— We invite you to complete the **loneliness scale** and to make good use of these items in your conversations with colleagues.

At the end, count the total (disagree = 1; slightly disagree = 2; neutral = 3; slightly agree = 4; agree = 5). The closer you are to 10, the less loneliness you experience; the closer you are to 50, the more loneliness you experience.

Statement	Disagree	Slightly disagree	Neutral	Slightly agree	Agree
1. I lack companionship					
2. There is no one i can turn to					
3. My interests and ideas are not shared by those around me					
4. There are no people I feel close to					
5. I feel left out					
6. My social relationships are superficial					
7. No one really knows me well					
8. I am unhappy being so withdrawn					
9. People are around me but not with me					
10. There are no people I can talk to					
Total score =					

ABOUT ISOLATION

Vested leaders understand how interactions and interdependencies are crucial. Where collisions occur, improvement and innovation follow. This can be among employees, customers, and partners. Consider what entrepreneur Frans Johansson dubbed *The Medici Effect*, named after the Medicis, the 15th century banking family in Florence, Italy.[226] The Medicis funded creators from a wide variety of disciplines (sculptors, poets, financiers, architects, and so on) and brought them together in the City of Florence. This intersectionality gave rise to breathtaking ideas and art, and heralded the beginning of the Renaissance, when knowledge and creativity flourished after what some called the Dark Ages. Furthermore, where genuine connection finds fertile ground, higher levels of job satisfaction and happiness follow. When employees think in terms of "us" and "them", Vested leaders are tasked with breaking down barriers, and they actively look for technology to help them do that appropriately. The Dalai Lama wrote the following,

> "I consider our tendency to see each other in terms of 'us' and 'them' as stemming from ignorance of our interdependence. As participants in the same global economy, we depend on each other, while changes in the climate and the global environment affect us all. What's more, as human beings, we are physically, mentally, and emotionally the same.
>
> Look at bees. They have no constitution, police, or moral training, but they work together in order to survive. Though they may occasionally squabble, the colony survives on the basis of cooperation. Human beings, on the other hand, have constitutions, complex legal systems, and police forces; we have remarkable intelligence and a great capacity for love and affection. Yet, despite our many extraordinary qualities, we seem less able to cooperate.
>
> In organisations, people work closely together every day. But despite working together, many feel lonely and stressed. Even though we are social animals, there is a lack of responsibility toward each other. We need to ask ourselves what's going wrong."[227]

Structural isolation happens when various parties lack access to something, which leaves them cut off from any relevant activities within the company. It could be, for example, that one department is not included in discussions about a new technological implementation or upgrade; it could be that digital fragmentation reigns within your organisation with different departments implementing different systems and platforms that are not (fully) integrated. As a consequence of these digital silos, employees struggle to share crucial information across these disconnected systems.

THE RISE OF THE SILO MENTALITY

Separation exists within most businesses. While this separation can occur in a visible manner – for example, entire departments are physically separated on different floors or buildings, or remote work amplification now only connects people through a virtual reality –, separation also exists in a more hidden way. Different roadmaps might appear, purposes become unaligned, IT systems are incompatible, and so on. In companies, the visible separation between teams and departments is referred to as *silos;* the invisible separation can be referred to as *silo mentality*.

The term "silo" originates from the grain silos that separate one type of grain from another and is frequently used as a metaphor for isolation within an organisation. Power, control, competition, hierarchy, and bureaucracy all contribute to the formation of silos. In this so-called "fiefdom of territories", silos can operate with efficiency and precision to deliver their agenda, but they often do so in isolation or without regard for others. Silos can form within, between, or beyond teams and departments. Silos are primarily made up of people who think and act similarly, who share a similar mentality.

Humans like silos because they provide comfort, reassurance, and a sense of certainty. They create structure and delineate authority and responsibility. Silos can be a practical way for businesses to operate more efficiently because they allow for focus, identity, and accountability, as well as pushing for faster decision making and the implementation of initiatives. Furthermore, silos offer psychological safety. Colleagues may feel more affinity within their tight-knit team or department. Collective norms and behaviours develop, resulting in a subculture that provides employees with a sense of security, safety, and predictability.

Despite the benefits that individual departments or teams might gain from focusing on their specialised goals, silos also nurture a *silo mentality*. At InnovTech, this started with groupthink and deteriorated further into genuine turf wars and cutthroat culture. In these silos, people are reluctant to share their skills, knowledge, or information with other silos, resulting in the creation of companies with companies – a fiefdom of territories where teams act independently and operate as their own mini empires. As history shows, the Western Roman Empire fell not only because of external threats but also because of a lack of internal alignment.[228] People were actively carving away at each other's positions and roles, leaving behind an empty vessel of an empire.

A lasting *silo mentality* brings certain dangers with it:
— **The parts eat the whole.** When teams operate in silos, they become focused solely on their own goals and objectives, ignoring the broader company strategy. For example, the marketing team at InnovTech may launch a campaign targeting a specific customer segment without coordinating this beforehand with the sales team, creating internal confusion and inefficiency.

— **The office is politics.** Siloed teams are traditionally followed by conflict and turf wars, each protecting their own interests. As each pursues their own agenda, teams now compete for resources, recognition, and influence. For example, the IT department at InnovTech withheld support for a project led by the marketing team, prioritising their own initiative. In such an "us vs. them" culture, trust between teams deteriorates and collaboration becomes a rare thing.

— **Customer focus is missing.** Teams are likely to lose sight of the bigger picture, including the customer experience. Without any clear coordination between departments, multiple teams may unknowingly target the same customer with different offers, causing confusion and frustration for the customer. For example, InnovTech's sales team strategically reached out to a potential client with one product pitch, while marketing bombards the same client with a different campaign, and customer service is unaware of either. The company's reputation is harmed as well.

— **Information isn't shared.** A siloed organisation struggles with poor communication and missing cooperation. Employees hoard valuable data, knowledge, or expertise, refusing or forgetting to share it with others. For example, the product development team at InnovTech had crucial information about a product's flaws, but this information wasn't reaching the customer support team that is now drowning in complaints without understanding the root cause. Not only does inefficiency skyrocket, innovation also suffers as fresh ideas are locked away behind individual teams' walls.

— **Motivation declines.** Employees in siloed organisations typically experience lower levels of motivation due to mixed messages and misaligned priorities. For example, one team at InnovTech was pursuing projects that were soon deprioritised and abandoned because other teams weren't even aware of them. Over time, silos become major sources of frustration, making it especially difficult for employees to form meaningful connections with colleagues.

REFLECTION

Do you ever feel as if you are working in a silo, or as if you are disconnected from others? How would you approach this? Does this apply more or less for digital transformation? Why?

While these days many transformative opportunities are found in the many interfaces between employees, teams, and companies, 83% of companies state that they have silos, and 97% say that silos negatively impact the company's performance.[229]

Furthermore, 61% of global operations managers consider cross-functional collaboration critical to helping the company achieve its strategic goals.[230] Michael Dell, CEO of Dell, says the following,

> "I think it is going to be very difficult to be a company in silos. I think the game has changed. We won't define our success by looking at the competitors, but at how satisfied are our customers, how engaged are our internal stakeholders, and how good is our product pipeline."

If you're wondering if you are caught in the invisible web of silos, consider the following questions:

THE ACT OF SILO BUSTING

When a *silo mentality* festers, or you notice you are on the verge of *siloing* the company, it is time to act before it reduces your company's agility and efficiency. The creation of coffee corners and the like will accomplish little, especially if there are no underlying structural mechanisms to help colleagues engage. Ideas can emerge during conversations at the coffee machine, but how will you ensure that these ideas are followed up on? How do you ensure that employees reach outside their silos to find colleagues with, for example, complementary expertise?

Vested leaders ask, "How many unbridgeable differences can we really have within our company, especially if we are de facto guided by the same corporate purpose?" When silos sprout like mushrooms on a drizzly autumn morning, it's time to go silo busting!

— **The common goal.** It's perfectly fine to have different objectives, as long as employees stay on task and have a strong overarching corporate purpose to relate to. Employees might lose sight of the corporate purpose. So, rather than creating goals for individual teams, Vested leaders collaborate with the Visionary leader and dare to work from shared goals that bring colleagues and teams together. This reminds employees that individual and team goals are secondary to the organisation. In *Systems Thinking Basics*, Virginia Anderson and Lauren Johnson write that recognising the interconnections between parts of the company and synthesising these into a unified view helps encourage collaboration.

Adil, as head of direct sales, gathers all department heads in a strategy workshop. Rather than each having their own goals, Adil first wants to make sure that people align on a common shared goal: enhancing customer satisfaction through a seamless integration of sales and marketing efforts, and by delivering product features that meet the needs of customers. Here, Adil reaches out to Hamza, a Visionary leader, to help with creating shared accountability.

— **Shared accountability.** Ignite ideas for collaboration and share successful examples – who has been collaborating with whom, both internally and externally? What went well?

Adil notices that InnovTech's departments still remain hyperfocused on their own metrics – Marketing tracks campaign success, Sales measures revenue, and Product Development looks at feature rollouts. Together with Hamza, they work on developing accountability metrics that tie each department's success to customer satisfaction.

— **Encourage questions and ask for input.** Working across boundaries is impossible without asking questions. Colleagues' feedback provides you with insights into how the company is performing in terms of silo-busting. Experiences on either side of the divide are not necessarily identical. Inquiry clarifies.

Adil senses a growing disconnect and discontent between the Product Development and Customer Success teams at InnovTech. While the first is rolling out new AI features, the latter struggles to support them due to a lack of technical understanding. Adil first listened to both teams individually before deciding to arrange a cross-department feedback session. The conversation uncovers certain gaps in training and documentation, and clearly highlighted that both teams hadn't really talked to each other in over a year.

— **Incentivise and connect.** Motivation is highly subjective, and Vested leaders try to identify people's individual drivers. They consider incentive systems that reward cross-unit collaboration; perhaps provide employees with trainings to improve their collaborative and networking skills; and support the celebration of cross-functional accomplishments. This creates belonging and attachment. To stimulate this further, it is worth considering joint task forces, joint meetings, focus groups, and cross-silo dialogues to help people meet others. Create a sounding board where everyone can share knowledge – what projects are they working on? What is their expertise? Their interests? What can they learn from each other?

As various teams remained reluctant to collaborate across departments, Adil and his change coalition connected with HR to introduce an incentive programme that rewards employees who contribute to cross-function projects. Recently, various joint task forces started addressing key issues – such as aligning product features with customer feedback –, and cross-silo dialogues are increasingly held. In doing so, the change coalition motivates employees to also look beyond their own direct borders.

— **Showcase behaviour.** Breaking down silos is not just a directive, but a behavioural shift. Vested leaders act as role models who demonstrate that cross-functional teamwork bears fruits. They can discuss shared goals with other teams, assign people on their teams to keep others in the loop, and spend time with others.

Adil leads by example at InnovTech. While he heads the Direct Sales team, he regularly attends Product Development meetings to share insights from customers. As he starts to actively mingle and participate in collaborative initiatives, Adil sets a clear example for others, encouraging them to follow suit.

— **Collaboration tools.** Technology can help you in facilitating the flow of ideas and information – consider integrated project and program management platforms with chat and virtual whiteboard capabilities embedded or data management software that integrates data from various sources. You might also use these whiteboards to prepare certain meetings and have colleagues answer certain questions beforehand.

InnovTech struggles with teams using different tools, leading to fragmented communication and a sense of technology overload. To fix this, Adil suggests introducing a centralised platform where everyone can collaborate on and share their updates in real-time.

— **Shift mindsets.** Inform colleagues about the dangers of silos – for example, how they not only stifle innovation but also prevent colleagues from benefiting from collaboration. People from different teams rarely see things in a similar way, which could lead to misunderstandings. With the right mindset, however, seeing things differently isn't necessarily perceived as a negative thing but rather as an opportunity for better solutions, this is where the help of Vigilant leaders comes comes in handy for the Vested leader, to open people's minds to alternative ways of seeing clearly.. A Vested leader is also aware that silos can exist *between* companies. They extend silo-busting beyond their company by, for example, making it easier for partners and customers to connect, collaborate, and co-create. To this end, they connect to the Voyager leader, and engage in co-creation activities.

At InnovTech, a mindset prevails that collaboration is risky and only invites more frustration to the equation. To solve this, Adil initiates a company-wide campaign to highlight the dangers of silo mentalities and how cross-functional collaboration impacts the company goals of strengthening the customer experience. Cross-departmental trainings expose colleagues to the perspectives and experiences of others, allowing them to see shared friction points.

The front-line paradox

Each of these practices is useful in its own way, and together they are mutually enhancing. The Vested leader creates conditions that make boundary-crossing easier and helps collaboration become second nature. Consider what Marketing Professor Carsten Lund Pedersen calls the *front-line paradox*: front-line employees are often the first within companies to sense impending change but the last to be heard within an organisation. As a result, companies often do not tap into a rich source of data. Pedersen explains this via the example of a call centre with 500 employees.[231]

Each employee gets an average of 160 incoming calls per week and over 600 calls per month. An average call lasts 380 seconds or over 6 minutes. When you do some quick math, this equals 320,000 customer calls per month and nearly 34.000 hours of customer conversation. Companies with a *silo mindset* miss out on that rich knowledge repository. The remedy is to use this *collective wisdom* instead. Leaders who turn to front-line workers for input gain a competitive edge over others who rely on historical data that might not necessarily reflect reality. For example, clothing company Zara relies upon front-line employees' input to decide which clothes to produce.

STORY CONTINUATION

The dramatic drop in customer satisfaction was as a wake-up call for Adil, revealing that the silos within InnovTech were not just an internal inconvenience but were putting the company at risk. Adil understands that InnovTech's **fragmented approach** had left them trailing behind competitors. He was also confronted with the fact that others have come to see the Direct Sales department as an impenetrable fortress. Especially eye-opening was the feedback from his own team – "What's the point, Adil? We're digitally transforming our sales department, but the other teams are ignoring our efforts. People don't even to talk to us during lunch breaks anymore." Adil knew he had to act quickly. The company's leadership expected him to address three key areas:

first, to **lead by example**; second, to tackle the emotional factors contributing to **isolation and misalignment**; and third, to implement structural solutions to **bridge the gaps** between departments.

Addressing the burning platform at InnovTech

As a Vested leader, Adil recognised it was his responsibility to actively engage in cross-functional activities and collaborate with other department heads. This **shift in his behaviour** would address one of the root causes of frustration within InnovTech. By demonstrating his commitment to breaking down barriers and working across teams, he set a powerful example for others to follow.

To further reduce the sense of isolation, Adil facilitated a **reconciliatory meeting**, encouraging open dialogue where colleagues could voice their struggles, doubts, and fears. He posed the same question to the group that had been asked of him, "What's the point?". Heads nodded in agreement, and Adil articulated what everyone was feeling, "We can't succeed alone". On top of that, Adil enlisted the help of Jessica – a strong Visionary leader – to **craft a shared vision** that all employees can rally behind, one that emphasises how working together would bring most value.

To **tackle the structural issues**, Adil and the department organised a brainstorming workshop. Together, they decided on several key initiatives to address isolation and misalignment:

— **Incentivise and align** cross-functional collaboration: HR was tasked with creating attractive incentives for employees to participate in cross-departmental initiatives.

— Create **shared accountability:** clear goals were established that require collaboration. One manager suggested tying product success metrics not only to customer satisfaction scores from the Product team but also from Marketing and Sales.

— **Promote open knowledge sharing:** collaborative tools like shared project management platforms and virtual whiteboards were put in place to improve real-time information and communication flows, making key data more accessible and transparent.

— **Develop cross-silo task forces:** these groups would tackle shared problems, and cross-functional innovation challenges were launched to solve company-wide problems and illustrate the benefits of diverse perspectives.

By attacking structural barriers through collaborative initiatives, addressing emotional needs and building trust, and showcasing exemplary leadership behaviour, Adil dismantled InnovTech's silos brick by brick.

Reflecting on InnovTech's case, how would you actively **bust the silos** within the organisation to increase the company's chances for a successful digital transformation journey? Part of the answer may lie with the configuration and deployment of certain technologies. Think about that too.

GIVING AND RECEIVING FEEDBACK

GREEN INNOVATIONS: MODERNISING IT INFRASTRUCTURE THROUGH FEEDBACK

Introduction

The CEO, Susan, recently attended an industry-wide seminar where she was introduced to several emerging technologies that could vastly improve the business – Green Future Labs, an SME focusing on developing sustainable solutions for various industries. Inspired, she returned with a clear goal: modernise the company's internal IT architecture. Arthur, a colleague with extensive experience in digital consultancy, was eager to spearhead the project. With Susan's support, Arthur was given the green light to assemble a new digital development team and lead this digital transformation journey.

Arthur, determined to make an impact, soon proposed Extreme Programming (XP) as the default methodology. He arranged a three-day deep dive to ensure that people were up to speed with XP from the beginning.

However, the IT department soon raised **concerns**. While they were open to new approaches, they **warned** that their current infrastructure wasn't yet equipped to handle a highly agile project. They expressed a willingness to evolve but clearly stressed the need for a more gradual transition, proposing a slower pace of implementation to avoid major disruptions to the company's legacy systems and day-to-day operations. "A few hiccups are always expected," the IT manager explained, "but we can't afford to jeopardise both the user and employee experience."

Despite these warnings, Arthur **remained focused** on speed and agility. He dismissed the IT team's feedback and concerns, and insisted on pushing forward. "You shouldn't shy away from a challenge," Arthur remarked confidently, pushing for an aggressive overhaul of the IT department. In his view, resistance was simply part of the transformation process, and the quicker they moved, the better.

The problem at Green Future Labs

As the weeks passed, the dissatisfaction across the company skyrocketed and voices grew **louder**. Colleagues complained about sluggish performance in the programs and systems they depended on. Many felt blindsided by the sudden and drastic changes, **struggling to understand** why such a sweeping overhaul was even necessary. The IT department felt increasingly alienated. While they had valuable feedback about the risks to the legacy systems and user disruptions, Arthur kept disregarding their concerns. Gradually, a cascade of problems started to appear. Not only did team members feel ignored and undervalued, resulting in tension and disengagement, but customers also started to complain about their diminished experiences. After all, the company's legacy systems, which still supported key functions and applications, were increasingly strained as delays and malfunctions spread at a rapid pace.

Susan, meanwhile, noticed the toll the project was taking on Green Future Labs and its operational efficiency. Productivity suffered, and clear tensions could be felt. The **disconnect** between Arthur's **vision** and **reality** had left the company in a state of dysfunction, with both employees and systems struggling to keep up.

THE GIFT OF FEEDBACK

Research on effective learning found that people need three things to improve their performance: a clear goal; a genuine desire to achieve that goal; and *feedback*. Seventy-five percent of people believe that feedback is valuable and 45% value feedback from sources other than their boss – peers and colleagues, clients and customers. Unfortunately, only 30% receive the feedback they desire.[232] The authors of *You Can Change Other People,* Peter Bregman and Howie Jacobson, formulate feedback as follows:

> "The objective of feedback is to help people improve performance. We want people to up their game. To live up to their potential. To contribute powerfully to their teams. To interact effectively with colleagues.

We want our organisations to become places where people can skilfully and candidly communicate with one another in the service of their growth and improved performance. Those are all worthy goals."[233]

Feedback is a vehicle to help people grow, improve, and change – hence it's often called *the gift of feedback* – sometimes in the shape of positive feedback or constructive feedback. In this chapter, we mostly focus on the latter. The advantages of feedback are manifold.

— A study of 530 work units found that team managers who received feedback showed 12.5% greater productivity after the feedback![234]
— Sixty-nine percent of employees say they would work harder if they felt their efforts were better recognised. In traditional workplace mindsets, the pay cheque is considered sufficient recognition, while it has been shown this does not entice most employees.[235]
— Feedback in short and helpful bursts helps employees to improve to a greater extent and more quickly, and 80% of Generation Y colleagues prefer on-the-spot recognition and feedback over delayed feedback during yearly formal review and appraisal talks.[236] Embedding frequent feedback helps you to take away negative feelings surrounding appraisal talks as these are often felt as stressful "do or die" moments.

Communication is often thought of as successfully conveying your message. But communication and feedback are more than this – they are two-way streets in which you provide information to people and search for and gather input from them. Feedback should, therefore, be approached as a process in which information flows equally between all parties. When you are preparing dinner, you sometimes ask family and friends whether more spices are needed.

It is interesting to note that people crave feedback but also dislike it. For instance, people fear questions from their partner about a new outfit. A similar dynamic can be noticed in the workplace.

RECEIVING FEEDBACK

What makes it so hard for people to receive feedback and criticism? When you are criticised, a reaction begins in your amygdalae – you have one on each side of the brain, beyond the eyes and the optical nerves. Bessel van der Kolk, a psychiatrist specialised in post-traumatic stress, calls the amygdalae the brain's "smoke detector" because it detects threats and prepares the body for an emergency response. When you perceive a threat, the amygdalae sound the alarm and release a cascade of chemicals. *Adrenaline* and *cortisol* – two stress hormones – prepare you to react.

Feedback might strike at the friction between two core human needs: our need to learn and grow; and our desire to be accepted just the way we are. People might experience feedback as a threat or personal attack. You might tighten your shoulders and, as in warfare, ready your defences, put up your shield, preparing for what will come over the horizon – you have your counterattack ready. This instant reaction induced by the *amygdala response* is deeply instinctive. In fact, it is so powerful that an *amygdala hijack* happens – you are *triggered* by something. You get sweaty palms, your heart rate increases, and your breathing becomes rapid and shallow. Perhaps your eyes narrow as well.

Hijacking your behaviour

To avoid the full impact of the amygdala response, it can help to consciously reflect on the feedback you receive. Three triggers can hijack your behaviour: truth, relationship, and identity.[237]

DID YOU KNOW?

The second our amygdala is activated, it shuts down the neural pathway to our prefrontal cortex. Because of this, we are disoriented in a heated discussion, our memory becomes less trustworthy, and we end up thinking from one perspective only – "I'm right; you are wrong".

When our memory is compromised by the amygdala, we cannot even recall things from the past that might help us calm down. For example, when you are in a conflict with your best friend, it becomes increasingly difficult to remember anything positive about them (even though they have been your best friend forever).

— **Truth.** Did the content of the feedback hurt, because deep within you knew it was true?

Initially, Arthur's responses are largely triggered by the truth of the feedback he receives. His deep drive to prove his expertise and make a lasting impact led him to dismiss the input from others. The communication that the negative consequences of his rigid approach to Extreme Programming (XP) were hurting the company and employees struck a chord. The truth was that he knew, deep down, that the approach was causing friction, but accepting this truth requires him to face himself and question his own behaviour.

— **Relationship.** Is your frustration related to the messenger rather than to the message?

Arthur's difficult relationship with feedback was also closely tied to his perception of the relationship with the people providing it. When he was mandated to steer the transformation, he saw himself as the expert and viewed others as less informed about the "right" methodology for a successful digital transformation. This led him to disregard feedback from the IT department, amongst others, perceiving it as resistance rather than genuine concern. The tension in these relationships made it difficult for Arthur to separate the message (that is, valid feedback) from the messenger (that is, what he believed to be employees who were challenging his authority). It wouldn't be until he consciously started to recognise his colleagues as partners that he could hear their concerns for what they truly were.

— **Identity.** Do you currently feel ill at ease?

The identity trigger was particularly powerful for Arthur. He derived a significant part of his self-worth and professional identity from being seen as a digital transformation expert. When faced with feedback that questioned his approach or suggested changes to his chosen methodology, Arthur felt his sense of self was under threat. It would take Arthur some time for introspection to reflect on his identity and find out how he could reposition himself in this journey to the betterment of Green Future Labs.

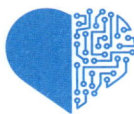

EXERCISE

Which of the three triggers recently made it hard for you to accept feedback? Can you pinpoint emotions that hijacked your responses? How did you handle the feedback? Could you derive any benefits?

These triggers cause you to feel, think, and perhaps act in a way that is not helpful. Even if feedback and critique set off one (or more) of these triggers, you can still derive value from it. Experts Sheila Heen and Douglas Stone formulate various techniques to become a better receiver and not discard valuable feedback.[238]

— **Know** your emotions, your responses, and your tendencies. Do you strike back or argue? Is your reaction fight, flight, or freeze? Why? Feedback will always evoke some emotions.

— **Disentangle** the "what" from the "who" and become less defensive. Do not allow relationships to determine how you interpret feedback. According to Roman law in the Middle Ages, envoys and their entourages enjoyed the right of safe passage during warfare because the envoy was just a bearer of news. Separate the message from the messenger.

— If the feedback is not clear to you, **unpack and reframe it.** Ask extra questions to make sure you understand the feedback. But do not ask for too much at once. This would create cognitive overload.

— There is nothing bad about **not accepting all feedback.** Because feedback is often just opinion, it can be worthwhile to gather multiple opinions – one colleague might call you impulsive while others call you spontaneous. The more you gather, the more rounded and objective feedback becomes.

— **Buy some time.** Sometimes it is hard to take in feedback on the spot. When you feel that you may react badly, say, "I hear your message, but I will need time to reflect on this otherwise I might say things I'd regret." It is natural to struggle with feedback at times.

— **Actively ask for feedback** and show that you are open to receive it. You might be required to give feedback, for example, as part of official evaluation talks. However, feedback is an act of giving and receiving.

— It is easier to take feedback knowing that **it is meant to help you.** People forget that feedback is about helping them learn and grow. Be glad that people take the time to give feedback. Not receiving any feedback is worse.

— **Notice the silver linings.** When people are in the wrong during a discussion, they are tempted to push this out of their minds and put additional effort into saving face. It's important to remember the silver lining: conceding an argument is to your credit and might even make you more credible. You have shown that you can reflect and put your blazing gun back in its holster. Rather than having lost, you learned something and acquired a new insight.

— **Focus on the future.** While it is useful to know what went wrong in the past, it is even more important to know how you can make things better and improve. Allow feedback to help you become better in the future, rather than just using it as a tool to reflect on (and stay in) the past.

— **Listen.** Listen. Listen. The quieter you become, the more you can hear. We sometimes feign listening – by nodding while being lost in our own thoughts – but this works counterproductively. When you "listen" to someone, make sure that you actually hear and register what they are saying. For example, at Green Future Labs, Arthur listens to the feedback of the IT department, without hearing them.

REFLECTION

The barrage of stress hormones like cortisol and adrenaline creates many different sensations. When you receive feedback, you might notice your face flush, your jaws clench firmly, the back of your neck tensing; maybe your throat constricts, or your voice starts quivering, your limbs tremble, and you feel a tightening sensation in your solar plexus.

When did you last experience this? What caused it and how did you react? And more importantly, perhaps, how did it feel, both during and after the experience?

These sensations are rarely pleasant – after all, they are designed to spur us into action. When we experience the amygdala response or hijack, we are the prisoners of a highly efficient, but also prehistoric response.

Invite people to give you feedback. It is easy to persuade someone to tell us about our positive contributions as people want to make others feel good. However, if you ask the same person to tell you about your shortcomings, they are reluctant. It requires immense effort to induce colleagues to share the truth about you, and some of your flaws. To effect this, ensure that they feel that they are in a safe space and clearly show that you are open to receiving their feedback. Consultant and author Scott Edinger writes that "You will need to get out of your way to invite opinions that others think you might not want to hear."[239] Taking this into consideration, it might be worthwhile to hold a weekly feedback round in which you source colleagues' input on pending issues.

GIVING FEEDBACK AND THE NEED FOR FEED-FORWARD

Receiving feedback is just one side of the coin. The other side – giving feedback – can be agonising. Positive feedback might feel easy, however, when you need to give feedback to someone who struggles and should do better, you would rather not give feedback at all – you do not want to hurt the other person. Giving feedback runs counter to our preference for conflict aversion; we try to avoid being in *conflict debt*. Still, Vested leaders would do well to provide such feedback, as it is considered essential for reinforcing desired behaviour and motivating people, strengthening relationships and contributing to a more supportive work environment.

One of the reasons for ineffective feedback is embedded in its name: it is *backward-looking*, which makes it difficult for the recipients to focus on the future.

FEED-FORWARD AND HOW TO GIVE SUPPORTIVE FEEDBACK

Consider feedback and critique as advice-giving that looks towards a preferable future. If the focus shifts to the time when change can be realised, feedback evolves into feedforward. One question is key: "What are we going to do, together, to reach the desired destination?".

DID YOU KNOW?

Research from Lauren Eskreis-Winkler showed that people feel more motivated when they can give advice instead of feedback. Advice comes from personal experience, which makes us more capable of giving useful insights about how to tackle issues and goals we struggle(d) with ourselves.[240]

Furthermore, giving advice helps the person offering it. Most people have never been asked for their insights. After offering advice, they would feel hypocritical if they didn't act on it themselves. This is called the "saying-is-believing effect". The key learning is this: harness the power of advice giving to help others and yourself.

Recipients of feedback may feel ashamed. Some deny the problem (no problem means no shame); some blame it on someone else (not my fault mean no shame). And colleagues who seem to accept your feedback might inwardly be experiencing the fight-flight-or-freeze mode. What can be done?

— Provide **regular** *on-the-spot feedback*. This feedback is likely to be more accurate as you minimise the time between the behaviour and the feedback; colleagues can adapt more quickly, which is beneficial for flexibility and performance; and employees and leaders are more likely to feel comfortable with the feedback process. Start with regular positive feedback and gradually move towards constructive feedback. This allows you to smooth the transition towards a feedback culture where constructive feedback is appreciated. Overall, employees who receive more feedback than average are better performers, have better evaluations, show a higher rate of job satisfaction, and have a stronger relationship with their boss.[241] However, excessively frequent feedback tends to increase the cognitive load of the recipient and decreases their sense of personal control. Cognitive load refers to the amount of mental effort that is being used in people's working memory. Managing cognitive load effectively prevents information overload and enables more efficient processing of new information.

— Understand that *giving feedback is less about the other person and more* **about you.** There is a constant battle between objectivity and subjectivity. Aim to be objective when you talk about someone else. Subjectivity in feedback-giving is permissible only when you talk about how something impacted you, how it made you feel. Liane Davey, author of *The Good Fight*, writes: "I can have all the adjectives in the world about my own experience because I own that, and that is my truth. But it is a big misconception that we should be using adjectives when we are describing the other person. None of those subjective statements about the other person are legit."[242] When you provide feedback, describe people's behaviour as neutrally as possible – through nouns and verbs, without adjectives. When you strive to anchor your feedback in a **situation**, rather than in a personal statement, you address the behaviour and its **impact** on you.

— Use the power of the 'I-message', which:

Reduces defensiveness: I-messages focus on the speaker's feelings and thoughts, rather than on criticising or blaming the listener. Framing the message from the perspective of "I feel..." or "I think..." reduces the likelihood that the listener will feel attacked, and encourages open and productive dialogue.

> "You always submit your reports late," becomes "I feel concerned when the reports are submitted late because of its impact on our workflow."

Promotes ownership: I-messages allow you to take ownership over your opinions and emotions and help the listener to better understand the impact of their actions.

> "You don't seem to care about this project," becomes "I feel frustrated because I think we have different levels of commitment to this project, and I'm not sure how to align our efforts."

Focuses on the issue rather than the person: I-messages keep the focus on the issue rather than on the person's character traits, intentions, or apparent flaws. This helps you to address certain behaviour or a situation that needs to change, instead of attributing negative qualities to the person. Otherwise, it is much more likely that the conversation will be derailed.

> "You are being too aggressive," becomes "I feel intimidated when the discussion gets heated like earlier because it makes it difficult for me to express my opinions."

Facilitates constructive feedback: I-messages make it easier to frame feedback in a constructive manner, which can then be directed towards finding solutions or making improvements.

> "Your presentation was confusing," becomes "I found some parts of the presentation hard to follow. Could we go over it together so I can understand the transitions better?"

Builds empathy and understanding: I-messages can help the listener understand the speaker's perspective and the emotional context of a situation.

> "You don't listen to what I'm saying," becomes "I don't feel heard when our conversations are interrupted, and it makes it tough for me to share my thoughts fully."

The result of good feedback is that the recipient *feels* something. If they do not feel anything, it means your message was not received. If they show some emotion, your message has caused them to reflect. Identify an outcome that leaves them energised.[243] Discover, together, the hidden opportunity. We are often tempted to default to the *sandwich method*, which *packages* the negative message between two buns of positive messages – sweetened with a spoonful of honeyed words. When your feedback is encoded in this manner, your message might not reach the person or they might hear only the negative message. Create conditions in which a colleague can take in, reflect on, and learn from feedback. *Practise with positive feedback*. When you get it wrong, they are less likely to react badly to praise.

FROM SILENCE TO INQUIRY

Providing feedback or speaking up is not considered an easy task, particularly in a professional environment. Research by occupational psychologist Peggy De Prins on the *employee silence* phenomenon found the following,

> "There is trepidation to give or ask for feedback. It's not just about bullying or transgressive behaviour, but also about professional dysfunctioning. You can give a sporadic remark about a small mistake, but how do you communicate that a colleague, or worse, your boss makes a mistake? Silence. Especially when the perception rules that the boss can make or break your career. People often remain silent out of cynicism or disappointment. They signalled that they provided input before, but that nothing was done with it – the so-called deaf ear syndrome. Really frustrating because an early feedback culture extinguishes fast as a result. To turn this around, companies need to invest in a culture of continuous listening".[244]

THE CEO DISEASE
The "CEO disease" is a vacuum in which you are isolated from honest feedback. The higher up you are in the company, the more likely you are to suffer from the disease and the more severe the symptoms. Katleen De Stobbeleir, Professor of Leadership, outlines a few of these symptoms.[245]

— You only hear positive things, rarely seem to receive any feedback, and no one seems to question you.
— You are surrounded by cheerleaders and "yes"-nodders. They are likely to sugarcoat any issues.
— You tend to take negative feedback personally. Feedback seems to affect your ego and you are not used to feedback that does not come from a cheerleader.

The longer you find yourself in such a vacuum, the stronger these symptoms become. After all, they reinforce one another. The consequences should not be underestimated. You disconnect from people and they no longer want to engage with you. You lose touch with reality, which negatively impacts the quality of your decision-making. If you find yourself floating in such a vacuum, it is time to act.

Gathering honest feedback about yourself is one of the most useful techniques. It is easy to step into a routine where you only speak to the same people, but dare to venture out, spend time with new people, and surface fresh ideas. Maintaining your support network is acceptable, but create a challenge network too. This consists of trusted critics who are honest and radically transparent with you.

As a Vested leader, like for all leaders, is it important to set an example. If people notice that you are looking for their input, everyone benefits. Not only are you more likely to find valuable feedback, but colleagues might start to change their own feedback-seeking and -giving behaviour.

STORY CONTINUATION

Arthur could not ignore the rising wave of criticism any longer, especially after Susan called him into her office for an honest discussion. The conversation left its mark, shaking his confidence to the extent that he mentioned his struggles during dinner at home. His partner, Marie-Laure, couldn't resist a sharp remark: "So, you're as deaf in the workplace as you are at home?" Arthur chuckled, but the comment cut deeper than he let on. It lingered, striking a chord – a feeling he couldn't shake.

That night, Arthur's thoughts churned as he reflected on the situation. Over the weekend, he began searching for answers. He remembered how a colleague at his previous job shared how she learned to **slow down, step back, and prioritise listening** to others before making decisions. This memory offered a glimmer of insight into what Arthur needed to do.

Addressing the burning platform at Green Future Labs

When the next week arrived, Arthur was noticeably quieter at work. He took a **monitoring** approach, observing more than he spoke. For the first time, he noticed the physical signs of frustration – slouched shoulders, tense faces, and exasperation – that seemed to permeate Green Future Labs. The disconnect between him and his team was palpable, and it was clear that his previous tactics had contributed to this environment.

Despite entering the first meeting of the week with a clear plan to adjust the project, Arthur found himself hesitating. Marie-Laure's voice echoed in his mind, and for the first time, he recognised how much he had been talking over others instead of listening to them. He resisted the urge to dominate the conversation, and instead leaned into a new approach: he opened the floor for **dialogue**, listening to **understand**, rather than to respond. As the meeting unfolded, he asked open-ended questions, giving his colleagues the **space to voice** their thoughts, and relied on active listening techniques: mirroring what he heard, summarising colleagues' points, and reflecting their concerns back to them. For the first time, his team felt as if their voices were truly being heard and they didn't refrain from giving sharp feedback. When Arthur acknowledged his mistake of wanting to move too fast, his colleagues understood that, rather than reacting defensively and listening passively, he was **actively engaging with their input.** Gradually, the tension in the office lessened. Shoulders lifted, scowls faded, and the team's energy began to shift toward collaboration rather than conflict.

Arthur increasingly saw the value of this **multidirectional** feedback process – not just as a tool for smoother communication, but to genuinely co-create solutions. He committed himself to this approach. A culture of **continuous** feedback informed every meeting and became a cornerstone of the project's success. Rather than pushing for a complete overhaul at once, Arthur understood that changes in smaller, incremental phases would allow for a more natural speed that didn't alienate people.

With each step, the digital transformation journey at Green Future Labs stabilised further, and the company's operational efficiency smoothened. What had once been a doomed transformation now had a fighting chance – because Arthur understood the power of feedback, which now helps to improve the introduction and use of technology.

Reflecting on Green Future Lab's situation, how would you **grow your feedback skills** as a Vested leader and improve the company's chances for a successful digital transformation journey? Is there any way you see digital technology help you give or receive better feedback?

ENERGY SCAN FOR VESTED DIGITAL TRANSFORMATION LEADERSHIP

The Vested leader enables the company to move beyond experiments and visionary tales and turn these into a productive, yet flexible, machinery. They put the organisation on a roadmap to successful digital transformation by creating organisational mechanisms to swiftly mobilise skills and resources from a variety of disciplines. They bring those resources together to plan, develop, improve, and redevelop the organisation. Vested leaders are champions in resolving obstacles and in stimulating collaboration across silos. They help people to trust and accept new technologies. In order to make change happen, learning and sharing best practices are key. They promote an agile culture that builds on employee empowerment.

Do you want to find out which of the Vested leader skills give you and your colleagues energy? Take this short test.

1 = never 2 = rarely 3 = sometimes 4 = very often 5 = always

Questions	Your response (1 – 5)
I like to make change happen	
I enjoy collaboration across silos (teams/departments/...)	
I like to build upon other people's work	
I like to mobilise the right skills and/or resources	
I enjoy resolving obstacles	
I like to solve conflicts between stakeholders (colleagues, customers,...)	
I enjoy helping people adopt technology-abled ways of working	
I like mobilising people to share best practices	

Total score:

CHECKLIST FOR VESTED DIGITAL TRANSFORMATION LEADERSHIP

If you now wonder whether signs of Vested digital transformation leadership can be spotted within your company, you can reflect on the following set of statements:

At [your company name], we **guide the change**, *as we...*

engage relevant internal parties.	
assist others in understanding the change.	
address resistance.	
build commitment.	
understand the individual nature of change.	
respond to concerns.	
respect the grief cycle.	
avoid inertia.	
balance accommodation with progression.	
avoid reverting to the old ways.	

... maintain capacity and avoid fatigue, *as we...*

take responsibility for the impacts of change.	
recognise signs of exhaustion.	
monitor morale.	
pace change.	
provide sufficient support.	
avoid prioritising speed.	
allow for recovery.	
maintain a willingness to change.	
have trustworthy leadership.	
understand people's limits.	

*... **bust silos**, as we...*

strive for genuine internal connection.	
strive for genuine external connection.	
avoid feelings and acts of isolation.	
battle silo mentality.	
have little to no office politics.	
share accountability.	
work from a shared goal.	
encourage open dialogues.	
address signs of loneliness.	
understand the need for people to belong.	

*... **rely on feedback**, as we...*

know how to ask for feedback and source advice.	
know how to give feedback.	
know how to receive feedback.	
listen genuinely.	
treat feedback as feedforward.	
empower colleagues' voices.	
interact in an empathic manner.	
pay attention to the CEO disease.	
understand that feedback is necessary for growth.	

CHAPTER 5

The combined power of digital leaders

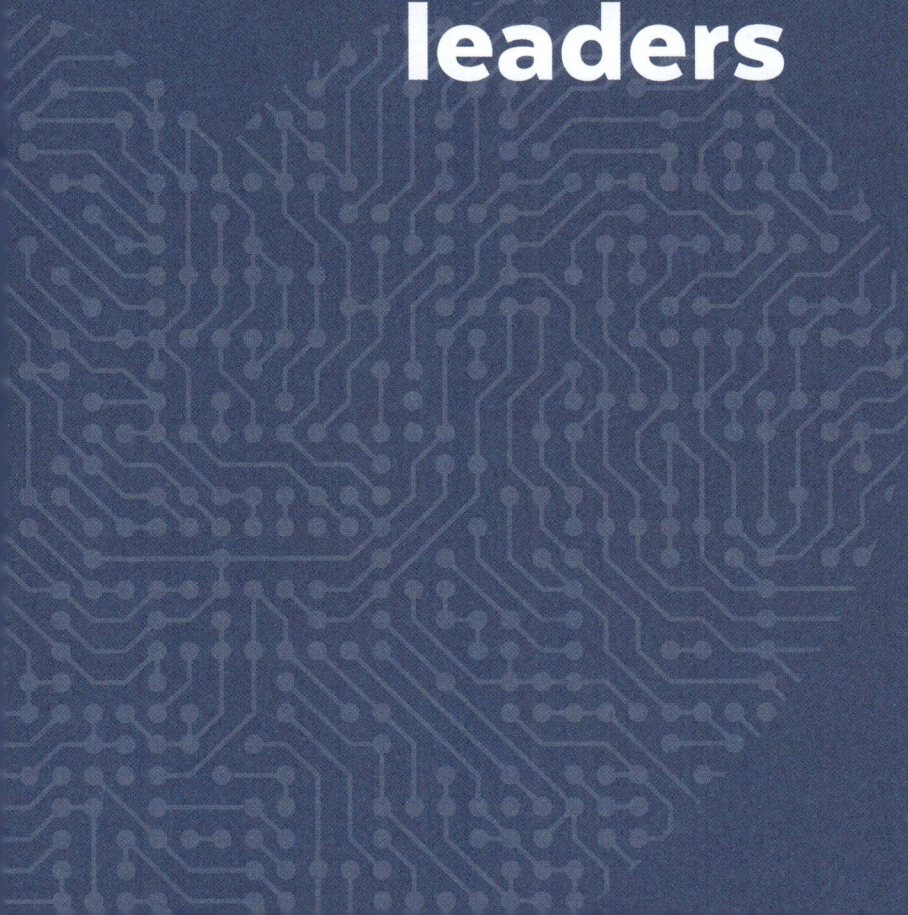

THE COMBINED POWER OF DIGITAL LEADERS

A digital transformation journey is fraught with moments of intense pressure and vulnerability. People who are familiar with the complexities of change in a fast-evolving digital landscape understand that leaders are vital in navigating these very moments.[246] Their combined efforts help employees safely cross that chasm between the current reality and a desired future state by offering guidance, structure, and reassurance. The digital leadership framework identifies four leadership types with their respective focuses, specialisations, and skillsets to support this.

The goal, however, is more than just helping people cross that divide. The digital transformation leaders establish strong foundations that connect internal and external stakeholders, even entire ecosystems, and allow ideas, data, and collaboration opportunities to flow freely across and beyond the organisational framework. Instead of having people focused on trying to survive – "We have to make it across" – the digital transformation leaders showcase and promote behaviours where people dare to lift their gaze towards exploring and exploiting new horizons.

More importantly, everyone in the organisation can take up the role of a Vigilant, Voyager, Visionary, and/or Vested leader. Strength-based leadership, in this regard, suggests that leaders can strive for and achieve organisational successes by finding and building on their own strengths and those of others.[247] Furthermore, the true power of digital transformation leaders is found in their ambition to collaborate, which allows them to transform the experience of digital transformation into an experience that cultivates and nurtures excitement and feelings of possibility.

This process requires more than just technical know-how, as we highlighted in the previous chapters. The organisation and the people therein must be supported in equipping themselves with a mindset that helps them deal and engage with digital transformation, that helps them move from survival to expansion.

FIXED VS. GROWTH MINDSET

A mindset is a mental operating system that constellates how you look at your own personal qualities and that guides your behaviours and your skills. Some people will consider their mindset, and therefore their behaviours and skills, as rather fixed; others consider these to be malleable. As such, your mindset, and the way you look at yourself, not only influences how you appraise effort but also influences how willing you are to exert that effort. In the context of digital transformation journeys,

> "[people] will have to accept that their [established] enterprises were not built to compete in a world that requires blending the physical and digital seamlessly. They'll need to open themselves to the digital space to rediscover the nature of value creation, the critical capabilities that need to be grown, and the new skills to be developed."[248]

Why does this matter? When psychologist Carol Dweck studied the effects of mindsets in children, she wondered why some got excited about complex problems while others got anxious, why some persisted where others gave up. What students believe about their brains – whether they see their intelligence as something that is fixed or something that can grow and change – has profound effects on their motivation, learning, and school achievement.[249] Furthermore, when people receive negative feedback on their performance, those with a growth mindset display different activation patterns in the brain than those who act from a fixed mindset.

Mindset	Fixed	Growth
Core belief	Our qualities and capacities are **etched in stone**.	Our qualities and capacities are **malleable** and can be cultivated.
Intelligence perception	Static	Developable
Desire	Look smart	Learn
5 tendencies		
	Avoid challenges	**Embrace** challenges
	Give up easily	**Persist** in the face of setbacks

	See effort as **fruitless** or worse	See effort as the path to **mastery**
	Ignore useful feedback	**Learn** from criticism
	Feel threatened by others' success	Find **lessons and inspiration** in the success of others
Result	May **plateau early** and achieve less than their full potential.	Reach ever-higher levels of **achievement**.
Confirmation	**Deterministic** world view.	Sense of **agency** and greater sense of **free will**.

— A **growth mindset** enhances learning from failure and helps you retain new information while fostering stronger resilience to setbacks – a boxer mentality. On a team-level, it is found that teams who show a collective growth mindset can openly express and solve disagreements, accept feedback, increase their confidence during trials and struggles, and are bolder in setting goals.

— A **fixed mindset**, in contrast, is often present in performance-driven cultures. Employees feel pressured to perform and fear failure. As a result, they avoid challenges, struggle to address mistakes, and are more vulnerable to setbacks. On the level of leadership, managers with a fixed mindset are less capable of changing their perceptions about colleagues and information – even when contrasting evidence is shown. What does this mean? If a colleague performs poorly, managers continue to see that colleague as a bad performer, even though that colleague might have substantially increased their performance in the meantime.

REFLECTIVE EXERCISE: FIXED MINDSET PERSONA

Do you recognise when a fixed mindset shows up? Why does it appear?
Do you recognise when a growth mindset shows up? Why does it appear?

What's more, a growth mindset is considered one of the core pillars of a strong digital culture. Within an organisational context, you might see individual employees or teams showcasing a fixed mindset of growth mindset, but you can also see entire companies operating (or not) with a mindset of growth (or fixedness). Carol Dweck and Tony Schwartz say:

> "When entire companies embrace a growth mindset, their employees report feeling far more empowered and committed; they also receive far greater organisational support for collaboration and innovation. In contrast, people at primarily fixed-mindset companies report more of only one thing: cheating and deception among employees, presumably to gain an advantage in the talent race [...] In a growth culture, people build their capacity to see through blind spots; acknowledge insecurities rather than unconsciously acting them out; and spend less energy defending their personal value so they have more energy available to create external value. How people feel – and make other people feel – becomes as important as how much they know."[250]

Unfortunately, the growth mindset is not always a clear-cut concept and might sometimes be rather elusive. How would you know in the first place whether a growth or fixed mindset is present or not? There are many questions we can ask ourselves and others that would help us better understand and frame how people and organisations engage with the future.

— **Fixed mindset:** Does your company play internal talent games, and are office politics present? Does it feel unsafe? Are growth attempts punished? Do you lack sufficient resources?
— **Growth mindset:** Does the company stimulate information sharing, collaboration and innovation, and feedback-seeking? Does it support employees in experimenting with new technologies and "failing fast"? Can they admit an error without getting the axe? Are you provided with opportunities to reskill/upskill? Are you rewarded for exploring and implementing new ideas?

REFLECTIVE EXERCISE: MINDSET AT SCALE

Would you say that your team, your department, and/or your entire company operates with a fixed mindset or rather a growth mindset? What do you see? What does it mean for digital transformation in your organisation?

Furthermore, people and entire companies might end up falling for certain lurking misconceptions regarding the growth mindset. Three bigger ones can be spotted:

— A growth mindset is eternal.

> **False.** A "pure" growth mindset does not exist. Everyone is a hybrid, and that mixture of fixed and growth mindsets evolves as we go through life. Considering this, people can lose their growth mindset but also regain it.

— A growth mindset is about praising and rewarding others for their effort.

> **False.** "Fuelling growth," writes Tony Schwartz, "requires a delicate balance between challenging and nurturing".[251]

— Espousing a growth mindset is sufficient.

> **False.** It is essential to actively embody a growth mindset in an organisation's culture and to encourage appropriate levels of risk-taking. While some risks won't work out, it is still worthwhile to reward colleagues for meaningful and valuable lessons learned.

Now, we don't always fully control for our own growth or fixed mindset. People who face challenges, experience severe setbacks, receive harsh criticism, or (seemingly) fare poorly compared to others, easily become insecure and defensive. This inhibits their learning and growth. Despite their own best efforts, their direct environment (work, school, home,…) might be filled with triggers that can activate a fixed mindset. Consider the following examples:

— You are constantly compared to others, which makes you feel like your abilities are judged against a certain fixed standard. People emphasise winning and outperforming others.
— Performance reviews are focused on highlighting mistakes and shortcomings. Little attention is given to effort or growth. Fear-based motivation results in anxiety and an overall fear of failure.
— Criticism is handed out easily, without any concrete suggestions for improvement or being offered a supportive hand.
— Being labelled and stereotyped (such as, "You are the logical one") makes you feel confined to a certain capability. You feel pressured to conform to the role, which could dissuade you from exploring new skills or interests.

— Praising someone for accomplishing something easily ("She's a natural") rather than working hard might create the impression that being naturally good at something is far more valuable than effort, which discourages people from taking on difficult tasks.
— Certain micro-aggressions, such as "I thought you were better at this", makes people feel that their abilities are fixed and that it might be better for them to avoid challenges.

REFLECTIVE EXERCISE: TRIGGERS

Which triggers do you identify in the company, in your team? Which ones push you into that fixed mindset? What is the impact of these triggers on your digital transformation journey?

Considering their pivotal role as digital transformation catalysts, our Vigilant, Voyager, Visionary, and Vested leaders ought to exercise their powers to stimulate people's growth mindset. However, they also hold the power to achieve the opposite by, hopefully unconsciously, triggering a fixed mindset on multiple levels – themselves, in colleagues and their teams, and the entire organisation and any external collaborations. Let us reflect on our four leadership types. Which kind of antipattern, red-flag behaviours might be identified, hinting towards a fixed mindset persona? Which kind of antipattern or red-flag behaviours could potentially hint towards people not sufficiently adopting the digital leaders' skills?

ANTIPATTERNS FOR THE VIGILANT DIGITAL TRANSFORMATION LEADER

LACKS CURIOSITY.

— ... prioritises immediate results over long-term learning opportunities.

— ... discourages acts of exploration and sharing new ideas.

— ... reacts negatively to new ideas or publicly dismisses suggestions.

Outcome: *The organisation grows disconnected from emerging technologies and industry trends. This can result in missed opportunities and an inability to anticipate or respond effectively to disruptions. Employees may become disengaged, resisting change, and become less open to adopting new technologies or ideas.*

FALLS VICTIM TO BIASED THINKING.

— ... cuts corners and rushes to conclusions.

— ... focuses only on successes and neglects the lessons from failure.

— ... favours existing or familiar beliefs over dissenting views.

Outcome: *The organisation is likely to make flawed decisions based on skewed or incomplete information. This could result in the adoption of technologies that are not suited to the company's needs or might result in the dismissal of valuable innovations. Resources are wasted.*

MISHANDLES INFORMATION.

— ... exaggerates in sharing data.

— ... communicates in an overly complex, abstract, or too technical manner.

— ... uses technology and tools impulsively.

Outcome: *Employees end up being overwhelmed and confused, resulting in a severe case of disengagement. Critical insights might be lost in the noise, which slows down decision-making, ultimately stalling or derailing digital transformation efforts. Leaders' credibility is undermined as they come across as unfocused and chaotic.*

ANTIPATTERNS FOR THE VOYAGER DIGITAL TRANSFORMATION LEADER

MAKES NO EFFORT TO CO-CREATE.
— ... fails to involve important stakeholders.
— ... does not acknowledge the input and value of other co-creation participants.
— ... prefers one-sided ideation.

Outcome: *The organisation risks developing solutions that are disconnected from real user needs and market demands. Products that have a limited relevance and effectiveness will suffer from lower adoption. Furthermore, the organisation might miss out on opportunities for innovation because of a lack of diverse perspectives.*

IS NOT OPEN TO VULNERABILITY.
— ... micromanages and dictates.
— ... never acknowledges personal errors.
— ... blames.

Outcome: *A culture of fear is spreading throughout the organisation. Employees avoid mistakes and failure, and do not feel empowered nor trusted to drive meaningful change. Teams are hesitant to take risks and instead opt for safer, less creative solutions to avoid criticism or blame. Innovation is stifled and collaboration drops.*

DOES NOT AIM FOR INCLUSION.
— ... avoids difficult conversations.
— ... neglects stakeholders' differences (e.g., communication style, work ethics, etc.).
— ... commits to diversity in a superficial manner.

Outcome: *Stakeholders' diverse backgrounds and tensions are left unattended. Open dialogues are missing, and escalation ensues, further disrupting teamwork and hindering momentum. The organisation misses out on critical insights that could drive digital innovation and boost overall creativity. The failure to embrace inclusivity jeopardises the organisation's competitiveness.*

ANTIPATTERNS FOR THE VISIONARY DIGITAL TRANSFORMATION LEADER

NEGLECTS PURPOSE.
— ... ignores personal values and motivations.
— ... causes feelings of disconnection between employees (and the organisation).
— ... approaches purpose from solely a strategic point of view.

Outcome: *The organisation continues with an unaligned or misaligned workforce that, after a while, struggles with decreased morale and motivation, making it difficult for leaders to achieve cohesive progress towards any digital transformation goals.*

PAYS NO ATTENTION TO STORYTELLING.
— ... confuses rather than clarifies.
— ... fails to build morale.
— ... does not frame the journey in a compelling way.

Outcome: *The organisation misses the opportunity for collective buy-in. Employees do not grasp the reason and benefits of the transformation. They don't feel inspired nor feel like they are part of a journey. Instead, confusion, apathy, and resistance emerge that erode morale further and slow down the digital transformation journey. Employees feel more and more disconnected from the organisation, making future change initiatives additionally challenging.*

MISMANAGES RISK.
— ... sticks rigidly to existing plans.
— ... fails to delegate responsibility and decision-making.
— ... considers bold risk taking to be all-or-nothing and does not hedge risk.

Outcome: *Unbalanced risk-taking has exposed the organisation to significant financial losses, operational disruptions, and failed initiatives. Over investment in unproven technologies harm the organisation, which ends up in reduced stakeholder confidence. It becomes gradually more difficult to drive additional innovation as future transformation efforts falter due to lack of buy-in and limited organisational capacity.*

FAILS TO PARTNER.
— ... only looks after the company's own interest.
— ... believes whatever the company does itself it does better.
— ... is secretive.

Outcome: *The organisation lacks strong partnerships that would provide access to essential resources and innovative ideas. This stalls its ability to adapt to rapidly changing landscapes and meet customer preferences. As the overall success of the digital transformation effort is compromised, the organisation starts to lose its competitive edge and market position.*

ANTIPATTERNS FOR THE VESTED DIGITAL TRANSFORMATION LEADER

FLIES SOLO.
— ... neglects key influencers.
— ... leaves passive resistance unaddressed.
— ... has a lone wolf attitude.

Outcome: *The organisation misses a leader that benefits from a strong support to effectively navigate challenges. Instead, fragmented efforts appear that further delay progress. Employees feel disconnected from the digital transformation journey and because of limited buy-in, growing resistance to change, and unaligned execution, the journey becomes rigid and more likely to falter.*

IS UNAWARE OF ABSORPTIVE CAPACITY.
— ... ignores concerns.
— ... doesn't allow for a breather.
— ... adheres rigidly to preset timelines and plans.

Outcome: *The organisation meets resistance to new technologies and processes as employees experience increasing symptoms of change fatigue. Employees now fail to effectively learn and integrate new systems, which has caused the transformation journey to hit an abrupt pause. The organisation has committed a broad range of resources, such as time and money, but without achieving any tangible return on their investments. New technological tools are left unused or remain stuck in development, gathering dust.*

DOES NOT BREAK SILO BEHAVIOUR.
— ... discourages cross-functional or -department initiatives.
— ... makes decisions in isolation.
— ... shows favouritism.

Outcome: *Colleagues catch each other in the act of actively hoarding information and guarding data access. Teams refrain from collaborating across silos. The organisation risks significant fragmentation and inefficiency. Decision making is being delayed week after week and departments hunt for misaligned objectives. These isolated acts* *undermine the digital transformation journey and cause any initiative to be disjointed and less effective. Organisational agility is reduced to a bare minimum and is expected to derail the journey.*

ENGAGES IN UNIDIRECTIONAL FEEDBACK.
— ... perceives feedback as a challenge to their authority and reacts defensively.
— ... prioritises their own vision and adopts a top-down approach.
— ... is unwilling to listen.

Outcome: *The organisation suffers from a pool of employees whose relationship with their leader is strained. They feel undervalued, disconnected, and often dismissed. As a result of not being open to colleagues' feedback, the organisation now grows a culture where learning is no longer taking place and, consequently, business is badly positioned to quickly adapt to changing market demands.*

It becomes clear that digital transformation leaders have three interconnected tasks to strive for:

1. Be aware of their **own actions and behaviours** and how these might act as clear triggers for fixed or growth mindsets in colleagues.
2. Foster a growth mindset **within colleagues** and other digital transformation **stakeholders**.
3. Build a growth mindset at the **organisational level**.

Such growth mindset culture starts by encouraging a work environment where employees feel safe to experiment, fail, and try again. **Psychological safety** in this regard refers to a shared belief among colleagues that they can take (inter)personal risks without fear of negative consequences to their reputation and career. In other words, in a psychologically safe work environment people are surrounded by a climate that is supportive of open dialogue, mistakes, and learning without fear. Colleagues can speak up, share ideas, ask questions, admit mistakes, and express concerns. A safety net is consciously woven by true digital transformation leaders who build on the strength of relationships, the power of feedback, the clarity of purpose, and more, resulting in a system supportive of continuous improvement, or growth.

STARTING FROM THE GROWTH MINDSET AS YOUR MENTAL OPERATING MODEL

The concept of the growth (or fixed) mindset can be considered instrumental to address deeper issues that influence a company's ability to change and innovate. In the context of digital transformation journey, leaders ought to master the skill of applying **system thinking** to diagnose change situations beyond the mere superficial observation. System thinking moves beyond a purely linear model of observation as it considers the organization as a whole with dynamic feedback loops between its various parts. In other words, as leaders are better equipped to spot interactions, they grasp the causes and true nature of a particular situation within the organisation in a more holistic manner.[252] The Iceberg Model,[253] visualises how we often approach certain situations in our private and professional lives. The iceberg model is a tool within the systems thinking tool case that helps to uncover the deeper, often hidden layers of a system and identify the hidden causes behind visible events. It consists of four levels:

— **Events:** the visible occurrences or outcomes.
— **Patterns:** recurring behaviours or trends over time.
— **System structure:** the relationship, rules, processes, and organisational dynamics driving these patterns.

— **Mental models:** the deeply held beliefs, assumptions, and values that shape how people think and behave.

As such, the Iceberg Model not only depicts various levels of a problem, but also provides us with numerous insights into how we can effect change within a system. These changes can be driven by means of certain *leverage points* – the locations within a system where a small shift in one level can result in changes in the overall system. The further below the surface you dive – and the deeper you go into the iceberg – the more impact a leverage point is likely to have. Given this, changing your *structures* and *mental models* has a greater impact than merely *reacting in the moment* and putting out fires as they arise. In a sense, events merely signal smoke and warn you that a fire might be burning somewhere. If you focus only on the smoke, you'll soon notice that the fire is burning even hotter.

Let's reflect on the Iceberg model and how to apply it to a digital transformation journey. In the following example, a manufacturing company recently rolled out a new AI-powered software tool to streamline operations. Things, however, aren't going as leadership expected – on the contrary. Issues have emerged and the successful adoption of the tool has stalled.

Event: A sharp drop is noticed in employee engagement soon after implementing the AI-powered tool. Several employees are frustrated with the new system, and some outright refuse to use the software, preferring to stick to their old ways of working.

Patterns: HR noticed that this is, in fact, not an isolated incident. Over the past year, multiple digital tools and systems were introduced. Each time, excitement seemed high at the initial launch, but was soon followed by confusion and dissatisfaction, resulting in technology un-adoption.

System Structures: Employees frequently mention that they feel overwhelmed. The pace of change is too fast, and they are not provided with sufficient training opportunities. What's more, employees are expected to learn about the system on the job. A formalised support or training process for new technology rollouts seems to be missing. Overall, tools are implemented without consulting teams, and there's limited opportunity for feedback. This leads to a lack of technology ownership and a general sense of being disconnected to the digital transformation journey.

Mental Models: Leadership considers digital transformation to be a disruptive force that people must simply cope with. "Those who can adapt, will adapt," they say, "those who resist change, simply do so out of laziness or fear". They struggle with changing their perceptions about colleagues. On the employee side, many employees consider the AI-powered tool a threat to their job and don't believe themselves capable of learning to work with it.

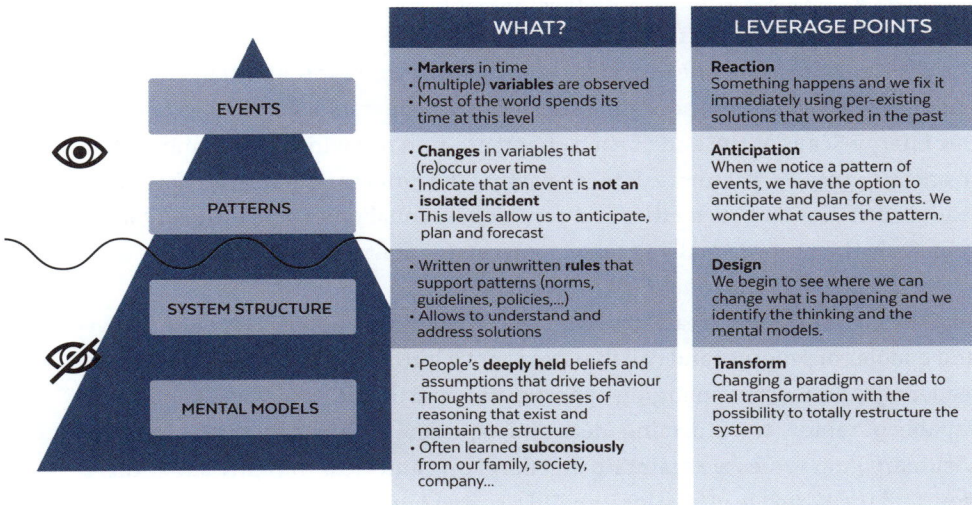

	WHAT?	LEVERAGE POINTS
EVENTS	• **Markers** in time • (multiple) **variables** are observed • Most of the world spends its time at this level	**Reaction** Something happens and we fix it immediately using per-existing solutions that worked in the past
PATTERNS	• **Changes** in variables that (re)occur over time • Indicate that an event is **not an isolated incident** • This levels allow us to anticipate, plan and forecast	**Anticipation** When we notice a pattern of events, we have the option to anticipate and plan for events. We wonder what causes the pattern.
SYSTEM STRUCTURE	• Written or unwritten **rules** that support patterns (norms, guidelines, policies,...) • Allows to understand and address solutions	**Design** We begin to see where we can change what is happening and we identify the thinking and the mental models.
MENTAL MODELS	• People's **deeply held** beliefs and assumptions that drive behaviour • Thoughts and processes of reasoning that exist and maintain the structure • Often learned **subconsiously** from our family, society, company...	**Transform** Changing a paradigm can lead to real transformation with the possibility to totally restructure the system

Iceberg analysis: By analysing issues through the Iceberg Model, the company can see that the visible event – employee disengagement – stems from deeper patterns of inadequate support during technology rollouts. These patterns are reinforced by system structures that neglect the importance of training, communication, and employee feedback and involvement. At the deepest level, biased mental models around self-change and technology hint at a strong fixed mindset spreading its roots.

Solution: To address this, the company must work on shifting the mental operating model of both leadership and employees from a fixed mindset to a growth mindset. Furthermore, system structures need to be shaped to include comprehensive training, involve employees early in the process, and create feedback loops.

The **four digital transformation leaders** – the Vigilant, Voyager, Visionary, and Vested leader – must collaborate, each bringing their unique perspective and approach to address the deeper issues identified in the Iceberg Model. They strive to nurture a growth mindset, which would act as a stronger lever for effective change. To address digital transformation challenges, cultivating a growth mindset within the organization can help the leaders break negative patterns and drive changes in system structures in more meaningful ways. Over time, this mindset fosters a culture where people are empowered to approach challenges proactively rather than reactively. As such, a growth mindset becomes a powerful lever for all digital leaders driving transformation across all levels of the Iceberg Model

People at all levels within the organisation can take on our different leadership roles. One person can even take on multiple roles, as long as they do so because the chosen jobs to be done energize them, align with their (potential) strengths, and they willingly accept accountability for their leadership. Remember to fill out our Energy Scans at the end of each chapter to find out which role is most likely to energise you. Furthermore, it is crucial that the different digital transformation leaders complement each other and consciously collaborate across the organisation. Only then can we really speak of a successful digital transformation.

Together, these leaders create an environment where technology is seen as a driver and enabler of progress and collaboration, not a burden nor a threat. The Vigilant leader ensures we spot emerging opportunities and threats; the Voyager makes us capable of rapidly transforming ideas and experiments into concrete results; the Visionary guarantees we maintain an energizing and clear digitally-savvy direction; and the Vested leader helps us build a strong foundation of trust and support. By combining their strengths, they transform the company's system structures and mental models, turning colleagues into a confident and collaborative team, ready to embrace the digital future.

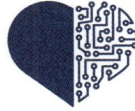

EXERCISE: THE ICEBERG MODEL IN PRACTICE

Think of a specific problem—past or present—that your organization has experienced as part of its digital transformation. Use the guiding questions below to unpack the issue beyond surface-level symptoms:

— **Event** – What specific incident or situation has occurred?
— **Pattern** – Do you notice recurring behaviors or outcomes that suggest this event is part of a larger pattern?
— **System Structure** – What underlying structures or processes might be reinforcing these patterns?
— **Mental Models** – Are there deeply held beliefs or assumptions within the organization that could be driving these structures?

Based on your analysis, what actions would you take to not only address the immediate issue but also prevent similar problems in the future?

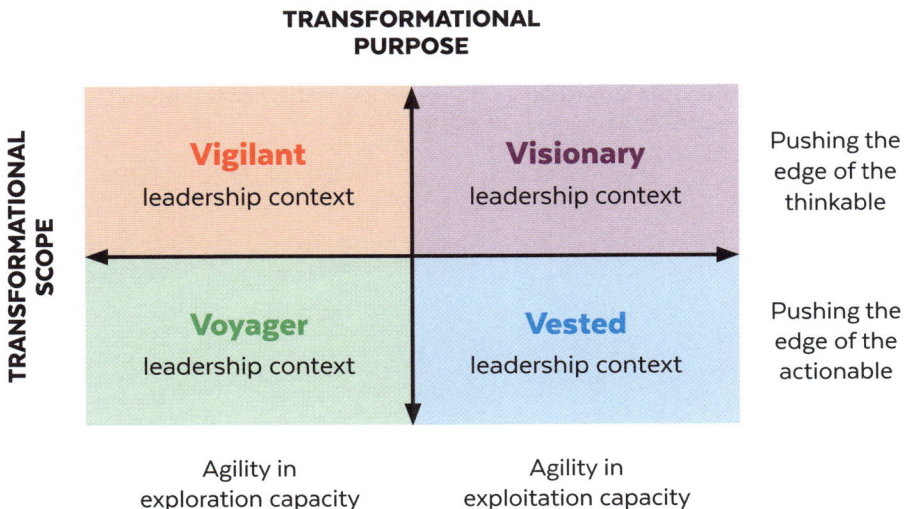

TRANSFORMATIONAL PURPOSE

Vigilant leadership context	**Visionary** leadership context
Voyager leadership context	**Vested** leadership context

TRANSFORMATIONAL SCOPE

Pushing the edge of the thinkable

Pushing the edge of the actionable

Agility in exploration capacity

Agility in exploitation capacity

1. WHAT OUR VIGILANT DIGITAL TRANSFORMATION LEADERS LEARNED

"Over the past few months, I've found out about so many interesting technologies, it's amazing! I did have to learn, however, to consciously take a step back and reflect on which ones are actually most relevant for the organisation and my colleagues to learn more about. I first checked things with my challenge network, and we boiled it down to sharing two technologies. Otherwise, as I've come to notice, colleagues won't read it. They'd just cling to the status quo and default option anyway." **– Larry, Digitize Consulting**

"I have to admit that I do have quite some innovation bias. I gobble up everything there is to know about the many potentials of new, innovative technologies. It sometimes makes me pay little to no attention to whether a technology is really that relevant for our business. I noticed that I also tend to neglect reading about potential risks. Whenever I learn about a new technological application, I now make sure that I give equal attention to the advantages and disadvantages of a technology, and try to position it more concretely within our company and within our industry." **– Brandon, Foresight Team at Fintrix**

"It's been eye-opening to understand that my colleagues might not necessarily be as enthusiastic about new ideas and technologies as I always am. Igniting their spark, however, is a new enticing challenge that I really love doing. I check for people's curiosity level and then tailor my approach accordingly. Just last week, I suggested that Louise, one of our in-house salespeople, could go and visit an innovative partner and see how they put technology to good use. She absolutely loved it! She even returned with some ideas of her own that she proposed to explore further." **– Hadrien, GalleryX**

2. WHAT OUR VOYAGER DIGITAL TRANSFORMATION LEADERS LEARNED

"The severe market reaction to our planning tool was a painful, but necessary confrontation with our usual modus operandi. We always believed that our partners wanted us to innovate for them – that's what they pay us for, right? –, but now we realise that they really want to innovate together with us. We've recently started involving customers in some of our other products. It's resulted in some remarkable ideas that could help reposition our products in the market!" **– Julio, SupplyTech**

"This definitely wasn't an easy journey for me. I always felt that I had to know everything and usually prefer to keep a tight ship at work. To be fair, I'm not like that, which felt like going against my nature. I was so happy when I dared to share some doubts and uncertainties. Gradually providing colleagues with opportunities to take on some ownership and involve them in decisions took a lot of unnecessary burdens from my shoulders. Plus, it is great to see the sparkle in colleagues' eyes when they talk about their projects."
– Jonathan, NexTalent

"I'll be honest, reaping the benefits of diversity... Way more complex than we thought it would be. It's already complicated between internal stakeholders, let alone if you add an external party to the mix. Still, the project proved to be a worthwhile learning curve for myself and for colleagues. Despite some big challenges, working with TechGears was a positive experience. What's more, we already brainstormed on launching a new project with them. There are still some struggles every now and then, both internally and externally, but everyone knows that we're headed in the same direction." **– Bram, Innovora**

3. WHAT OUR VISIONARY DIGITAL TRANSFORMATION LEADERS LEARNED

"We had really underestimated how connected many colleagues are to our school and how energised they feel as a result. By only concentrating on the future, and paying less heed to the past and present, we stole that from them. People felt increasingly disconnected, which left our school in a perilous situation. I was most happy to drill down into the essence of what we've always done and what we've always been most proud of: mentoring our students. This hasn't changed, digital or not." – **Tom, Farbright School of Trade and Commerce**

"We had clearly missed something crucial when translating our vision and Vincent had us cornered with his questions. We were of the impression that people would build their own story of why the company was gunning for these changes. Seeing what went wrong, it's now safe to say that was probably our most important assignment. Even though we might not have handled things properly in the beginning, it was still a great experience for us to see how a story could bring people, and the entire organisation, back to life. What's even more interesting, some of our colleagues now also actively think in terms of telling a story – when they're doing a meeting or reaching out to potential new customers! People really seem to appreciate it." – **Saim and Sophie, Family & Co. Mart**

"I'm glad that Benjamin stopped me that day in the hallway. I had perhaps thought about taking risks in a too black-and-white manner, which gave rise to some fears. I really didn't want to jeopardise or burden the company with excessive exposure to risk. But reflecting on it from a different angle helped. 'Thoughtful risk-taking', Benjamin called it. I liked that! We recently spread our wings and engaged in some exploratory conversations with some unique startups. We even decided to go for a pilot project with one of them. It seems promising. Meanwhile we keep building and strengthening our core business." – **Matthias, Müller & Sons Construction**

"It's clear that we had skipped some crucial steps in the beginning. We've worked a lot with HBN before, but since then things have considerably changed outside and inside both companies. Some of our usual pappenheimers had retired or left for someplace else. Maybe we were simply a bit naïve about what it takes to properly collaborate with one another. We had shied away from the formal talks and sometimes painful conversations, believing that these were signals of a bad partnership. Now we know that these are in fact crucial ingredients for a successful or, at least, smoother way of doing things together. We'd set this in practice with EtnAI, for example. And, indeed, that was an entirely different reality from the very beginning." – **Jürgen, Atlas Newspaper**

4. WHAT OUR VESTED DIGITAL TRANSFORMATION LEADERS LEARNED

"It was only when our customers started to lash out that I understood how badly I had handled this. Our isolated, siloed approach to a digital transformation had found its way to the outside world. When I first tried to reconcile with other teams, I had to catch a lot of headwinds – people were frustrated. Rightfully so. Luckily, InnovTech has always been a place where lessons can be learned and where people can sometimes run headfirst into a wall. We smoothed things over, and we have taken a different route. Information and helping hands are now easily flowing across teams, people are talking once more, and I also feel that colleagues have started to regain their trust in me." – **Adil, InnovTech**

"We went too fast. There's no other way to put it. We went too fast, and more and more people dropped out the further we went. Can't really blame them either. It's good to be ambitious but there was too much of a speed divergence between what we thought was possible and what was truly possible. When Dominique suggested that I read about the bank account principle, it really hit me: people were running on empty savings accounts, and we were constantly asking them to make more withdrawals. No matter how you look at it, we had to give people time and opportunity to rebuild those accounts. We decided to slow down, which didn't feel comfortable at first, but now we keep moving steadily. Have you read Aesop's fable of the hare and the tortoise? Guess this was similar: in our eagerness and, well, maybe overconfidence, we believed we could push to the finish line." – **Maria, EcoGoods**

"I've always been a bit of a lone wolf, I'd say. But reflecting now on what happened, I must admit that I couldn't keep this up. It had become too much, and I lost track of things. When I first involved some other colleagues to help me, I remained hesitant and I for sure wasn't convinced. Still, over time, this way of working started to feel natural, and we now have this organic flow going on between our coalition and other colleagues. I feel very supported by the people around me and colleagues also seem to appreciate the way things are being handled. In the end, we keep things as simple as possible and we communicate proactively." – **Will, Fortura**

Yeah... My partner still jokes about my work situation every now and then, but I can really see how deaf I was to colleagues' ideas and needs. I just talked and talked and talked, never taking the time to listen. My relationship with colleagues has vastly improved and the rough edges are smoothed. They now feel comfortable coming to my office with questions and suggestions. I always make sure to take the time to listen and be a good conversational sparring partner." – **Arthur, Green Future Labs**

REFERENCE LIST

INTRODUCTION

Agasisti, T. (2022), "Corporate training: digital transformation tops the list", *EFMD Global*.

Anseel, F. (2022), "Lucinda Brogden: how leaders can improve workplace mental health", *UNSW Business School*.

Apotheker, J., Duranton, S., Lukic, V., de Bellefonds, N., Iyer, S., Bouffault, O., and de Laubier, R. (2024), "From Potential to Profit with GenAI", *Boston Consulting Group*.

Barsade, S. (2002), "The Ripple Effect: Emotional Contagion and Its Influence on Group Behavior", *Administrative Science Quarterly,* Vol. 47, No. 4, pp. 644-675.

Basking, K. (2018), "5 reasons companies struggle with digital transformation", *MIT Management*.

Beard, A. (2022), "Can Big Tech Be Disrupted?", *Harvard Business Review*.

Bloomberg, J. (2022, 14 April). "Digitization, Digitalization, And Digital Transformation: Confuse Them At Your Peril", *Forbes*.

Bonnet, D. and Westerman, G. (2020), "The New Elements of Digital Transformation", *MIT Sloan*.

Breque, M., De Nul, L. and Petridis, A., (2021), "Industry 5.0 – Towards a sustainable, human-centric and resilient European industry", *Publications Office of the European Union*.

Brown, S. (2020), "How to master two different digital transformations", *Harvard Business Review*.

Clark, T.R., (2022), "Agile Doesn't Work Without Psychological Safety", *Harvard Business Review*.

Clear, J. (2018), *Atomic Habits*, Random House Business.

Coleman, J. (2017), "Make Learning a Lifelong Habit", *Harvard Business Review*.

Coleman, J. (2022), "So, what is organizational agility? 2022 UPDATE", *Scrum*.

Dagan, N., Baz-Sanchez, L., and Weddle, B. (2020), "Driving organizational and behavior changes during a pandemic", *McKinsey Organization Blog*.

Dries, N., Luyckx, J., and Rogiers, P. (2024), "What 570 Experts Predict the Future of Work Will Look Like", *Harvard Business Review*.

Eyrich, N.W., Quinn, R.E., and Fessell, D.P. (2019), "How One Person Can Change the Conscience of an Organization", *Harvard Business Review*.

Garcia, J. (2022), "Common pitfalls in transformations: A conversation with Jon Garcia", *McKinsey & Company*.

Gartner (2024), "Digital Transformation: How to Scope and Execute Strategy".

Gates, L.A. (2018), "Agile Strategy: Short-Cycle Strategy Development and Execution", *SEI Blog*.

Gherson, D., and Gratton, L. (2022), "Managers Can't Do It All", *Harvard Business Review*.

Grebe, M., Hunke, N., Kataeva, N., Lenhard, E., Backx, J., Rehberg, B., and Gardelli, V. (2024), "Why Companies Get Agile Right – and Wrong", *Boston Consulting Group*.

Harbert, T. (2021), "Digital transformation has evolved. Here's what's new.", *MIT Management*.

Hemerling, J. (2016), "5 ways to lead in an era of constant change", *TEDx*.

Hemerling, J., Kilmann, J., and Matthews, D. (2018), "The Head, Heart, and Hands of Transformation", *Boston Consulting Group*.

Hill, L.A., Le Cam, A., Menon, S., and Tedards, E. (2022), "Digital Transformation: A New Roadmap for Success", *Harvard Business School Working Knowledge*.

Hill, L.A., Le Cam, A., Menon, S., and Tedards, E. (2022), "Curiosity, Not Coding: 6 Skills Leaders Need in the Digital Age", *Harvard Business School*.

Hougaard, R., and Carter, J. (2018), "Ego Is the Enemy of Good Leadership", *Harvard Business Review*.

Jesuthasan, R, and Boudreau, J. (2022), *Work without Jobs, How to Reboot Your Organisation's Work Operating System*, The MIT Press.

Kurzweil, R. (2010), "10 Questions for Ray Kurzweil", *Time*.

Lehnis, S. (2021), "Human-centric digital transformation", *Open Access Government*.

Marckstadt, F., Laamanen, T., and Dimke, M. (2020), "Transformation Champions, Turning Opposites into Complements", *Deloitte*.

N.,N., "Did Peter Drucker Say That?", *Drucker Institute*.

Prause, J. (2020), "Digitization vs Digitalization", *SAP Insights*.

Ready, D.A., Cohen, C., Kiron, D., and Pring, B. (2020), "The New Leadership Playbook for the Digital Age, Reimagining What IT Takes to Lead", *MITSloan Management Review*.

Relihan, T. (2018), "Agile at scale, explained", *MIT Management*.

Schrage, M., Muttreja, V., and Kwan, A. (2022), "How the Wrong KPIs Doom Digital Transformation", *MIT Sloan Management Review*.

Somers, M. (2021), "The 3 leadership types in a nimble organization", *MIT Management*.

van Heuven, D. (2022), "Je baan of je leven (aflevering 17): Hoe empathisch mag je zijn als leider?" *MTSprout*.

Viaene, S. (2020), *Digital Transformation Know-How*, Acco.

Viaene, S. (2024), "Leading Successful Digital Transformations", *Ivey Business Journal*.

Viaene, S, & Sen, K. (2024). Leading digital transformation for organizational agility: a substantive practice-based framework. Working paper 20241212. Vlerick Business School.

Visnjic, I., Birkinshaw, J., and Linz, C. (2022), "When Gradual Change Beats Radical Transformation", *MIT Sloan Management Review*.

Westerman, G. (2022), "The Questions Leaders Should Ask in the New Era of Digital Transformation", *MIT Sloan Management Review*.

Yin, Y., Mueller, J., and Wakslak, C. (2024), "Understanding How People React to Change: A Domain of Uncertainty Approach", *Academy of Management Annals*, Vol. 18, No. 2.

Zucker, R. (2019), "Why Highly Efficient Leaders Fail", *Harvard Business Review*.

CHAPTER 1 – VIGILANT LEADERSHIP

STIMULATING CURIOSITY

Angner, E. (2020), "Epistemic Humility – Knowing Your Limits in a Pandemic", *Behavioral Scientist*.

Barco (2022), "The new museum experience: When culture and technology come together", *Barco*.

Brown, B. (2021), *Atlas of the Heart – Mapping Meaningful Connection and the Language of Human Experience*, Random House.

Capozzi, M.M., and Tiffany Vogel (2021), "Advance learning to shape the future – and deliver today", *McKinsey Organisation Blog*.

Chamorro-Premuzic, T., and Josh Bersin (2018), "4 Ways to Create a Learning Culture on Your Team", *Harvard Business Review*.

Chang, Y.-Y., and Shih, H.-Y. (2019), "Work curiosity: A new lens for understanding employee creativity", *Human Resource Management Review*, Vol. 29, No. 4, pp. 100672.

Conn, Charles, and Robert McLean (2020), "Six problem-solving mindsets for very uncertain times", *McKinsey Quarterly*.

Day, H.I. (1982), "Curiosity and the interested explorer", *Performance & Instruction*, Vol. 21, No.4, pp.19-22.

Fessell, D.P., and Karen Reivich (2021), "Why You Need to Protect Your Sense of Wonder – Especially Now", *Harvard Business Review*.

Furr, N., Nel, K., and Tomas Zoëga, Ramsoy (2018), "If Your Innovation Effort Isn't Working, Look at Who's on the Team", *Harvard Business Review*.

Grant, A. (2016), *Originals, How Non-Conformists Move The World*, Penguin Random House LLC.

Grossman, R.J. (2015), "How to Create a Learning Culture, " *SHRM Better Workplaces Better World*.

Ive, J. (2021), "Jony Ive on What He Misses Most About Steve Jobs", *Wall Street Journal News Exclusive*.

Kashdan, T.B. (2015), "Companies value curiosity but stifle it anyway", *Harvard Business Review*.

Kashdan, T.B., Stiksma, M.C., Disabato, McKnight, P.E., Bekier, J., Kaji, J., and Lazarus, R. (2018), "The five-dimensional curiosity scale: capturing the bandwith of curiosity and identifying four unique subgroups of people", *Journal of Research in Personality*, Vol. 73, pp. 130-149.

Kashdan, T. B., Rose, P., & Fincham, F. D. (2004), "Curiosity and exploration: Facilitating positive subjective experiences and personal growth opportunities"n Journal of Personality Assessment, Vol. 82, No.3, pp. 291–305.

Moore, D.A. (2018), "Overconfidence: The mother of all biases", *Psychology Today*.

Oskamp, S. (1965), "Overconfidence in case-study judgments", *Journal of Consulting Psychology*, Vol. 29, No. 3, pp. 261–265

Zao-Sanders, M. (2021), "Identify – and Hire – Lifelong Learners", *Harvard Business Review*.

UNMASKING BIASES AND NOISE

Acton, C. (2022), "Are You Aware of Your Biases", *Harvard Business Review*.

Beard, A. *(2021),* "Why Smart People (Sometimes) Make Bad Decisions", *HBR IdeaCast*.

Brown, S. (2021), "6 trends in data and artificial intelligence for 2021 and beyond", *MIT Sloan*.

Coene, S. (2021), "Psychologische inertie in organisatieverandering", *LinkedIn*.

Cuofano, G. "What Are Biases Really and Why We Got It All Wrong About Biases", *FourWeekMBA*.

Eastwood, B. (2021), "Who owns digital innovation? Who cares?", *MIT Sloan*.

Galef, J. (2016), "Why you think you're right – even if you're wrong", *TEDx*.

Kahneman, D., Sibony, O., and Sunstein C.R. (2021), *Noise: A Flaw in Human Judgment*, Little, Brown Spark.

Kahneman, D., and Sibony, O. (2021), "Sounding the alarm on system noise", *McKinsey Quarterly*.

Kahneman, D. (2017), *Thinking, Fast and Slow*, Penguin Group.

Kittelstad, K., "17 Examples of Bias", YourDictionary.

Morse, G. (2016), "Designing a Bias-Free Organisation", *Harvard Business Review*.

N.,N., "Reducing Workplace Bias: Hyperbolic Discounting", *Mindfulnessexercises*.

N.,N., "Reducing Workplace Bias: Confirmation Bias", *Mindfulnessexercises*.

N.,N., "Reducing Workplace Bias: The Optimism Bias", *Mindfulnessexercises*.

N.,N., "Reducing Workplace Bias: Shared Information Bias", *Mindfulnessexercises*.

N.,N., "Reducing Workplace Bias: Sunk Cost Fallacy", *Mindfulnessexercises*.

N.,N., "Reducing Workplace Bias: Backfire Effect", *Mindfulnessexercises.*

Offut-Kleider, H., Meacham, A.M., Branum-Martin, L., and Capodanno, M. (2021), "What's in a face? The role of facial features in ratings of dominance, threat, and stereotypicality", *Cognitive Research: Principles and Implications* Vol. 6, No.53.

Relihan, T. (2019), "Fixing a toxic work culture: Dealing with 'toxic superstars'", *MIT Sloan.*

Relihan, T. (2019), "Fixing a toxic work culture: Guarding against the 'dark triad'", *MIT Sloan.*

Sibony, O., and Kahneman, D. (2021), "Bias is a big problem. But so is 'noise'", *The New York Times.*

Taylor, S. (2017), "The Three Most Important Truths to Know About Unconscious Bias", *Forbes.*

Tugend, A. (2010), "Too Many Choices: A Problem That Can Paralyse", *The New York Times.*

van Neerven, S. (2022), "Oh jee, een rebel in je team! Maar is dat wel zo'n ramp?", *MT Sprout.*

Williams, J.C., and Mihaylo, S. (2019), "How the Best Bosses Interrupt Bias on Their Teams", *Harvard Business Review.*

MASTERING INFORMATION OVERLOAD

Anseel, F. (2014), "Altijd bereikbaar zijn is verslavend en ongezond, maar niet verboden", *De Morgen*

Berinato, S. (2019), "Data Science and the Art of Persuasion", *Harvard Business Review.*

Brinton, W. (1914), *Graphic Methods for Presenting Facts*, The Engineering Magazine Company.

Buckingham, M. (2021), "Becoming a More Critical Consumer of Information", *Harvard Business Review.*

Compernolle, T. (2014), "Brain-Hostile Open Offices: The Fifth BrainChain", *Brainchains.*

De Smet, A., Hewes, C., Luo, M., Maxwell, J.R., and Simon, P. (2020), "If we're all so busy, why isn't anything getting done?", *McKinsey & Company.*

Edmunds, A., and Morris, A. (2000), "The problem of information overload in business organisations: a review of the literature", Vol. 20, No.1, 0-28.

Hafenbrack, A.C, Kinias, Z., and Barsade, S.G. (2013), "Debiasing the Mind Through Meditation: Mindfulness and the Sunk-Cost Bias", *Psychological Science*, Vol. 25, No.1, pp. 369-376.

Hart, S.M. (2022), "Het Onrustige Brein", *Susan Marletta Hart.*

Klausegger, C., Sinkovics, R.R., and Zou, H. (2007), "Information overload: a cross-national investigation of influence factors and effects", *Marketing Intelligence & Planning*, Vol. 25, No. 7, pp. 691-718.

Laker, B., Pereira, V., Budhawar, P., and Malik, A. (2022), "The Surprising Impact of Meeting-Free Days", *MIT Sloan Management Review*.

Lancefield, D. (2022), "Stop Wasting People's Time with Meetings", *Harvard Business Review*.

N.,N., "De Tegenwoordige Tijd van Bieke Depoorter: "Mijn mailbox is een grote stressfactor in mijn leven", *De Tijd*.

N.,N., "Op zoek naar concentratie: Ontwikkel je eigen interne keukenwekker", *De Tijd*.

Newport, C. (2016), *Deep Work: Rules for Focused Success in a Distracted World*, Grand Central Publishing.

Northrup, K. (2020), "Want to Be More Productive? Try Doing Less.", *Harvard Business Review*.

Pasricha, N. (2018), "Why You Need an Untouchable Day Every Week", *Harvard Business Review*.

Pozen, R.C., and Downey, K. (2019), "What Makes Some People More Productive Than Others", *Harvard Business Review*.

Sawhney, V. (2020), "Why Your Brain Dwells on Unfinished Tasks", *Harvard Business Review*.

Schin, L. (2014), "10 Steps To Conquering Information Overload", *Forbes*.

Schmitt, J.B., Debbelt, C.A., and Schneider, F.M. (2016), "Too much information? Predictors of information overload in the context of online news exposure", *Information, Communication & Society*, Vol. 21, No.8, 1151-1167.

Sinclair, H.C. (2021), "7 ways to avoid becoming a misinformation superspreader", *ideas.ted.com*

Van Bergen, A. (2015), "Theo Compernolle ontmaskert de multitask hype", *Focus Learning Journeys*.

van Noort, W. (2021), "Mobiel diet: minder op je smartphone", *Psychologie Magazine*.

Zorn, J.T., and Marz, L. (2017), "The Busier You Are, the More You Need Quiet Time," *Harvard Business Review*.

CHAPTER 2 – VOYAGER LEADERSHIP

CO-CREATING FOR INNOVATION

Abrahams, R., and Groysberg, B. (2021), "How to Become a Better Listener", *Harvard Business Review*.

Adams, R. (2021), "The Righting Reflex, its dangers, and how we can avoid it", *Aspen Psychology Services*; Miller, W., and Rollnick, S. (2002), *Motivational Interviewing: Preparing People for Change*, New York: The Guilford Press.

Angner, E. (2020), "Epistemic Humility – Knowing Your Limits in a Pandemic", *Behavioral Scientist*.

Ashton, K. (2015), *How to Fly a Horse: The Secret History of Creation, Invention, and Discovery*, Doubleday.

Brugmann, J., and Prahalad, C.K. (2007), "Cocreating Business's New Social Compact", *Harvard Business Review*.

Ćirić, J. (2020), "Nearly 60% of Icelanders Want a New Constitution," *Iceland Review*.

Claman, P. (2017), "How to Spark Creativity When You're in a Rut", *Harvard Business Review*.

Conn, C., and McLean, R. (2020), "Six problem-solving mindsets for very uncertain times", *McKinsey Quarterly*.

Gilbert, E. (2009), "Your elusive creative genius", TEDx.

Gouillart, F. (2011), "Engagement Platforms Must Enable Co-creation", *Harvard Business Review*.

Gouillart, F. (2012), "Co-Creation: The Real Social-Media Revolution", *Harvard Business Review*.

Gouillart, F., and Billings, D. (2013), "Community-Powered Problem Solving", *Harvard Business Review*.

Grant, A. (2021), "How to Argue With Someone Who Has Different Views", *PBS*.

Grant, A. (2021), *Think Again: The Power of Knowing What You Don't Know*. WH Allen.

Gregersen, H. (2018), "Better Brainstorming: Focus on questions, not answers, for breakthrough insights", *Harvard Business Review*.

Grenny, J. (2019), "How to Be Creative on Demand", *Harvard Business Review*.

Harbert, T. (2021), "Digital transformation has evolved. Here's what's new", *MIT Management*.

Hill, L.A., Le Cam, A., Menon, S., and Tedards, E. (2022), "Where Can Digital Transformation Take You? Insights from 1,700 Leaders", *Harvard Business School Working Knowledge*.

Hunsaker, B.T., Knowles, J., Baris, R., and Ettenson, R. (2021), "Great Strategy Consider More Than Customers and Investors", *MIT Sloan Management Review*.

Hunsaker, T.B., and Knowles, J. (2021), "Most Businesses Should Neither 'Pivot' nor 'Double Down'", *MIT Sloan Management Review*.

IKEA (2017), "Press Release: IKEA opens up to co-create the future range with the world".

Ive, J. (2021), "Jony Ive on What He Misses Most About Steve Jobs", *Wall Street Journal News Exclusive*.

LaBarre, P. (2011), "Inventing the Future of Management is Everybody's Job", *Harvard Business Review*.

Ospina, N.S. et al. (2019), "Eliciting the Patient's Agenda – Secondary Analysis of Recorded Clinical Encounters", *Journal of General Internal Medicine*, Vol. 34, pp. 26-40.

Prahalad, C.K., & Ramaswamy, V. (2004). Co-creation experiences: the next practice in value creation. *Journal of Interactive Marketing, Vol.18, Issue 3,* 5-14.

Ramaswamy, V., and Gouillart, F. (2010), "Building the Co-Creative Enterprise", *Harvard Business Review*.

Ramaswamy, V., and Gouillart, F. (2010), "The Power of Co-creation: Build it with them to boost growth, productivity, and profits", *Free Press*.

Relihan, T. (2018), "Here's how 'questions bursts' make better brainstorms", *MIT Management*.

Satell, G. (2018), "Set the Conditions for Anyone on Your Team to Be Creative", *Harvard Business Review*.

Saunders, E.G. (2018), "How to Be Creative When You're Feeling Stressed", *Harvard Business Review*.

Scharmer, O. (2016). Theory U: leading from the future as it emerges. Berrett-Koehler Publishers.

Shambaugh, R. (2019), "How to Unlock Your Team's Creativity", *Harvard Business Review*.

Somers, M. (2021), "How 8 innovative leaders keep track of ideas", *MIT Management*.

Stackpole, B. (2021), "Innovating in existing markets: 3 lessons from LEGO", *MIT Management*.

Stern, S. (2011), "A Co-creation Primer", *Harvard Business Review*.

Uzzi, B., Mukherjee, S., Stringer, M., and Jones, B. (2013), "Atypical Combinations and Scientific Impact", *Science*, Vol. 342, pp. 468-472.

Verhoef, P.C., van Doorn, J., and Beckers, S.F.M. (2013), "Understand the Perils of Co-Creation", *Harvard Business Review*.

Zaki, M., McColl-Kennedy, J.R., and Neely, A. (2021), "Using AI to Track How Customers Feel – In Real Time", *Harvard Business Review*.

Zomorodi, M. (2017), "How boredom can lead to your most brilliant ideas", *TEDx*.

EMBRACING VULNERABILITY AND AUTHENTICITY

Barsade, S., and O'Neill, O.A. (2016), "Managing Your Emotional Culture", *Harvard Business Review*, 2016.

Barsade, S., Coutifaris, C.G.V., and Pillemer, J. (2018), "Emotional contagion in organizational life", *Research in Organizational Behavior*, Vol. 38, pp. 137-151.

Barsade, S., and Klotz, F. (2019), "Employee Emotions Aren't Noise – They're Data", *MITSloan Management Review*.

Barsade, S. (2020), "The Contagion We Can Control", *Harvard Business Review*.

Batista, E. (2015), How Great Coaches Ask, Listen, and Empathize", *Harvard Business Review*.

Bregman, P. (2019), "The Best Leaders Aren't Afraid to Ask for Help", *Harvard Business Review*.

Brown, B. (2019), "Netflix Special, Brené Brown, the call to courage", *Netflix*.

Brown, B. (2021), *Atlas of the Heart*.

Burris, E., and Sinha, R. (2022), "Don't Let "Being New" Stop You From Speaking Up", *Harvard Business Review*.

Corlett, S., Mavin, S., and Beech, N. (2019), "Reconceptualising Vulnerability and its Value for Managerial Identity and Learning", *Management Learning*, Vol 50, No. 5, pp. 556–575.

De Prins, P. (2022), "Straffe HR-uitspraak: Schaamte op de werkvloer", *HR Square*.

Fosslien, L., and Duffy, M.W. (2019), "How Leaders Can Open Up to Their Teams Without Oversharing", *Harvard Business Review*.

Grant, A. (2022), "Sigal Barsade Taught Me That Emotions Have a Place in the Workplace", *Adam Grant Thinks Again*.

Ibarra, H. (2015), "The Authenticity Paradox", *Harvard Business Review*.

Leberecht, T. (2017), "The lost art of losing", *ideas.ted.com*.

Miner, A.G., Glomb, T.M. & Hulin, C. (2005), "Experience sampling mood and its correlates at work", *Journal of Occupational and Organisational Psychology*, Vol. 78, pp. 171-195.

Satama, S., Seeck, H., & Garcia-Lorenzo, L. (2023), "Embracing relational vulnerabilities at the top: a study of managerial identity work amidst the insecurities of the self", *Culture and Organization*, Vol. 30, No. 4, pp. 442–461.

Soenens, B. (2022), "Giving a compliment is harder than it seems", *Dare To Think*.

Timms, M. (2022), "Blame Culture Is Toxic. Here's How to Stop It", *Harvard Business Review*.

Thomas, M. (2021), "How to Get Your Team to Stop Asking You Every Little Question", *Harvard Business Review*.

Wainwright, S, and Williams, C. (2005), "The Embodiment of Vulnerability: A Case Study of the Life and Love of Leoš Janáček and his Opera The Makropulos Case." *Body & Society* Vol, 11, No. 3, pp. 27–41.

Williams, P. (2018), "The Importance of Being Courageously Vulnerable At Work", *Forbes*.

N.,N. (2021), "Interview with Adam Grant," *Happinez Magazine*.

N.,N., (2022), "Een complimentje geven is niet zo evident als het lijkt", *Universiteit Gent Durf Denken*.

BUILDING UPON DIVERSITY AND INCLUSION

Anni, K., Vainik, U., and Mõttus, R. (2024), "Personality Profiles of 263 Occupations", *Journal of Applied Psychology*. Advance online publication.

Anseel, F. (2022), "Het wordt nog spannend op de werkvloer", *De Tijd*.

Auger-Domínguez, D. (2021), "How to make diversity, equity and inclusion a reality at work – not just a mission statement", *ideas.ted.com*.

Bell, G. (2021), "Moving From Safe Space to Brave Space", *Mindful*.

Bersin, J. (2019), "Why Diversity and Inclusion Has Become a Business Priority", *Josh Bersin*.

Bourke, J., and Titus, A. (2019), "Why Inclusive Leaders Are Good For Organizations, and How to Become One", *Harvard Business Review*.

Bregman, R. (2019), *De meeste mensen deugen, een nieuwe geschiedenis van de mens*, De Correspondent.

Bresman, H., and Edmondson, A.C. (2022), "Research: To Excel, Diverse Teams Need Psychological Safety", *Harvard Business Review*.

Brown, K. (2018), "To Retain Employees, Focus on Inclusion – Not Just Diversity", *Harvard Business Review*.

Brownlee, D. (2019), "4 Common Diversity and Inclusion Myths In The Workplace", *Forbes*.

Dimovski, A. (2020), "24 Captivating Workplace Diversity Statistics", *GoRemotely*.

Ellsworth, D., Goldstein, D., and Schaninger, B. (2021), "Inclusion doesn't happen by accident: Measuring inclusion in a way that matters", *McKinsey Organization Blog*.

Ferdman, B.M., and Deane, B.R. (2013), *Diversity at Work: The Practice of Inclusion*, Jossey-Bass.

Fotaki, M. (2021), "Diversity in the workplace must be matched with an atmosphere of genuine inclusion", *The Conversation*.

Garcia-Alonso, J., Krentz, M., Tracey, C., and Tsusaka, M. (2017), "Getting the Most from Your Diversity Dollars", *Boston Consulting Group*.

Georges, L. (2018), "How generational stereotypes hold us back at work", *TEDx*.

Hill. L.A., Le Cam, A., Menon, S., and Tedards, E. (2022), "Digital Transformation: A New Roadmap for Success", *Harvard Business School Working Knowledge*.

Jones, G., Chace, B.C., and Wright, J. (2020), "Cultural diversity drives innovation: empowering teams for success", *International Journal of Innovation Science*, Vol. 12, No. 3, pp. 323-343.

Little, B. (2016), "Who are you, really? The puzzle of personality", *TEDx*.

Meyer, E., "How to lead a successful international team", *Scottish Enterprise*.

Miller, J. (2023). The power of diversity and inclusion: driving innovation and success. *Forbes*, August 16, 2023.

N.,N., (2018), "Trends in High-Performing Global Virtual Teams," *RW3 CultureWizard*.

N.,N., "Diversity & Inclusion Knowledge Maps", *PRISM*.

N.,N., "Increase Your Team's Performance with The Culture Map", *Agents Of Awareness*.

N.,N., (2013), "Waiter, is that inclusion in my soup? A new recipe to improve business performance", *Deloitte*.

N.,N., (2022), "Diversiteit? Met alleen een ander aannamebeleid ben je er nog niet", *MTSprout*.

N.,N., (2022), "Reducing identity threat to promote an inclusive environment", *Stone Soup Consulting*.

Perna, M.C. (2023), "5 Marks Of A Toxic Work Culture – And How You Know It's Time To Leave", *Forbes*.

Romansky, L., Garrod, M., Brown, K., and Deo, K. (2021), "How to Measure Inclusion in the Workplace", *Harvard Business Review*.

Satell, G., and Windschitl, C. (2021), "High-Performing Teams Start with a Culture of Shared Values", *Harvard Business Review*.

Somers, M. (2022), "The former IBM CEO on diversity and the discomfort of good ideas", *MIT Management*.

Sperling-Magro, J., Almond, A., and Fitzgerald, M. (2021), "Building inclusion at scale, one nudge at a time", *McKinsey Blog*.

Sull, D., Sull, C., Cipolli, W., and Brighenti, C. (2022), "Why Every Leaders Needs to Worry About Toxic Culture", *MIT Sloan Management Review*.

Taras, V., Baack, D., Caprar, D., Jiménez, A., and Froese, F. (2021), "Research: How Cultural Differences Can Impact Global Teams", *Harvard Business Review*.

Vangronsvelt, K. (2022), "Wat zegt de wetenschap over diversiteit", *HRmagazine*.

Wheeless, N. (2021), "4 Lessons for Building Diverse Teams", *Harvard Business Review*.

Woods, A. (2021), "The Great Resignation Doesn't Have to Threaten Your DE&I Efforts", *Harvard Business Review*.

Zheng, W., Kim, J., Kark, R., and Mascolo, L. (2023), "What Makes an Inclusive Leader?", *Harvard Business Review*.

CHAPTER 3 – VISIONARY LEADERSHIP

CRAFTING ORGANISATIONAL AND INDIVIDUAL PURPOSE

Achor, S., Reece, A., Rosen Kellerman, G., and Robichaux, A. (2018), "9 out of 10 People Are Willing to Earn Less Money to Do More-Meaningful Work", *Harvard Business Review*.

Alma, H. (2020), *Het verlangen naar zin – de zoektocht naar resonantie in de wereld*, ten have.

Bailey, C., and Madden, A. (2016), "What Makes Work Meaningful – Or Meaningless", *MIT Sloan Management Review*.

Barrick, M.R., Mount, M.K., and Li, N. (2013), "The Theory of Purposeful Work Behavior: The Role of Personality, Higher Order Goals, and Job Characteristics", *The Academy of Management Review*, Vol. 38, No. 1, pp. 132-153.

Blount, S., and Leinwand, P. (2019), "Why Are We Here?", *Harvard Business Review*.

Bulgarella, C. (2018), "Purpose-Driven Companies Evolve Faster Than Others", *Forbes*.

Bolino, M.C., and Klotz, A.C. (2017), "How to Motivate Employees to Go Beyond Their Jobs", *Harvard Business Review*.

Bromley, T., Lauricella, T., and Schaninger, B. (2021), "Making work meaningful from the C-suite to the frontline", *McKinsey Organization Blog*.

Bromley, T., Lauricella, T., and Schaninger, B. (2021), "Running on all five sources: Actions leaders can take to create more meaningful work", *McKinsey Organization Blog*.

Cartwright, S., and Holmes, N. (2006), "The meaning of work: The challenge of regaining employee engagement and reducing cynicism", *Human Resource Management Review*, Vol. 16, No. 2, pp. 199-208.

Carucci, R., Clark, D., and Chamorro-Premuzic, T. (2022), "The Upside of Feeling Uncertain About Your Career", *Harvard Business Review*.

Carver, C., "How to Make a Love List", *bemorewithless*.

Clark, R.E., and Saxberg, B. (2019), "4 Reasons Good Employees Lose Their Motivation", *Harvard Business Review*.

Croneberger, J. (2021), "Vision, Mission And Purpose: The Difference", *Forbes*.

De Smet, A., Dowling, B., Mugayar-Baldocchi, M., and Schaninger, B. (2021), "'Great Attrition' or 'Great Attraction'? The choice is yours", *McKinsey*.

De Smet, A., Dowling, B., Mugayar-Baldocchi, M., and Spratt, J. (2022), "It's not about the office, it's about belonging", *McKinsey Organization Blog*.

De Smet, A., Dowling, B., Mugayar-Baldocchi, M., and Schaninger, B. (2022), "Gone for now, or gone for good? How to play the new talent game and win back workers", *McKinsey Quarterly*.

Dhingra, N., Samo, A., Schaninger, B., and Schrimper, M. (2021), "Help your employees find purpose – or watch them leave", *McKinsey*.

Dhingra, N., and Schaninger, B. (2021), "The search purpose at work, how to unleash the power of purpose at work and in life", *McKinsey*.

Dewettinck, K., and Defever, E. (2020), "The Case for Purpose", *Vlerick Business School*.

Eyrich, N.W., Quinn, R.E., and Fessel, D.P. (2019), "How One Person Can Change the Conscience of an Organization", *Harvard Business Review*.

Furini, M., Gaggi, O., Mirri, S., Montangero, M., Pelle, E., Poggi, F., and Prandi, C. (2022), "Digital Twins and Artificial Intelligence as Pillars of Personalised Learning Models", *Communications of the ACM*.

Garton, E., and Mankins, M. (2015), "Engaging Your Employees Is Good, but Don't Stop There", *Harvard Business Review*.

Gast, A., Probst, N., and Simpson, B. (2020), "Purpose, not platitudes: A personal challenge for top executives", *McKinsey Quarterly*.

Grant, A. (2021), "Post-Covid Happiness Comes in Groups", *The New York Times*.

Happiness@Work Study (2022), "Werkplezier is het meest onderschatte wapen in de strijd om talent", *De Tijd*.

Hawke, E. (2020), "Give yourself permission to be creative", *TEDx*.

Hunsaker, T., and Knowles, J. (2020), "The Essence of Strategy Is Now How to Change", *MIT Sloan Management Review*.

Johnson, W. (2018), "You Have to Stop Canceling and Rescheduling Things. Really.", *Harvard Business Review*.

Koe, D. (2021), "How to create a life of meaning, money, and impact (as fast as humanly possible)", *Twitter*.

Lai, L. (2017), "Motivating Employees Is Not About Carrots or Sticks", *Harvard Business Review*.

Malnight, T.W., Buche, I., and Dhanaraj, C. (2019), "Put Purpose at the Core of Your Strategy", *Harvard Business Review*.

N.,N., "Job Security and Meaningful Work in High Demand for Today's Workforce", *Net Impact*.

N.,N., "Intangible Asset Market Value Study", *Ocean Tomo*.

N.,N., (2024), "What is Digital Twin and How can it be used in Education?", *TheCodeWork*.

N.,N., "The Ultimate Wheel of Life Interactive Assessment", *WheelOfLife*.

Onderick-Harvey, E. (2018), "5 Behaviors of Leaders Who Embrace Change", *Harvard Business Review*.

Partena Professional, "Met startgeld alleen wint niemand de oorlog om talent", *De Tijd*.

Pfau, B. N. (2015), "How an Accounting Firm Convinced Its Employees They Could Change the World", *Harvard Business Review*.

PWC (2016), "Putting Purpose to Work: A study of purpose in the workplace".

Quataert, S., and Buyens, D. (2020), "Careers are not dead – we're just traveling different roads", *Vlerick Business School*.

Ritter, D. and Chim, L. (2019), "Why Agile Works", *Boston Consulting Group*.

Schwartz, T., and Porath, C. (2014), "Why You Hate Work", *The New York Times*.

Smith, I.H., and Kouchaki, M. (2023), "Narrow the Gap Between Company and Employee Purpose", *Harvard Business Review*.

Tiggelaar, B. (2018), *De ladder, Waarom veranderen zo moeilijk is én welke 3 stappen wel werken*, Tyler Roland Press.

Turner, C. (2023), "Unleashing the potential of Digital Twins in Education – A Revolution in Learning", *LinkedIn*.

Viaene, S., & Sen, K. (2024). Leading digital transformation for organizational agility: a substantive practices-based framework. *Working paper 20241212*. Vlerick Business School.

Wade, C. (2020), "Don't have a single purpose or passion? That's ok", *ideas.ted.com*.

Zmuda, C. (2024), "Bridging the Purpose Gap: A Leadership Imperative", *LinkedIn Pulse*.

HARNESSING THE POWER OF STORYTELLING

Anderson, C. (2013), "How to Give a Killer Presentation", *Harvard Business Review*.

Ashkenas, R., and Manville, B. (2019), "You Don't Have to Be CEO to Be a Visionary Leader", *Harvard Business Review*.

Bonigala, M., "Symbol Based Logos That Stand For Something", *SpellBrand*.

Britton, C. (2021), "People Synchronize Heart Rates While Listening Attentively to Stories", *Neuroscience News*.

Duarte, N. (2018), "How to Identify and Tell Your Most Powerful Stories", *Harvard Business Review*.

Duarte, N., "Five motivating story plots every leaders needs to know", *Duarte*.

Eber, F. (2020), "How your brain responds to stories – and why they're crucial for leaders", *TEDx*.

Fell, A. (2021), "Hippocampus Is the Brain's Storyteller", *Neuroscience News*.

Gershman, S. (2019), "To Overcome Your Fear of Public Speaking, Stop Thinking About Yourself", *Harvard Business Review*.

Goman, C.K., (2013), "What Leaders Don't Know About The Rumor Mill", *Forbes*.

Johnson, C., "What is story?", *Pressbooks*.

Kanitz, R., Gonzalez, K., Briker, R., and Straatmann, T. (2023), "Augmenting Organizational Change and Strategy Activities: Leveraging Generative Artificial Intelligence", *The Journal of Applied Behavioral Science*, Vol. 59, No. 3, pp. 345-363.

Knight, R. (2017), "How to Improve Your Sales Skills, Even If You're Not a Salesperson", *Harvard Business Review*.

N.,N., (2019), "Storytelling, How to reset an organisation's narrative to inspire change", *TheStorytellers*.

N.,N., "The Art of Rekindling Your Work Motivation", *Calm*.

Pesechkian, N. (1990), *De Koopman en De Papegaai*, Ad Donker

Sanchez, P., "The Right Story at the Right Time: Motivate Your Team when They're In a Slump", *Duarte*.

Sinek, S. (2009), *Start With Why*.

EMBRACING RISK WITH CONFIDENCE

Brassey, J., De Smet, A., Kothari, A., Lavoie, J., Mugayar-Baldocchi, M., and Zolley, S. (2021), "Future proof: Solving the 'adaptability paradox' for the long term", *McKinsey*.

Cespedes, F.V., and Hoyne, N. (2022), "How Managers Can Build a Culture of Experimentation", *Harvard Business Review*.

Furr, N., Nel, K., and Ramsøy, T.Z. (2018), "If Your Innovation Effort Isn't Working, Look at Who's on the Team", *Harvard Business Review*.

Galton, F. (1907), "The Ballot-Box", *Nature*, Vol 75, pp. 509-510.

Galton, F. (1907), "Vox Populi", *Nature*, Vol. 75, pp. 450-451.

García-Granero, A., Llopis, Óscar, Fernández-Mesa, A., and Alegre, J. (2015), "Unraveling the link between managerial risk-taking and innovation: The mediating role of a risk-taking climate", *Journal of Business Research*, Vol. 68, No. 5, pp. 1094-1104.

Grant, A. (2017), *Originals: How Non-Conformists Move the World*, Penguin Books.

Grant, H. (2013), "The Hidden Danger of Being Risk-Averse", *Harvard Business Review*.

Ibarra, H. (2004), *Working Identity: Unconventional Strategies for Reinventing Your Career*, Harvard Business School Press.

Klein, G. (2008), "Performing a Project Premortem", *Harvard Business Review*.

Kreamer, A. (2015), "Not Taking Risks Is the Riskiest Career Move of All", *Harvard Business Review*.

Levitin, D. (2015), "How to stay calm when you know you'll be stressed", *TEDx*.

Lovallo, D., Koller, T., Uhlaner, R., and Kahneman, D. (2020), "Your Company Is Too Risk-Averse", *Harvard Business Review*.

N.,N., "What is a Kaospilot?", *Kaospilot*.

Pallotta, D. (2011), "Taking a Risk Is Not Immoral", *Harvard Business Review*.

Peeters, C. (2019), "The three horizons of growth, video transcript for Take The Lead 2019", *Vlerick Business School*.

Rabin, M., and Bazerman, M. (2019), "Fretting about Modest Risks is a Mistake", *California Management Review*, Vol. 61, No. 3, pp. 34-48.

Reich, T., Fulmer, A.G., and Dhar, R. (2022), "Nervous About Taking a Risk? Write a List of Pros and Cons", *Harvard Business Review*.

Rosen, R.J. (2016), "The Art of Recognizing Good Ideas", *The Atlantic*.

Schumpeter, J.A. (1994 [1942]), *Capitalism, Socialism, and Democracy*, Routledge.

Somers, M. (2022), "The former IBM CEO on diversity and the discomfort of good ideas", *MIT Management*.

Stackpole, B. (2021), "Innovating in existing markets: 3 lessons from LEGO", *MIT Management*.

Surowiecki, J. (2004), *The Wisdom of Crowds: Why the Many are Smarter Than the Few and How Collective Wisdom Shapes Business, Economies, Societies, and Nations*, Doubleday.

DEVELOPING PARTNERSHIPS

Baer, M.D., Dhensa-Kahlon, R.K., Colquitt, J.A., Rodell, J.B., Outlaw, R., and Long, D.M. (2014), "Uneasy Lies the Head that Bears the Trust: The Effects of Feeling

Trusted on Emotional Exhaustion", *Academy of Management Journal*, Vol. 58, No. 6, pp. 1637-1657.

Baer, M.D., Frank, E.L., Matta, F.K., Luciano, M.M., and Wellman, N. (2021), "Undertrusted, Overtrusted, or Just Right? The Fairness of (In)Congruence between Trust Wanted and Trust Received", *Academy of Management Journal*, Vol. 64, No. 1, pp. 180-206.

Basque, A. (2023), "Tips For A Successful Media Partnerships & Collaboration: Avoiding Common Pitfalls", *K6*.

Brown, S., Henz, T., Sibanda, T., and Wang, M. (2021), "Collaborations between corporates and start-ups", *McKinsey*.

Carnevale, J.B. (2022), "If You Think Trusting Your Employees More is the Answer, You Might Want to Think Again", *Entrepreneur Europe*.

Chiappa, C. (2023), "Media company Axel Springer and OpenAI launch global partnership", *Politico*.

Cross, R., Rebele, R., and Grant, A. (2016), "Collaborative Overload", *Harvard Business Review*.

Hill, L.A., Le Cam, A., Menon, S., and Tedards, E. (2022), "Digital Transformation: A New Roadmap for Success", *Harvard Business School Working Knowledge*.

Mayer, R. C., Davis, J.H., and Schoorman, F.D. (1995), "An Integrative Model of Organizational Trust." *The Academy of Management Review* Vol. 20, no. 3, pp. 709–734.

Nye, J.S. Jr. (2005), *Soft Power: The Means to Success in World Politics*, Public Affairs New York.

Onderick-Harvey, E. (2018), "5 Behaviors of Leaders Who Embrace Change", *Harvard Business Review*.

OpenAI (2024), "Global news partnerships: Le Monde and Prisa Media".

PWC (2016), "19th Annual Global CEO Survey – Redefining business success in a changing world", *PWC*.

Sahay, B.S. (2003), "Understanding trust in supply chain relationships", *Industrial Management & Data Systems*, Vol. 103, No. 8, pp. 553-563.

Sloan, P., and Oliver, D. (2013), "Building Trust in Multi-Stakeholder Partnerships: Critical Emotional Incidents and Practices of Engagement", *Organisation Studies*, pp. 1-34.

Sucher, S.J., and Gupta, S. (2019), "The Trust Crisis", *Harvard Business Review*.

Tejpal, G., Garg, R.K. and Sachdeva, A. (2013), "Trust among supply chain partners: a review", *Measuring Business Excellence*, Vol. 17, No. 1, pp. 51-71.

The Economist Intelligence Unit (2008), "The role of trust in business collaboration, an EIU briefing paper sponsored by Cisco Systems", pp. 1-28.

Wu, M-Y., Weng, Y-C., and Huang, I-C. (2012), "A study of supply chain partnerships based on the commitment-trust theory", *Asia Pacific Journal of Marketing and Logistics*, Vol. 24, No. 2, pp. 690-707.

Yoffie, D.B., and Kwak, M. (2006), "With Friends Like These: The Art of Managing Complementors", *Harvard Business Review*.

Zak, P.J. (2017), "The Neuroscience of Trust", *Harvard Business Review*.

CHAPTER 4 – VESTED LEADERSHIP

BUILDING A CHANGE COALITION

Anderson, L.A., and Anderson, D. (2003), "How to Build a Critical Mass of Support to Accelerate Your Change", *Being First*.

Dans, E. (2021), "The Pandemic Has Changed Business Structures: There's No Going Back", *Forbes*.

Fowler, F. (2015), "Dominant Coalition Perceptions in Health-Oriented, Non Profit Public Relations". *Thesis*.

Haelle, T. (2020), "Your 'Surge Capacity' Is Depleted – It's Why You Feel Awful", *Elemental*.

Ho, S. (2022), "Pandemic anniversary: COVID-19 lessons after year two", *CTV News*.

Kübler-Ross, E. (1969), *Death and Dying*, MacMillan.

Lucchini, L., Centellegher, S., Pappalardo, L., Gallotti, R., Privitera, F., Lepri, B., and De Nadai, M. (2021), "Living in a pandemic, changes in mobility routines, social activity and adherence to COVID-19 protective measures", *Scientific Reports*, Vol. 11, No. 24452.

Malik, N.K., Khalil, G.I., Al Amoodi, A.Y., Bakhsh, M.A.S., and Sahwan, M.R. (2021), "Combatting Resistance to Change During the COVID19 Pandemic with Design Thinking Approach: Making a Case for the Public Sector", *2021 International Conference on Innovation and Intelligence for Informatics, Computing, and Technologies*.

Maxik, K., Kimble, C., and Coustasse, A. (2021), "Change Management Is a Consideration Beyond the Pandemic", *Health-System Edition*, Vol. 10, No. 3.

N.N., (2024), "How do you build a change coalition?", *LinkedIn*

N.,N., (2020), "Beyond COVID-19: From Resistance to Change to a Culture of Proactively Seeking Change within Franchise Networks", *Fasken*.

N.,N., "How to Help Families and Staff Build Resilience During the COVID-19 Outbreak", *Center on the Developing Child Harvard University*.

N.,N., (2021), "How The Recruitment Industry Has Changed During the Covid Pandemic", *Digital Information World*.

Pritchard, R.S., Davis, D., and Filak, V.F. (2009), "The impact of the dominant coalition on health care public relations practitioners", *That Matters to the Practice*, pp. 571.

Stouten, J., Rousseau, D.M., and De Cremer, D. (2018), "Successful Organizational Change: Integrating the Management Practice and Scholarly Literatures", *The Academy of Management Annals*, Vol. 12, No. 2, pp. 1-93.

Uohara, M.Y., Ward, W.H., Goel, N., Atchley, K., and Esnaola, N.F. (2019), "Managing Change", *Springer,* pp. 197-205.

Viaene, S., & Sen, K. (2024). Leading digital transformation for organizational agility: a substantive practices-based framework. *Working paper* 20241212. Vlerick Business School.

COPING WITH CHANGE FATIGUE

Antliff, S. (2021), "Workplace overwhelm: how to protect your team from change fatigue", *Atlassian.*

Baker, M. (2020), "How to Reduce the Risk of Employee Change Fatigue", *Gartner.*

Boroditsky, L. (2017), "How language shapes the way we think", *TEDx.*

Cohen, W.M., and Levinthal, D.A. (1990), "Absorptive Capacity: A New Perspective on Learning and Innovation", *Administrative Science Quarterly*, Vol. 35, No. 1, pp. 128-152.

Haelle, T. (2020), "Your 'Surge Capacity' Is Depleted – It's Why You Feel Awful", *Elemental.*

Heath, C., and Heath, D. (2010), *Switch: How to Change Things When Change Is Hard*, Crown Business.

Hobraft, P. (2018), "How Absorptive Capacity, Knowledge, and Idea Management Builds Innovation Capacity", *Hype Innovation Blog.*

Innis, J., and Berta, W. (2016), "Routines for change: how managers can use absorptive capacity to adopt and implement evidence-based practice", *Journal of Nursing Management*, Vol. 24, No. 6, pp. 718-724.

N.,N., "Ditch Change Fatigue and Embrace Continual Evolution", *Center for Creative Leadership.*

N.,N., "Change Comes at a Cumulative Cost", *Center for Creative Leadership.*

N.,N., (2016), "6 Blind Men And The Elephant", *Journey To The Center Of You.*

Smith, C. (2021), "4 Ways to Solve Change Fatigue", *The Change Management Blog.*

BREAKING DOWN SILOS

Bernstein, E.S., and Turban, S. (2018), "The impact of the 'open' workspace on human collaboration", *Philosophical Transactions of the Royal Society B: Biological Sciences*, Vol. 373, No. 1753.

Bryan, B.T., Andrews, G., Thompson, K.N., Qualter, P., Matthews, T., and Arseneault, L. (2023), "Loneliness in the workplace: a mixed-method systematic review and meta-analysis", *Occupational Medicine*, Vol. 73, No. 9, pp. 557-567.

de Waal, A., Weaver, M., Day, T., and van der Heijden, B. (2019), "Silo-Busting: Overcoming the Greatest Threat to Organizational Performance", *Sustainability*, Vol. 11, No. 23, 6860.

De Smet, A., Dowling, B., Mugayar-Baldocchi, M., and Spratt, J. (2022), "It's not about the office, it's about belonging", *McKinsey Organization Blog*

Edmondson, A.C., Jan, S., and Casciaro, T. (2019), "Cross-Silo Leadership", *Harvard Business Review*.

Eisenberger, N., Lieberman, M.D., and Williams. K.D. (2003), "Does rejection hurt? An FMRI study of social exclusion", *Science*, Vol. 302, No. 5643, pp. 290-292.

Gleeson, B., "5 Ways to Destroy the Pesky Silos in Your Organization", *Inc*.

Hadley, C.N. (2021), "Employees Are Lonelier Than Ever. Here's How Employers Can Help", *Harvard Business Review*.

Hickman, A. (2019), "How to Manage the Loneliness and Isolation of Remote", *Gallup*.

Johansson, F. (2017), *The Medici Effect: What Elephants and Epidemics Can Teach Us About Innovation*, Harvard Business Review Press.

Lencioni, P. (2006), *Silos, Politics, and Turf Wars*, Jossey-Bass.

Little, B. (2016), "Who are you, really? The puzzle of personality", *TEDx*.

McMurray, C. (2022), "Loneliness Has a Different Neural Basis Than Social Anxiety", *Neuroscience News*.

Mena, Y.S. (2018), "Summary The Loneliness of The Interconnected", *Scribd*.

Moens, E., Baert, S., Verhofstadt, E., and Van Ootegem, L. (2021), "Does loneliness lurk in temp work? Exploring the associations between temporary employment, loneliness at work and job satisfaction", *IZA Discussion Paper*, No. 12865.

N.,N., "Working from home and lonely", *Conquering Loneliness in NZ*.

N.,N., "6 Strategies for Breaking Down Silos in Your Organization", *Eagles Flight*.

N.N., (2022), "Loneliness affect mental health of millions, yet many feel ashamed to talk about it", *Mental Health Foundation*.

Pedersen, C.L. (2021), "Gain Competitive Advantage by Transcending the Front-Line Paradox", *MIT Sloan Management Review*.

Piore, A. (2020), "Why do you feel lonely? Neuroscience is starting to find answers", *MIT Technology Review*.

PWC (2015), "Reimagining Operations".

Seife, C., "The Loneliness of the Interconnected", *Archive.org*.

Seppälä, E., and King, M. (2017), "Burnout at Work Isn't Just About Exhaustion. It's Also About Loneliness", *Harvard Business Review*.

Statista (2024), "Feeling of loneliness among adults 2021, by country".

Sull, D., Sull, C., Cipolli, W., and Brighenti, C. (2022), "Why Every Leader Needs to Worry About Toxic Culture", *MIT Sloan Management Review*.

Timmer, A. (2019), "Loneliness in the workplace: Scaling the problem", *The Great Indoors*.

The Dalai Lama, and Hougard, R. (2019), "The Dalai Lama on Why Leaders Should Be Mindful, Selfless, and Compassionate", *Harvard Business Review*.

Varella, S. (2021), "Feeling of loneliness among adults 2021, by country", *Statista*.

Wilson, B. (2016), "Critical Reading of The Loneliness of the Interconnected by Charles Seife", *VT English*.

GIVING AND RECEIVING FEEDBACK

Asplund, J., and Blacksmith, N. (2011), "Strengthening Your Company's Performance", *Gallup Business Journal*.

Batista, E. (2015), How Great Coaches Ask, Listen, and Empathize", *Harvard Business Review*.

Bregman, P., and Jacobson, H. (2021), "Feedback Isn't Enough to Help Your Employees Grow", *Harvard Business Review*.

Bregman, P., and Jacobson, H. (2021), "You Can Change Other People, The Four Steps to Help Your Colleagues, Employees – Even Family – Up Their Game", *Wiley*.

Brink, K.E., and Costigan, R.D. (2015), "Oral Communication Skills: Are the Priorities of the Workplace and AACSB-Accredited Business Programs Aligned?", *Academy of Management Learning & Education*, Vol. 14, No. 2, pp. 205-221.

Buckingham, M., and Goodall, A. (2019), "The Feedback Fallacy", *Harvard Business Review*

De Prins, P. (2022), "Bedek niet alles met de mantel der liefde", *De Standaard*.

De Stobbeleir, K. (2019), "CEO Disease: Diagnosis, Symptoms and a Few Treatments", *Vlerick Business School Insights*.

Edinger, S. (2021), "Encourage Your Employees to Give You Critical Feedback", *Harvard Business Review*.

Edmondson, E.C., Jang, S., and Casciaro, T. (2019), "Cross-Silo Leadership", *Harvard Business Review*.

Eskreis-Winkler, L., Fischbach, A., and Duckworth, A.L. (2018), "Dear Abby: Should I Give Advice or Receive It?", *Psychological Science*, Vol. 29, No. 11, pp. 1797-1806.

Fischer-Lokou, J., Lamy, L., Guéguen, N., and Dubarry, A. (2016), "Effects of Active Listening, Reformulation, and Imitation on Mediator Success: Preliminary Results", *Psychol. Rep.*, Vol. 118, No. 3, pp. 994-1010.

Frey, L., "Diplomatic immunity, international law", *Britannica*.

Galef, J. (2010), "3 healthier ways to cope with criticism, disappointment and defeat", *ideas.ted.com*.

Gallo, A. (2016), "How to Disagree with Someone More Powerful than You", *Harvard Business Review*.

Goldstein, J. (2019), "The Feedback Triggers: Why Some People Respond Negatively to Feedback", *The Leadership Laboratory*.

Grant, A. (2021), "The lost art of listening", *ideas.ted.com*.

Grant, A. (2022), "Sigal Barsade Taught Me That Emotions Have a Place in the Workplace", *Adam Grant Thinks Again*.

Grenny, J., and Maxfield, B. (2019), "How Leaders Can Ask for the Feedback No One Wants to Give Them", *Harvard Business Review*.

Hamilton, D.M. (2015), "Calming Your Brain During Conflict", *Harvard Business Review*.

Hattie, J., and Timperley, H. (2007), "The Power of Feedback", *Review of Educational Research*, Vol. 77, No. 1, pp. 81-112.

Heen, S., and Stone, D. (2014), "Find the Coaching in Criticism", *Harvard Business Review*.

Hogan, M. (2016), "5 Employee Feedback Stats That You Need to See", *LinkedIn Talent Blog*.

Imber, A. (2020), "Stop Asking for Feedback", *Harvard Business Review*.

Itzachkov, G., and Kluger, A.N. (2017), "Can holding a stick improve listening at work? The effect of Listening Circles on employees' emotions and cognitions", *European Journal of Work and Organizational Psychology*, Vol. 26, No. 5, pp. 663-676.

Lam, C.F., DeRue, D.S., Karam, E.P., Hollenbeck, J.R., (2011), "The impact of feedback frequency on learning and task performance: Challenge the "more is better" assumption", *Organizational Behavior and Human Decision Processes*, Vol. 116, No. 2, pp. 217-228.

Liu, C. (2021), "Christine vs. Work: How to Give Feedback – Especially When You're Dreading it", *Harvard Business Review*.

MacLaren, N.G., et al. (2020), "Testing the babble hypothesis: Speaking time predicts leader emergence in small groups", *The Leadership Quarterly*, Vol. 31, No. 5.

Melwani, S., and Barsade, S. G. (2011), "Held in contempt: The psychological, interpersonal, and performance consequences of contempt in a work context", *Journal of Personality and Social Psychology*, Vol. 101, No. 3, pp. 503-520.

Mertenss, S., Schollaert, E., and Anseel, F. (2021), "How much feedback do employees need? A field study of absolute feedback frequency reports and performance", *International Journal of Selection and Assessment*, Vol. 29, No. 3-4, pp. 326-335.

Milkman, K. (2021), "One simple way to build someone's confidence: Ask for their advice", *ideas.ted.com*.

Miller, W., and Rollnick, S. (2002), *Motivational Interviewing: Preparing People for Change*, New York: The Guilford Press.

Nunez, K., and Legg, T.J. (2020), "Fight, Flight, Freeze, What This Response Means", *Healthline*.

Porath, C. (2022), "Nine Tips for Giving Better Feedback at Work", *Greater Good Magazine*.

Porter, J. (2019), "How Leaders Can Get Honest, Productive Feedback", *Harvard Business Review*.

N.,N., (2021), "Katleen De Stobbeleir: "De meeste mensen hebben de neiging zichzelf te gaan overschatten", *Radio 1 Select: De wereld van Sofie*.

So, Y., Lee, K., and Oah, S. (2013), "Relative Effects of Daily Feedback and Weekly Feedback on Customer Service Behavior at a Gas Station", *Journal of Organizational Behavior Management*, Vol. 33, No. 2, 137-151.

Spataro, S.E., and Bloch, J. (2018), "'Can You Repeat That?' Teaching Active Listening in Management Education", *Journal of Management Education*, Vol. 42, No. 2, pp. 168-198.

Svenson, O. (1981), "Are we all less risky and more skillful than our fellow drivers?", *Acta Psychologica*, Vol. 47, No. 2, pp. 143-148.

Valcour, M. (2015), "How to Give Tough Feedback That Helps People Grow", *Harvard Business Review*.

Zenger, J., and Folkman, J. (2016), "What Great Listeners Actually Do", *Harvard Business Review*.

CHAPTER 5 – THE COMBINED POWER OF DIGITAL LEADERS

AlNuaimi, B.K., Singh, S.K., Ren, S., Budhwar, P., and Vorobyev, D. (2022), "Mastering digital transformation: The nexus between leadership, agility, and digital strategy." *Journal of Business Research*, Vol. 145, pp. 636-648.

Balle, M. (1996), *Managing With Systems Thinking: Making Dynamics Work for You in Business Decision-making*, McGraw-Hill Book Co. Ltd.

Burkus, D., (2011), "Building the Strong Organization: Exploring the Role of Organizational Design in Strength-Based Leadership", *Journal of Strategic Leadership*, Vol. 3, No. 1, pp. 54-66.

Cabrera, D., and Cabrera, L. (2020), "Systems Thinking in Seven (7) Images", *Cabrera Research Club*.

Cabrera, D., and Cabrera, L. (2020), "The Four Simple Rules of Systems Thinking", *Cabrera Research Club*.

Derler, A. (2019), "Growth Mindset Culture", *Neuroleadership Institute New York*.

Dweck, C.S. (2008), "Brainology", *National Association of Independent Schools*.

Dweck, C.S. (2016), "What Having a "Growth Mindset" Actually Means", *Harvard Business Review*.

Dweck, C.S. (2017), *Mindset, changing the way you think to fulfil your potential*, Robinson.

Dweck, C.S., and Yeager, D.S. (2018), "Mindsets Change the Imagined and Actual Future", in Oettingen, G., Sevincer, A.T., and Gollwitzer, P.M (eds.), *The Psychology of Thinking about the Future*.

Gonzalez, K., Kanitz, R., and Briker, R. (2024), "'AI Can't Steal My Soul': In the Age of AI, the Human Touch is Paramount for the Craft of Managing Change", *The Journal of Applied Behavioral Science*, Vol. 60, No. 4, pp. 589-602

Holey-Weber, J. (2016), "Growth Mindset Interventions: Lessons from Across Domains", Master's thesis.

Ly, B. (2023), "The Interplay of Digital Transformation Leadership, Organizational Agility, and Digital Transformation", *Journal of the Knowledge Economy*.

Monat, J., Amissah, M., and Gannon, T. (2020), "Practical Applications of Systems Thinking to Business", *Systems*, Vol. 8, No. 2, pp. 14.

Monat, J.P., and Gannon, T.F. (2015), "What is Systems Thinking? A Review of Selected Literature Plus Recommendations", *American Journal of Systems Science*, Vol. 4, No. 1, pp.11–26.

Mrazek, A.J., et al., (2018), "Expanding minds: Growth mindsets of self-regulation and the influences on effort and perseverance", *Journal of Experimental Social Psychology*, Vol. 79, pp. 164-180.

Schwartz, T. (2018), "Create a Growth Culture, Not a Performance-Obsessed One", *Harvard Business Review*.

Schwartz, T. (2018), "Leaders Focus Too Much on Changing Policies, and Not Enough on Changing Minds", *Harvard Business Review*.

Sisk, V.F., et al. (2018), "To what extent and under which circumstances are growth mindsets important to academic achievements? Two meta-analyses", *Psychological Science*, Vol. 29, No. 4, pp. 549-574.

Viaene, S. (2020), *Digital Transformation Know-How*, Acco.

Weber, E., Krehl, E-H., Buettgen, M., and Schweikert, K. (2019), "The Digital Leadership Framework: Insights into New Leadership Roles Facing Digital Transformation", *Academy of Management Proceedings*.

Yeager, D.S., and Dweck, C.S. (2020), "What can be learned from growth mindset controversies?", *American Psychological Association*, Vol. 75, No. 9, pp. 1269-1284.

NOTES

1   Kurzweil, R. (2010), "10 Questions for Ray Kurzweil", Time.
2   Dries, N., Luyckx, J., and Rogiers, P. (2024), "What 570 Experts Predict the Future of Work Will Look Like", Harvard Business Review.
3   Hemerling, J. (2016), "5 ways to lead in an era of constant change", TEDx.
4   Gates, L.A. (2018), "Agile Strategy: Short-Cycle Strategy Development and Execution", SEI Blog.
5   N.,N., "Did Peter Drucker Say That?", Drucker Institute.
6   Coleman, J. (2022), "So, what is organizational agility? 2022 UPDATE", Scrum.
7   Bloomberg, J. (2022, 14 April). Digitization, Digitalization, And Digital Transformation: Confuse Them At Your Peril. Forbes.
8   Viaene, S (2024). Leading successful digital transformations. Ivey Business Journal, Sept-Oct.
9   Gartner (2024), "Digital Transformation: How to Scope and Execute Strategy".
10 Apotheker, J., Duranton, S., Lukic, V., de Bellefonds, N., Iyer, S., Bouffault, O., and de Laubier, R. (2024), "From Potential to Profit with GenAI", Boston Consulting Group.
11 Marckstadt, F., Laamanen, T., and Dimke, M. (2020), "Transformation Champions, Turning Opposites into Complements", Deloitte.
12 Garcia, J. (2022), "Common pitfalls in transformations: A conversation with Jon Garcia", McKinsey & Company.
13 Grebe, M., Hunke, N., Kataeva, N., Lenhard, E., Backx, J., Rehberg, B., and Gardelli, V. (2024), "Why Companies Get Agile Right – and Wrong", Boston Consulting Group.
14 Agasisti, T. (2022), "Corporate training: digital transformation tops the list", EFMD Global.
15 Clark, T.R. (2022), "Agile Doesn't Work Without Psychological Safety", Harvard Business Review.
16 Schwartz, T. (2018), "Leaders Focus Too Much on Changing Policies, and Not Enough on Changing Minds", Harvard Business Review.
17 Westerman, G. (2022), "The Questions Leaders Should Ask in the New Era of Digital Transformation", MIT Sloan Management Review.

18 Lehnis, S. (2021), "Human-centric digital transformation", Open Access Government.

19 Bonnet, D., and Westerman, G. (2020), "The New Elements of Digital Transformation", MIT Sloan.

20 Barsade, S. (2002), "The Ripple Effect: Emotional Contagion and Its Influence on Group Behavior", Administrative Science Quarterly, Vol. 47, No. 4, pp. 644-675.

21 Hemerling, J., Kilmann, J., and Matthews, D. (2018), "The Head, Heart, and Hands of Transformation", Boston Consulting Group.

22 Clark, T.R. (2022), "Agile Doesn't Work Without Psychological Safety", Harvard Business Review.

23 Ready, D.A., Cohen, C., Kiron, D., and Pring, B. (2020), "The New Leadership Playbook for the Digital Age: Reimagining What It Takes to Lead", MITSloan Management Review.

24 Hill, L.A., Le Cam, A., Menon, S., and Tedards, E. (2022), "Curiosity, Not Coding: 6 Skills Leaders Need in the Digital Age", Harvard Business School.

25 Hill, L.A., Le Cam, A., Menon, S., and Tedards, E. (2022), "Curiosity, Not Coding: 6 Skills Leaders Need in the Digital Age", Harvard Business School.

26 Ready, D.A., Cohen, C., Kiron, D., and Pring, B. (2020), "The New Leadership Playbook for the Digital Age, Reimagining What IT Takes to Lead", MITSloan Management Review

27 Somers, M. (2021), "The 3 leadership types in a nimble organization", MIT Management.

28 Viaene, S, & Sen, K. (2024). Leading digital transformation for organizational agility: a substantive practice-based framework. Working paper 20241212. Vlerick Business School.

29 Yin, Y., Mueller, J., and Wakslak, C. (2024), "Understanding How People React to Change: A Domain of Uncertainty Approach", Academy of Management Annals, Vol. 18, No. 2.

30 Adam Grant (2016), Originals, How Non-Conformists Move The World, Penguin Random House LLC.

31 Adam Grant (2016), Originals, How Non-Conformists Move The World, Penguin Random House LLC.

32 Brené Brown (2021), Atlas of the Heart, Mapping Meaningful Connection and the Language of Human Experience, Random House, 64.

33 Ibid., Atlas of the Heart, 65.

34 Ive, J. (2021), "Jony Ive on What He Misses Most About Steve Jobs", Wall Street Journal News Exclusive.

35 Chang, Y-Y., and Shih, H-Y. (2019), "Work curiosity: A new lens for understanding employee creativity", Human Resource Management Review, Vol. 29, No. 4, pp. 100672.

36 Loewenstein, G. (1994). The psychology of curiosity: A review and reinterpretation. Psychological Bulletin, 116(1), 75–98.

37 Suzuki, S., Dixon, T., and Baker, R. (1970). Zen Mind, Beginner Mind. Weatherhill, New York.

38 Angner, E. (2020), "Epistemic Humility – Knowing Your Limits in a Pandemic", Behavioural Scientist.

39 Moore, D.A. (2018), "Overconfidence: The mother of all biases", Psychology Today.

40 Grossman, R.J. (2015), "How to create a learning culture, The Society for Human Resource Management.

41 Berlyne, D.E. (1954), "A theory of human curiosity", *British Journal of Psychology*, General Section, Vol. 45, No. 3, pp. 180-191.

42 Kashdan, T., Disabato, D.J., Goodman, F.R., and Naughton, C. (2018), "The Five Dimensions of Curiosity", *Harvard Business Review*.

43 Kahn, H. (1979), "The Expert and Educated Incapacity", *Hudson.org*.

44 Rouse, C., and Goldin, C. (2000), "Blind orchestra auditions better for women, study finds", *Princeton University*.

45 Iyengar, S.S., and Lepper, M.R. (2000), "When choice is demotivating: can one desire too much of a good thing?", *J. Pers. Soc. Psychol.*, Vol. 79, No. 6, pp. 995-1006.

46 Williams, J.C., and Mihaylo, S. (2019), "How the Best Bosses Interrupt Bias on Their Teams", Harvard Business Review.

47 Haliburton, L., Leusmann, J., Welsch, R., Ghebremedhin, S., Isaakidis, P., Schmidt, A., and Mayer, S. (2024), "Uncovering labeler bias in machine learning annotation tasks", *AI and Ethics*.

48 Chen, Y., Jean, G.Y., and Kim Y-M. (2013), A Day without a Search Engine: An Experimental Study of Online and Offline Search", *Experimental Economics*, Vol. 17, No. 4, pp. 512-536.

49 World Health Organization (2020), "Let's flatten the infodemic curve", *WHO*.

50 Ehrlich, R. (2022), "Podcast: Jocelyn Brewer: Why It's Time to Rethink Your Digital Habits", *Dr. Ron Ehrlich*.

51 Berinato, S. (2019), "Data Science and the Art of Persuasion", Harvard Business Review.

52 Sinclair, H.C. (2021), "7 ways to avoid becoming a misinformation superspreader", *ideas.ted.com*

53 De Smet, A., Hewes, C., Luo, M., Maxwell, J.R., and Simon, P. (2020), "If we're all so busy, why isn't anything getting done?", McKinsey & Company.

54 Waytz, A. (2023), "Beware a Culture of Busyness", Harvard Business Review.

55 De Smet, A., Hewes, C., Luo, M., Maxwell, J.R., and Simon, P. (2020), "If we're all so busy, why isn't anything getting done?", *McKinsey & Company*.

56 Brinton, W. (1914), Graphic Methods for Presenting Facts, The Engineering Magazine Company.

57 Sawhney, V. (2020), "Why Your Brain Dwells on Unfinished Tasks", Harvard Business Review

58 Zeigarnik, B. (1927). Über das Behalten von erledigten und uneredigten Handlungen. Psychologische Forschung. Vol 9, pp. 1-85.

59 Ogden, R., et al. (2023), "Technology Is Secretly Stealing Your Time, Here's How to Get It Back", *Scientific American*.

60 Hill, L.A., Le Cam, A., Menon, S., and Tedards, E. (2022), "Where Can Digital Transformation Take You? Insights from 1,700 Leaders", Harvard Business School Working Knowledge.

61 Prahalad, C.K., & Ramaswamy, V. (2004). Co-creation experiences: the next practice in value creation. Journal of Interactive Marketing, Vol.18, Issue 3, 5-14.

62 https://ideas.lego.com/, accessed 31 03 2025

63 Julkowski, R. (2018), "How Starbucks Turned Crowdsources Ideas into New Products", *Stanford Technology Ventures Program*.

64 IKEA (2017), "Press Release: IKEA opens up to co-create the future range with the world".

65 Hunsaker, T.B., and Knowles, J. (2021), "Most Businesses Should Neither 'Pivot' nor 'Double Down'", MIT Sloan Management Review.

66 Harbert, T. (2021), "Digital transformation has evolved. Here's what's new", MIT Management.

67 Hill, L.A., Le Cam, A., Menon, S., and Tedards, E. (2022), "Where Can Digital Transformation Take You? Insights from 1,700 Leaders", Harvard Business School Working Knowledge.

68 Angner, E. (2020), "Epistemic Humility – Knowing Your Limits in a Pandemic", Behavioral Scientist.

69 Shambaugh, R. (2019), "How to Unlock Your Team's Creativity", Harvard Business Review.

70 Claman, P. (2017), "How to Spark Creativity When You're in a Rut", Harvard Business Review.

71 Grenny, J. (2019), "How to Be Creative on Demand", Harvard Business Review.

72 Parry, D., and London Philharmonic Orchestra (2009), "The 50 Greatest Pieces of Classical Music".

73 Grant, A. (2016), Originals: How Non-Conformists Move the World. Viking; Simonton, D.K., and Lebuda, I. (2019), "A Golden Age for Creativity Research: Interview with Dean Keith Simonton", Creativity, Vol. 6, No. 1, pp. 140-146.

74 Grant, A. (2021), "How to Argue With Someone Who Has Different Views", PBS.

75 N.N. (2012), "Study Reveals Global Creativity Gap", Adobe News

76 Boynton, A. (2014), "Pixar Chief: Protect Your 'Ugly Babies'", *Forbes*.

77 Ashton, K. (2015), How To Fly A Horse: The Secret History of Creation, Invention, and Discovery, Doubleday, pp. 61.

78 Ive, J. (2021), "Jony Ive on What He Misses Most About Steve Jobs", Wall Street Journal News Exclusive.

79 Klyve, D. (2014), "Darwin, Malthus, Süssmilch, and Euler: The Ultimate Origin of the Motivation for the Theory of Natural Selection", *Journal of the History of Biology*", Vol. 47, pp. 189-212.

80 Relihan, T. (2018), "Here's how 'question bursts' make better brainstorms", *MIT Management Sloan School*.

81 Abrahams, R., and Groysberg, B. (2021), "How to Become a Better Listener", Harvard Business Review.

82 Ospina, N.S. et al. (2019), "Eliciting the Patient's Agenda – Secondary Analysis of Recorded Clinical Encounters", Journal of General Internal Medicine, Vol. 34, pp. 26-40.

83 Grant, A. (2021), Think Again: The Power of Knowing What You Don't Know. WH Allen.

84 MacLaren, N.G., Yammarino, F.J., Dionne S.D., et al., (2020), "Testing the babble hypothesis: Speaking time predicts leader emerge in small groups", *The Leadership Quarterly*, Vol. 31, No. 5, pp. 101409.

85 Scharmer, O. (2016). Theory U: leading from the future as it emerges. Berrett-Koehler Publishers.

86 Adams, R. (2021), "The Righting Reflex, its dangers, and how we can avoid it", Aspen Psychology Services; Miller, W., and Rollnick, S. (2002), Motivational Interviewing: Preparing People for Change, New York: The Guilford Press.

87 FedEx (2020), "FedEx to Transform Package Tracking with SenseAware ID, the Latest Innovation in FedEx Sensor Technology".

88 IBM (2018), "TradeLens, a Maersk and IBM solution", delivers a blockchain-enabled visibility and document management solution for container shipping that promotes more efficiency and secure global trade", *official statement IBM*.

89 Philips (2021), "Philips introduces new HealthSuite solutions to drive healthcare's digital transformation", *Philips Official Statement*.

90 Stern, S. (2011), "A Co-creation Primer", Harvard Business Review.

91 Stackpole, B. (2021), "Innovating in existing markets: 3 lessons from LEGO", MIT Management.

92 Leberecht, T. (2017), "The lost art of losing", ideas.ted.com.

93 Barsade, S., and Klotz, F. (2019), "Employee Emotions Aren't Noise – They're Data", MITSloan Management Review.

94 Soenens, B. (2022), "Giving a compliment is harder than it seems", Dare To Think.

95 Bregman, P. (2019), "The Best Leaders Aren't Afraid to Ask for Help", Harvard Business Review.

96 Corlett, S., Mavin, S., and Beech, N. (2019), "Reconceptualising Vulnerability and its Value for Managerial Identity and Learning", Management Learning, Vol 50, No. 5, pp. 556–575.

97 Wainwright, S, and Williams, C. (2005), "The Embodiment of Vulnerability: A Case Study of the Life and Love of Leoš Janáček and his Opera The Makropulos Case." Body & Society Vol, 11, No. 3, pp. 27–41.

98 Brown, B. (2021), Atlas of the Heart, pp. 13.

99 Satama, S., Seeck, H., & Garcia-Lorenzo, L. (2023), "Embracing relational vulnerabilities at the top: a study of managerial identity work amidst the insecurities of the self", Culture and Organization, Vol. 30, No. 4, pp. 442–461.

100 Taras, V., Baack, D., Caprar, D., Jiménez, A., and Froese, F. (2021), "Research: How Cultural Differences Can Impact Global Teams", Harvard Business Review.

101 Wolters Kluwer (2014), "CEO Nancy McKinstry addresses diversity at Wolters Kluwer".

102 Somers, M. (2022), "The former IBM CEO on diversity and the discomfort of good ideas", MIT Management.

103 Jones, G., Chace, B.C., and Wright, J. (2020), "Cultural diversity drives innovation: empowering teams for success", International Journal of Innovation Science, vol. 12, No. 3, pp. 323-343.

104 Vangronsvelt, K. (2022), "Wat zegt de wetenschap over diversiteit", HR-magazine.

105 Vangronsvelt, K. (2022), "Wat zegt de wetenschap over diversiteit", HR-magazine.

106 Audre Lorde, "Quotes", *GoodReads*.

107 Anni, K., Vainik, U., and Mõttus, R. (2024), "Personality Profiles of 263 Occupations", Journal of Applied Psychology. Advance online publication.

108 Little, B. (2016), "Who are you, really? The puzzle of personality", TEDx.

109 Meyer, E., "How to lead a successful international team", *Scottish Enterprise*.

110 Wheeless, N. (2021), "4 Lessons for Building Diverse Teams", Harvard Business Review; Brownlee, D. (2019), "4 Common Diversity and Inclusion Myths In The Workplace", Forbes.

111 Wheeless, N. (2021), "4 Lessons for Building Diverse Teams", Harvard Business Review.

112 Meyer, E. (2016). The Culture Map: Decoding How People Think, Lead, and Get Things Done Across Cultures". *PublicAffairs*.

113 Meyer, E. (2016). The Culture Map: Decoding How People Think, Lead, and Get Things Done Across Cultures". *PublicAffairs*.

114 Anseel, F. (2022), "Het wordt nog spannend op de werklvoer", De Tijd.

115 Perna, M.C. (2023), "5 Marks Of A Toxic Work Culture – And How You Know It's Time To Leave", Forbes.

116 Fotaki, M. (2021), "Diversity in the workplace must be matched with an atmosphere of genuine inclusion", The Conversation.

117 Bersin, J. (2019), "Why Diversity and Inclusion Has Become a Business Priority", Josh Bersin.

118 Zheng, W., Kim, J., Kark, R., and Mascolo, L. (2023), "What Makes an Inclusive Leader?", Harvard Business Review.

119 Miller, J. (2023). The power of diversity and inclusion: driving innovation and success. Forbes, August 16, 2023.

120 Auger-Domínguez, D. (2021), "How to make diversity, equity and inclusion a reality at work – not just a mission statement", ideas.ted.com.

121 N.,N., (2022), "Reducing identity threat to promote an inclusive environment", Stone Soup Consulting.

122 Bregman, R. (2021), *Humankind. A Hopeful History*. Bloomsbury Publishing.

123 Mor Barak, M.E. (2022). Managing Diversity. Toward a Globally Inclusive Workplace. *Sage Ltd*.

124 Ferdman, B.M., and Deane, B.R. (2013), Diversity at Work: The Practice of Inclusion, Jossey-Bass, pp. 44.

125 Viaene, S., & Sen, K. (2024). Leading digital transformation for organizational agility: a substantive practices-based framework. Working paper 20241212. Vlerick Business School.

126 Onderick-Harvey, E. (2018), "5 Behaviors of Leaders Who Embrace Change", Harvard Business Review.

127 Clark, R.E., and Saxberg, B. (2019), "4 Reasons Good Employees Lose Their Motivation", Harvard Business Review.

128 Cartwright, S., and Holmes, N. (2006), "The meaning of work: The challenge of regaining employee engagement and reducing cynicism", Human Resource Management Review, Vol. 16, No. 2, pp. 199-208.

129 De Smet, A., Dowling, B., Mugayar-Baldocchi, M., and Schaninger, B. (2021), "'Great Attrition' or 'Great Attraction'? The choice is yours", McKinsey Quarterly.

130 De Smet, A., Dowling, B., Mugayar-Baldocchi, M., and Schaninger, B. (2021), "'Great Attrition' or 'Great Attraction'? The choice is yours", McKinsey Quarterly.

131 Partena Professional (2022), "Met startgeld alleen wint niemand de oorlog om talent", De Tijd.

132 Smith, I.H., and Kouchaki, M. (2023), "Narrow the Gap Between Company and Employee Purpose", Harvard Business Review.

133 Dhingra, N., Samo, A., Schaninger, B., and Schrimper, M. (2021), "Help your employees find purpose – or watch them leave", McKinsey & Company.

134 Dhingra, N., Samo, A., Schaninger, B., and Schrimper, M. (2021), "Help your employees find purpose – or watch them leave", McKinsey & Company.

135 Scheibe, S., Freund, A.M., and Baltes, P.B. (2007), "Toward a Developmental Psychology of Sehnsucht (Life Longings): The Optimal (Utopian) Life", Developmental Psychology, Vol. 43, No. 3, pp. 778-795.

136 Ritter, D. and Chim, L. (2019), "Why Agile Works", Boston Consulting Group.

137 Dhingra, N., and Schaninger, B. (2021), "The search for purpose at work", McKinsey Podcast.

138 Zmuda, C. (2024), "Bridging the Purpose Gap: A Leadership Imperative", LinkedIn Pulse.

139 Hawke, E. (2020), "Give yourself permission to be creative", TEDx.

140 Celestine, N. and Nash, J. (2024), "Abraham Maslow, His Theory & Contribution to Psychology", Positive Psychology.

141 Locke, E.A., and Latham, G.P. (2006), "New Directions in Goal-Setting Theory", Current Directions in Psychological Science, Vol. 15, No. 5, pp. 265-268.

142 van Dam, A., Noordzij, G., and Born, M. (2020), "Social workers and recovery from stress", Journal of Social Work, Vol. 21, No. 5, pp. 999-1018.

143 Dweck, C. (2016), "What Having a 'Growth Mindset' Actually Means", Harvard Business Review.

144 de Saint-Exupery, A. (2018). The Little Prince (I. Testot-Ferry, Trans.). Wordsworth Editions.

145 Both-Nwabuwe, J.M.C., Dijkstra, MT.M., and Beersma, B. (2017), "Sweeping the Floor or Putting a Man on the Moon: How to Define and Measure Meaningful Work", Frontiers in Psychology, Vol. 8, 1658.

146 PWC (2016), "Putting Purpose to Work: A study of purpose in the workplace".

147 Rimé, B., and Páez, D. (2023), "Why We Gather: A New Look, Empirically Documented, at Émile Durkheim's Theory of Collective Assemblies and Collective Effervescence", *Perspectives on Psychological Science*, Vol. 18, No. 6, pp. 1306-1330.

148 Grant, A. (2021), "There's a Specific Kind of Joy We've Been Missing", *The New York Times*.

149 N.N., (2010), "Organization Culture at Walmart", Case Study Inc.

150 Eyrich, N.W., Quinn, R.E., and Fessell, D.P. (2019), "How One Person Can Change the Conscience of an Organization", *Harvard Business Review*.

151 Fickess, J. (2016), "KPMG - Appeals to Hearts of Employees & Reaps the Rewards", *Workspan*.

152 Gast, A., Probst, N., and Simpson, B. (2020), "Purpose, not platitudes: A personal challenge for top executives", McKinsey & Company.

153 Blount, S., and Leinwand, P. (2019), "Why Are We Here?", Harvard Business Review.

154 Interview with the authors", 2020.

155 Bailey, C., and Madden, A. (2016), "What Makes Work Meaningful – Or Meaningless", MIT Sloan Management Review.

156 PWC (2016), "Putting Purpose to Work: A study of purpose in the workplace".

157 Blount, S., and Leinwand, P. (2019), "Why Are We Here?", Harvard Business Review.

158 Smith, I.H., and Kouchaki, M. (2023), "Narrow the Gap Between Company and Employee Purpose", Harvard Business Review.

159 Hebb, D.O. (1949). The Organization of Behavior. Wiley, New York.

160 Knight, R. (2017), "How to Improve Your Sales Skills, Even If You're Not a Salesperson", Harvard Business Review.

161 Johnson, C., "What is story?", Pressbooks.

162 Adler, J.M., Dunlop, W.L., et al. (2017), "Research Methods for Studying Narrative Identity: A Primer", *Social Psychological and Personality Science*, Vol. 8, No. 5, pp. 519-527.

163 Pesechkian, N. (1990), De Koopman en De Papegaai, Ad Donker, pp. 14; 18.

164 Zak, P.J. (2015), "Why Inspiring Stories Make Us React: The Neuroscience of Narrative", *Cerebrum*.

165 Goman, C.K. (2020), "I Heard It Through the Grapevine", *Amanet*.

166 Duarte, N. (2018), "How to Identify and Tell Your Most Powerful Stories", Harvard Business Review.

167 Eber, K. (2021), "How your brain responds to stories - and why they're crucial for leaders", TedX Talks.

168 Anderson, C. (2013), "How to Give a Killer Presentation", Harvard Business Review.

169 Cespedes, F.V., and Hoyne, N. (2022), "How Managers Can Build a Culture of Experimentation", Harvard Business Review.

170 Cespedes, F.V., and Hoyne, N. (2022), "How Managers Can Build a Culture of Experimentation", Harvard Business Review.

171 Kreamer, A. (2015), "Not Taking Risks Is the Riskiest Career Move of All", Harvard Business Review.

172 Lovallo, D., Koller, T., Uhlaner, R., and Kahneman, D. (2020), "Your Company Is Too Risk-Averse", Harvard Business Review.; Grant, H. (2013), "The Hidden Danger of Being Risk-Averse", Harvard Business Review.

173 Rosen, R.J. (2016), "The Art of Recognizing Good Ideas", The Atlantic.

174 Lovallo, D., Koller, T., Uhlaner, R., and Kahneman, D. (2020), "Your Company Is Too Risk-Averse", Harvard Business Review.

175 Rabin, M., and Bazerman, M. (2019), "Fretting about Modest Risks is a Mistake", California Management Review, Vol. 61, No. 3, pp. 34-48.

176 Somers, M. (2022), "The former IBM CEO on diversity and the discomfort of good ideas", MIT Management.

177 Grant, A. (2016), Originals. *How Non-Conformists Move the World*. Viking.

178 Baer, D. (2015), "In 1982, Steve Jobs presented an amazingly accurate theory about where creativity comes from", *Business Insider*.

179 Rabin, M., and Bazerman, M. (2019), "Fretting about Modest Risks is a Mistake", California Management Review, Vol. 61, No. 3, pp. 34-48.

180 Rabin, M., and Bazerman, M. (2019), "Fretting about Modest Risks is a Mistake", *California Management Review*, Vol. 61, No. 3, pp. 34-48.

181 Kahneman, D., and Klein, G. (2009), "Conditions for intuitive expertise: a failure to disagree", Am. Psychol., Vol. 64, No. 6, pp. 515-526.

182 Kahneman, D. (2012), "Thinking, Fast and Slow", *Penguin*.

183 Kreamer, A. (2015), "Not Taking Risks Is the Riskiest Career Move of All", Harvard Business Review.

184 Insead Knowledge (2007), "Networking is vital for succesful managers", *Insead*.

185 Beswick, C. (2024), "Overcoming the innovation paradox: three key reasons why large organisations struggle to stay ahead", *Outcome*.

186 Webley, K. (2010), "The Happy Meal", *Time*.

187 Galton, F. (1907), "The Ballot-Box", Nature, Vol 75, pp. 509-510; Galton, F. (1907), "Vox Populi", Nature, Vol. 75, pp. 450-451.

188 Surowiecki, J. (2005), "The Wisdom of Crowds: Why the Many Are Smarter Than the Few", *Abacus*.

189 Kaospilot, "Our History", accessed 31 03 2025.

190 Lovallo, D., Koller, T., Uhlaner, R., and Kahneman, D. (2020), "Your Company Is Too Risk-Averse", Harvard Business Review; Rabin, M., and Bazerman, M. (2019), "Fretting about Modest Risks is a Mistake", California Management Review, Vol. 61, No. 3, pp. 34-48; Brassey, J., De Smet, A., Kothari, A., Lavoie, J., Mugayar-Baldocchi, M., and Zolley, S. (2021), "Future proof: Solving the 'adaptability paradox' for the long term", McKinsey.

191 Klein, G. (2007), "Performing a Project Premortem", *Harvard Business Review*.

192 Brown, S., Henz, T., Sibanda, T., and Wang, M. (2021), "Collaborations between corporates and start-ups", McKinsey podcast.

193 Hill, L.A., Le Cam, A., Menon, S., and Tedards, E. (2022), "Digital Transformation: A New Roadmap for Success", Harvard Business School Working Knowledge.

194 Mayer, R. C., Davis, J.H., and Schoorman, F.D. (1995), "An Integrative Model of Organizational Trust." The Academy of Management Review Vol. 20, no. 3, pp. 709–734.

195 Wu, M-Y., Weng, Y-C., and Huang, I-C. (2012), "A study of supply chain partnerships based on the commitment-trust theory", Asia Pacific Journal of Marketing and Logistics, Vol. 24, No. 2, pp. 690-707; Tejpal, G., Garg, R.K. and Sachdeva, A. (2013), "Trust among supply chain partners: a review", Measuring Business Excellence, Vol. 17, No. 1, pp. 51-71; The Economist Intelligence Unit (2008), "The role of trust in business collaborations, an EIU briefing paper sponsored by Cisco Systems", pp. 1-28.

196 Sloan, P., and Oliver, D. (2013), "Building Trust in Multi-Stakeholder Partnerships: Critical Emotional Incidents and Practices of engagement", Organization Studies, Vol. 34, No. 12, pp. 1835-1868.

197 Zak, P.J. (2017), "The Neuroscience of Trust", Harvard Business Review.

198 Zak, P.J. (2017), "The Neuroscience of Trust", Harvard Business Review.

199 Viaene, S., & Sen, K. (2024). Leading digital transformation for organizational agility: a substantive practices-based framework. Working paper 20241212. Vlerick Business School.

200 N.N., (2024), "How do you build a change coalition?", LinkedIn

201 Uohara, M.Y., Ward, W.H., Goel, N., Atchley, K., and Esnaola, N.F. (2019), "Managing Change", Springer, pp. 197-205.

202 Uohara, M.Y., Ward, W.H., Goel, N., Atchley, K., and Esnaola, N.F. (2019), "Managing Change", Springer, pp. 197-205.

203 Uohara, M.Y., Ward, W.H., Goel, N., Atchley, K., and Esnaola, N.F. (2019), "Managing Change", Springer, pp. 197-205.

204 Anderson, L.A., and Anderson, D. (2002), "How to Build a Critical Mass of Support to Accelerate Your Change", Being First Inc, pp.1.

205 Malik, N.K., Khalil, G.I., Al Amoodi, A.Y., Bakhsh, M.A.S., and Sahwan, M.R. (2021), "Combatting Resistance to Change During the COVID19 Pandemic with Design Thinking Approach: Making a Case for the Public Sector", 2021 International Conference on Innovation and Intelligence for Informatics, Computing, and Technologies, pp. 658.

206 Kübler-Ross, E. (1969), "On Death and Dying", Routledge, London.

207 Dans, E. (2021), "The Pandemic Has Changes Business Structures: There's No Going Back", *Forbes*.

208 Haelle, T. (2020), "Your 'Surge Capacity' Is Depleted – It's Why You feel Awful", Elemental.

209 N.,N., "Change Comes at a Cumulative Cost", Center for Creative Leadership.

210 Haelle, T. (2020), "Your 'Surge Capacity' Is Depleted – It's Why You feel Awful", Elemental.

211 Baker, M. (2020), "How to Reduce the Risk of Employee Change Fatigue", Gartner.

212 Baker, M. (2020), "How to Reduce the Risk of Employee Change Fatigue", *Gartner*.

213 Antliff, S. (2021), "Workplace overwhelm: how to protect your team from change fatigue", Atlassian.

214 Smith, C. (2021), "4 Ways to Solve Change Fatigue", The Change Management Blog; Innis, J., and Berta, W. (2016), "Routines for change: how managers can use absorptive capacity to adopt and implement evidence-based practice", Journal of Nursing Management, Vol. 24, No. 6, pp. 718-724; Baker, M. (2020), "How to Reduce the Risk of Employee Change Fatigue", Gartner.

215 Fiske, S., Cuddy, A., & Glick, P. (2007). Universal dimensions of social cognition: warmth and competence. Trends in Cognitive Sciences, vol.11, no.2, 77-83.

216 Heath, C., and Heath, D. (2010). Switch: How to Change Things When Change Is Hard. *Crown Currency*.

217 Bryan, B.T., Andrews, G., Thompson, K.N., Qualter, P., Matthews, T., and Arseneault, L. (2023), "Loneliness in the workplace: a mixed-method systematic review and meta-analysis", Occupational Medicine, Vol. 73, No. 9, pp. 557-567.

218 Hickman, A. (2019), "How to Manage the Loneliness and Isolation of Remote", Gallup.

219 Eisenberger, N., Lieberman, M.D., and Williams, K.D. (2003), "Does rejection hurt? An FMRI study of social exclusion", *Science*, pp. 290-292.

220 Timmer, A. (2019), "Loneliness in the workplace: Scaling the problem", the Great Indoors.

221 Bernstein, E.S., and Turban, S. (2018), "The impact of the 'open' workspace on human collaboration", Philosophical Transactions of the Royal Society B: Biological Sciences, Vol. 373, No. 1753.

222 Piore, A. (2020), "Why do you feel lonely? Neuroscience is starting to find answers", *Technology Review*.

223 Statista (2024), "Feeling of loneliness among adults 2021, by country".

224 N.N., (2022), "Loneliness affect mental health of millions, yet many feel ashamed to talk about it", Mental Health Foundation.

225 N.N., (2022), "Loneliness affect mental health of millions, yet many feel ashamed to talk about it", Mental Health Foundation.

226 Johansson, F. (2004). The Medici Effect: Breakthrough Insights at the Intersection of Ideas, Concepts, and Cultures. *Harvard Business School Press*.

227 The Dalai Lama, and Hougaard, R. (2019), "The Dalai Lama on Why Leaders Should be Mindful, Selfless, and Compassionate", Harvard Business Review.

228 Wasson, D.L. (2018), "Fall of the Western Roman Empire", *World History Encyclopedia*.

229 de Waal, A., Weaver, M., Day, T., and van der Heijden, B. (2019), "Silo-busting: Overcoming the greatest threat to organizational performances", Sustainability, Vol. 11, No. 23, pp. 6860.

230 PWC (2015), "Reimagining Operations".

231 Pedersen, C.L. (2021), "Gain Competitive Advantage by Transcending the Front-Line Paradox", MIT Sloan Management Review.

232 Hogan, M. (2016), "5 Employee Feedback Stats That You Need to See", LinkedIn Talent Blog.

233 Bregman, P., and Jacobson, H. (2021), "Feedback Isn't Enough to Help Your Employees Grow", Harvard Business Review.

234 Asplund, J., and Blacksmith, N. (2011), "Strengthening Your Company's Performance", Gallup Business Journal.

235 Hogan, M. (2016), "5 Employee Feedback Stats That You Need to See", LinkedIn Talent Blog.

236 Hogan, M. (2016), "5 Employee Feedback Stats That You Need to See", LinkedIn Talent Blog.

237 Goldstein, J. (2019), "The Feedback Triggers: Why Some People Respond Negatively to Feedback", The Leadership Laboratory.

238 Heen, S., and Stone, D. (2014), "Found the Coaching in Criticism", Harvard Business Review.

239 Edinger, S. (2021), "Encourage Your Employees to Give You Critical Feedback", Harvard Business Review.

240 Eskreis-Winkler, L., Fischbach, A., and Duckworth, A.L. (2018), "Dear Abby: Should I Give Advice or Receive It?", Psychological Science, Vol. 29, No. 11, pp. 1797-1806.

241 Porath, C. (2022), "Nine Tips for Giving Better Feedback at Work", Greater Good Magazine.

242 Liu, C. (2021), "Christine vs. Work: How to Give Feedback – Especially When You're Dreading it", Harvard Business Review.

243 Bregman, P., and Jacobson, H. (2021), You Can Change Other People: The Four Steps to Help Your Colleagues, Employees – Even Family – Up Their Game, Wiley.

244 De Prins, P. (2022), "Bedek niet alles met de mantel der liefde", De Standaard.

245 De Stobbeleir, K. (2019), "CEO Disease: Diagnosis, Symptoms and a Few Treatments", Vlerick Business School Insights.

246 AlNuaimi, B.K., Singh, S.K., Ren, S., Budhwar, P., and Vorobyev, D. (2022), "Mastering digital transformation: The nexus between leadership, agility, and digital strategy." Journal of Business Research, Vol. 145, pp. 636-648; Ly, B. (2023), "The Interplay of Digital Transformation Leadership, Organizational Agility, and Digital Transformation", Journal of the Knowledge Economy; Weber, E., Krehl, E-H., Buettgen, M., and Schweikert, K. (2019), "The Digital Leadership Framework: Insights into New Leadership Roles Facing Digital Transformation", Academy of Management Proceedings.

247 Burkus, D., (2011), "Building the Strong Organization: Exploring the Role of Organizational Design in Strength-Based Leadership", Journal of Strategic Leadership, Vol. 3, No. 1, pp. 54-66.

248 Viaene, S. (2020), Digital Transformation Know-How, Acco.

249 Dweck, C.S. (2008), "Brainology", National Association of Independent Schools.

250 Dweck, C. (2016), "What Having a "Growth Mindset" Actually Means", Harvard Business Review; Schwartz, T. (2018), "Create a Growth Culture, Not a Performance-Obsessed One", Harvard Business Review.

251 Schwartz, T. (2018), "Create a Growth Culture, Not a Performance-Obsessed One", Harvard Business Review.

252 Gonzalez, K., Kanitz, R., and Briker, R. (2024), "'AI Can't Steal My Soul': In the Age of AI, the Human Touch is Paramount for the Craft of Managing Change", The Journal of Applied Behavioral Science, Vol. 60, No. 4, pp. 589-602.

253 Hall, E.T. (1976). Beyond Culture. Anchor Press.

D/2022/45/346 – ISBN 9789401487740– NUR 800/808

Cover design: Gert Degrande | De Witlofcompagnie
Interior design: Joost van Lierop

LannooCampus Publishers is a subsidiary of Lannoo Publishers, the book and multimedia division of Lannoo Publishers nv.

LannooCampus Publishers
Vaartkom 41 box 01.02
3000 Leuven
Belgium
www.lannoocampus.com

P.O. Box 23202
1100 DS Amsterdam
The Netherlands